PETER'S
PREACHING

Text copyright © Jeremy Duff 2015
The author asserts the moral right
to be identified as the author of this work

Published by
The Bible Reading Fellowship
15 The Chambers, Vineyard
Abingdon OX14 3FE
United Kingdom
Tel: +44 (0)1865 319700
Email: enquiries@brf.org.uk
Website: www.brf.org.uk
BRF is a Registered Charity

ISBN 978 0 85746 350 0

First published 2015

10 9 8 7 6 5 4 3 2 1 0

Cover images:
Front: Leonardo Correa Luna/Gettyimages
Back: troyka/Shutterstock

A catalogue record for this book is available from the British Library

Printed and bound by CPI Group (UK) Ltd, Croydon CR0 4YY

PETER'S
PREACHING
THE MESSAGE OF MARK'S GOSPEL

JEREMY DUFF

For Jesus' disciples in Widnes

CONTENTS

CHAPTER 1

PETER'S PREACHING

'Who told you that?' is an important question. The office gossip and, even worse, the 'Twittersphere', are constantly producing crises, scandals and conspiracies, but most of them melt quickly away as soon as you ask, 'Who told you this?' Of course, this is nothing new: the courts have long since known not to accept evidence that starts, 'A friend of mine met this man in the pub who said…'

So what about Mark's Gospel? Who is this Mark? He doesn't introduce himself in the Gospel, and he certainly isn't one of the twelve disciples. Was he there when Jesus went around doing all those miracles, or is he the first-century equivalent of a 'friend of a friend who met a man in the pub'?

Fortunately, we have a revealing piece of evidence about the identity of Mark, the man responsible for Mark's Gospel. It's a shaft of light from the very earliest days of Christianity, which illuminates the origins of this Gospel and, as we shall see, of all the Gospels. Furthermore, there is intriguing evidence from the very way in which early Christians wrote—creating a system of abbreviations and adopting the latest technology (which could be described as the ancient world's equivalent of the ebook). When all this evidence is put together with the surprising way that the earliest church used and honoured Mark's Gospel, there is a fascinating story to be unearthed.

Our starting point is a revealing snippet of information directly about Mark. It comes from a man called Papias, who was bishop of the city of Hierapolis, Turkey, in the early years of the second century AD. (Hierapolis is close to Colosse and is mentioned in Colossians 4:13. It's the modern-day town of Pamukkale, a popular tourist site because of its hot springs.) Scholars normally date Papias's life to about AD60–130. In comparison, Jesus was most probably crucified in AD30, and Mark's Gospel written AD60–65. So Papias was a young man around the time when Mark's Gospel began to circulate.

Sadly, Papias's own writings have not been preserved. Much from the ancient world is lost to us, long since having rotted away or been destroyed in one disaster or another. Other than in chance finds, like the Dead Sea Scrolls, authors from that era reach us only if, throughout the many centuries before printing was invented, monks dutifully copied and recopied their work as the originals wore out. That only happened if the writings were highly valued. Unfortunately, Papias seems to have fallen out of favour, condemned by a key authority—the first 'church historian', Eusebius (who finished his work in AD324)—probably because Papias wrote interpretations of the book of Revelation that linked 'the beast' with Rome. This use of symbolic language did not go down well in the Roman imperial church in Eusebius' time.

All is not lost, though, for, in his historical works, the same Eusebius twice quoted Papias's words. First, we can read Papias's description of how he was always seeking out information from Jesus' disciples and those who had personally learnt from them.

*Whenever anyone who had been a follower of the elders came,
I would investigate the elders' words—what Andrew or what
Peter said, or what Philip or what Thomas or James or what
John or Matthew or any other of the Lord's disciples said, and
the things which Aristion and John the elder, the disciples of
the Lord, were saying.*

PAPIAS' WORDS RECORDED IN EUSEBIUS, *HISTORY OF THE CHURCH*, 39.4

Papias wanted to know! This is hardly surprising: people
in the ancient world were just as curious as we are today.
Furthermore, this was still about a century before any real
concept of the 'New Testament' emerged, so a man like
Papias had no ready-made source of accepted, authoritative
books to rely on. For comparison, we see a similar focus on
seeking out accurate sources for what Jesus did and said in
the opening four verses of Luke's Gospel: Luke searched out
the eyewitnesses to Jesus, so that his readers could be assured
that they were hearing the truth.

You'll notice that the word 'elder' occurs three times in
this quotation. It's a difficult word to pin down. It really
means an 'old respected man' but the word was also used
for a Christian leader, and, when you read what Papias says,
it is clear that he is using it to talk about Jesus' disciples—
Andrew, Peter, James and John and others. Peter uses the
same word to describe himself in 1 Peter 5:1–2, where he also
exhorts the 'elders' of the churches to shepherd God's flock
willingly and eagerly.

So whenever someone who had learnt from one of Jesus'
disciples (a 'follower of the elders') came to Hierapolis,
Papias would ask them about what the disciples had said.
This makes sense, for some of Jesus' disciples would certainly
have lived until about AD60 or 70, and there would have

been people still around in AD100, who had heard them. By AD100, Papias himself would perhaps have been 30 or 40. Indeed, if he was born in AD60, he himself would have been just contemporary with Jesus' disciples, although he would have been only a child and perhaps none of them ever came to Hierapolis in person. (There was a tradition in the early church that Papias heard the apostle John, who is said to have been the last apostle to die. Maybe he did, but Papias' own words here don't make this claim: he states only that he listened to the people who had learnt from the disciples.)

So far, so good in this detective story. Papias got his information from good sources—but what did he say?

> *The elder also said this: after Mark became Peter's translator, he wrote down accurately, though not in order, everything he remembered that the Lord had said or done. For he neither heard the Lord nor followed him, but afterward he followed Peter, as I said. Now Peter used to shape his teaching according to what was needed, and was not making an ordered arrangement of the Lord's sayings. So Mark did nothing wrong when he wrote down the individual stories as he remembered them. For he did pay careful attention to one thing—to leave out nothing that he heard, nor to include anything false.*

PAPIAS' WORDS RECORDED IN EUSEBIUS, *HISTORY OF THE CHURCH*, 39.15

So Papias is quoting 'the elder'—one of these foundational figures from the earliest days of Christianity, perhaps one of Jesus' disciples or perhaps one from the same generation. He is quoting someone who was there when Mark was writing—and what does he say?

Perhaps surprisingly to the cynical mind, he doesn't tell us that Mark was a super-accurate eyewitness to what Jesus did and said; nor does he claim that Mark was inspired by some heavenly vision. His report is somewhat more modest. Mark himself, so Papias tells us, did not hear Jesus or follow him before his resurrection. However, he became a follower of Peter. Presumably that means he became a Christian in response to Peter's preaching, becoming one of his supporters and looking to him for leadership. Twice in this passage we read that Mark wrote down 'as/everything *he* remembered'. Technically we could argue about whether 'he' is Mark or Peter. However, since the passage also tells us that Mark wasn't an eyewitness but got his information from hearing Peter, it comes to the same thing: Mark wrote down Peter's account of what Jesus had said or done.

Papias also tells us that Mark was Peter's translator or interpreter. The Greek word used here can mean a translator in the straightforward sense, but it can also mean someone who helps by explaining someone else's words. Indeed, the word 'interpreter' in English can carry both meanings: for example, 'the foreign diplomat was accompanied by her interpreter' and 'the BBC is offering an interesting interpretation of the Prime Minister's speech'.

Why did Peter need a translator/interpreter? Well, because he was, as the book of Acts puts it, 'an uneducated, ordinary man' (Acts 4:13). More to the point, he was a Galilean fisherman, so his first language would have been Aramaic (the language of the region in Jesus' time). He may have been able to speak some Greek; people often do learn enough of the language of the ruling classes and of international trade to 'get by'. Peter spent his later years preaching to Greek speakers and even Latin speakers in Rome, and guiding the Greek-speaking church there. More generally, he was a central figure in the Jesus movement, which, during Peter's lifetime, became mainly Greek-speaking. So maybe he learnt some more Greek, but it would be no surprise if he used translators or interpreters.

Perhaps you are wondering about the two letters Peter wrote in the New Testament. Were they written in Greek? Yes, they were, but look at the way 1 Peter ends:

> *I have written these few words to you **through Silvanus**, whom I consider a faithful brother, to encourage you and to testify that this is the true grace of God. Take your stand on it. The church in Babylon, chosen alongside you, sends greetings, as does Mark my son.*
> 1 PETER 5:12–13

Peter has written 1 Peter 'through Silvanus'. He didn't write the clear, attractive Greek that we find in the letter himself: he had a helper, a secretary—quite possibly a translator—called Silvanus, presumably because he couldn't have managed it himself. We are used to this sort of writing in our own context. When we see the published autobiography of a famous footballer or pop star, we all know that they will probably have been helped by a ghostwriter. Someone more adept at writing will have listened to them and worked with them to produce a good-quality written product that communicates what the famous person wants to say.

Did you notice that final reference in 1 Peter 5:13 to Mark as 'my son'? It is a tantalising glimpse into the circle of people around Peter. While we cannot be sure, this may well be the same 'Mark' that Papias tells us about. Peter certainly seems close to him, as he would be to the one who acted as his translator/interpreter when he preached. Interestingly, 2 Peter is written in a Greek style very different from the style of 1 Peter. This may seem surprising, until we remember that both letters would have been written with the assistance of a secretary/translator/interpreter, and different helpers could well have produced different styles of language.

So the jigsaw fits together. Peter needed a translator/ interpreter. He could probably order his breakfast in Greek, just as some of us can 'get by' in another language on holiday, and, by the time he was preaching and teaching in Rome, his Greek may have become much better. He probably wasn't reliant on Mark to translate his message word for word. Sometimes we just need someone to help put the complicated concepts into the other language, or to help interpret what we are saying for our foreign hearers. Even so, as Peter's translator/interpreter, Mark would have been intimately familiar with Peter's message, words and meaning.

How Mark wrote

Papias tells us something more. If you look back to the second quotation ('The elder also said this...'), you will see that he seems to be trying to convey something slightly tricky about the way Mark and Peter handled the stories of Jesus. Papias says that Mark wrote down 'accurately, though not in order', that he had no intention of giving an 'ordered arrangement of the Lord's sayings'. He tells us that, in this respect, Mark was following in Peter's footsteps, for Peter 'used to shape his teaching according to what was needed'. Nevertheless, Papias tells us that Mark's account of Peter's preaching is trustworthy: he omitted nothing and included nothing false.

So Mark's Gospel contains the preaching of Peter, in a

written form. It is genuine preaching—stories about Jesus and accounts of his teaching, recounted by Peter for a particular audience on a particular day. Mark has put the material together into his Gospel, without any attempt to give the material a particular historical order. This stands to reason. For example, Mark will have heard and remembered Peter telling the parable of the sower, and he will have heard and remembered Peter speaking about the time when Jesus healed Jairus's daughter. However, it is extremely unlikely that Peter would have said, 'Jesus told this parable shortly before he met Jairus and healed his daughter, who you might remember I told you about last week.' Peter would have preached about different incidents and different pieces of Jesus' teaching, without indicating a precise chronology. Then Mark, we are told, wrote it all down without attempting to go back and piece together an accurate 'order' (although, of course, it would be obvious that the crucifixion came at the end).

If we are on the right lines here, we should find Mark's Gospel to be slightly disjointed, made up of separate stories rather loosely stitched together (except for the final days in Jerusalem leading up to Jesus' death and resurrection, when the story has an intrinsic flow). We might expect to find the material grouped by topic or theme, as Mark writes down, for example, all the parables he remembers Peter retelling. We might also expect a particular sort of honesty, as Peter would have remembered how bewildering it felt to have actually been one of Jesus' disciples: he knew he wasn't a saint from a stained-glass window. Also, of course, we might expect the sort of little details that Peter would have included in his preaching—since, after all, he had been there.

All of that is exactly what we find.

Look at chapters 2—4 in Mark's Gospel. They present a series of very loosely connected stories.

- 2:1–12: 'A few days later, when Jesus again entered Capernaum...' (healing the paralysed man).
- 2:13–17: 'Once again Jesus went out beside the lake...' (calling Levi; eating with tax collectors).
- 2:18–22: 'Now John's disciples and the Pharisees were fasting...' (new wineskins for new wine).
- 2:23–27: 'One sabbath Jesus was going through the cornfields...' (Son of Man is Lord of the sabbath).
- 3:1–6: 'Another time he went into the synagogue...' (healing on the sabbath).
- 3:7–12: 'Jesus withdrew with his disciples to the lake...' (summary of healings).
- 3:13–19: 'Jesus went up on a mountainside and called to him...' (calling the twelve disciples).
- 3:20–35: 'Then Jesus entered a house...' (Jesus' family and the claim that he is working for Satan).
- 4:1–20: 'Again Jesus began to teach by the lake...' (parable of the sower).
- 4:21–23: 'He said to them, "Do you bring in a lamp..."' (what is hidden should be disclosed).
- 4:24–25: '"Consider carefully what you hear," he continued...' (the measure you use will be measured to you).
- 4:26–29: 'He also said, "This is what the kingdom of God is like..."' (parable of seed growing secretly).
- 4:30–34: 'Again he said, "What shall we say the kingdom of God is like...?"' (parable of the mustard seed).

None of these stories has a proper link to the story before. They begin with vague phrases such as 'Once again...' or

'One sabbath...' yet the stories themselves are anything but vague, capturing many details and the emotions involved. It is as if those remembering the stories have focused on their key points, not on how they fit into a timeline or specific locations. This is, in fact, how human memory works. We remember what is important. Most married people can remember what they wore on their wedding day—because it mattered—but not what they wore the day before. This means that, while we remember individual incidents well, we tend not to remember which order they came in. Just think back to a holiday a few years ago: you can probably remember a number of great days, or meals you had, but you would struggle to remember which day was which. The sequence doesn't matter, so our brains don't remember.

The different passages in Mark seem to be arranged thematically. For example, from Mark 1:21 there is a steadily building tension between Jesus and the religious authorities, which culminates in 3:6: 'Then the Pharisees went out and began to plot with the Herodians how they might kill Jesus.' Immediately we start to see this plot in action, when in verse 22 Jesus is accused of working for Satan, but then it all goes quiet: there are no further significant clashes with the authorities until chapter 12. Is this because, historically, Jesus clashed with the religious authorities repeatedly at the beginning of his ministry, then changed so that he got on well with them, and then changed again near the end so that the tension re-emerged? Possibly, but it is perhaps more likely that this bunching of passages on a particular theme comes from Mark. He gathered together at the beginning of his Gospel a number of stories that highlighted the tension between Jesus and the religious system of his day. This established the theme and allowed it to overshadow the rest of the story.

Similarly, Mark 4 is a collection of parables about the kingdom of God, joined by phrases like 'he also said', yet there are no parables in chapters 1—3 or 5—6. It can't be that Jesus wasn't teaching in those chapters because we are explicitly told that he was. At the same time, chapter 4 doesn't read as if it is an account of what Jesus said on a particular day. The natural conclusion is that Mark has grouped Jesus' parables about the kingdom together in one chapter.

Scholars sometimes use the phrase 'pearls on a string' to describe Mark's Gospel. It's a good description. The individual stories and pieces of teaching are like pearls, carefully preserved from Jesus and polished in the telling (or, we might say, as Peter preached them over the years), but their arrangement is a different matter. It is probably too flippant to say that they have just been 'strung together': as we will see throughout the book, and particularly in chapter 10, the sequence does seem to reveal a plan. Nevertheless, the order of the stories or teaching (how the pearls are arranged) is a separate matter from their content (the pearls themselves). We might say that in Mark we find pearls of Peter's preaching, arranged in an order by Mark, his translator/interpreter.

Mark's Gospel is also sprinkled with details that are not found in Matthew and Luke when they tell the same stories. For example, Mark alone tells us that the grass on which the 5000 sat for their meal was 'green' (6:39). Only he records the Aramaic words that Jesus said to Jairus's daughter: 'Talitha koum' (5:41). It's only from Mark that we hear how Jesus, healing someone who was deaf, 'put his fingers into the man's ears. Then he spat and touched the man's tongue. He looked up to heaven and, with a deep sigh, said to him, "Ephphatha!"' (7:33–34).

Mark also pulls no punches in the way he describes the Twelve. Only he describes the disciples as having 'hardened hearts' (6:52; 8:17), the same description used in the Old Testament of Pharaoh when he refused to let the Hebrews leave Egypt (for example, in Exodus 11:10) and, by Mark himself, of Jesus' enemies who were plotting to kill him (Mark 3:5–6). Similarly, Mark admits that James and John asked Jesus if they could have the places of honour for themselves, while Matthew saves their reputations by saying that it was their mother who did the asking (compare Mark 10:35–37; Matthew 20:20–21.) Even Jesus is presented as speaking more bluntly by Mark, whose account of Jesus' encounter with the brave and clever Syro-Phoenician woman (7:25–30) makes Jesus appear rude and inconsistent. (Jesus heals the daughter only because her mother makes a clever reply.) When Matthew tells the story (15:21–28), this aspect is very much toned down.

So we do find exactly the sort of snippets of detail and honesty that we would expect if Mark's account was fundamentally Peter's story. Although Mark's Gospel is shorter overall than Matthew's and Luke's, time and time again, when Mark, Matthew and Luke record the same incident, Mark's version is longer because it is full of detail. At the same time, the way Jesus and the disciples are portrayed fits well with the view that Peter himself was 'telling it how it was', rather than being a suitably presentable version of events written by someone for whom Peter is a great 'saint'.

Thus, we find that the words of Mark's Gospel themselves confirm the early evidence of Papias. The Gospel does appear to be Peter's preaching, written down 'not in order' by his translator/interpreter Mark.

Wider confirmation

All good TV detectives want to build up a number of pieces of evidence that point to the identity of the murderer. Not only was the blood found on his clothes, but he was seen leaving the area and was known to be jealous of the victim! We can do the same here. At the heart of our understanding is the evidence from Papias, which matches well with what we find in Mark's Gospel, but there are other supporting factors.

First, scholars have long recognised that Matthew and Luke appear to have used Mark's Gospel in some fashion (they call this 'Marcan priority'). There is a significant overlap in the wording: 50 per cent of the words of Mark occur in Luke and a massive 90 per cent of Mark's words appear in Matthew. You really can see Matthew as 'Mark with additions' or even 'the revised expanded version of Mark'. Seen from a different angle, Matthew and Luke are noticeably close to each other when Mark tells the same story too. It's as if, when Mark has the story, they both use him as a base.

You could suggest that these similarities are present just because people remembered the stories and Jesus' teaching well—so naturally they would remember the same words. However, that will not quite do, for two reasons. Firstly, of course, Jesus taught in Aramaic, but the similarity of wording is in Greek: the writers agree on the same *translation* of Jesus' words. More importantly, Matthew and Luke present the material in the same order as Mark does. As we saw earlier, Mark's order seems to be artificial—pearls on a string. The stories' content was remembered well because it mattered, but the comparative chronology (which parable was taught before which other) was not remembered because it was unimportant. Matthew and Luke put the stories and teaching in basically the same order as in Mark, but that order—the way in which the pearls were strung together—was Mark's creation. Hence, if Matthew and Luke also use it, that strongly points to their having based the material on Mark itself.

This fits with what Luke says in the opening of his Gospel.

> *Many have undertaken to draw up an account of the events which have been fulfilled among us, just as those who were eyewitnesses and servants of the word from the beginning have handed them down to us. Therefore it seemed good to me to investigate everything carefully from the beginning and to write an orderly account for you, most excellent Theophilus.*
> LUKE 1:1–3

Luke seems to be implying that he knows of other written accounts of Jesus' life which were based on eyewitness testimony handed down, but that, in comparison, his work will be 'orderly'. Although we can't be certain what Luke was referring to, it certainly fits our emerging understanding of Mark—material known to Luke, not written by an eyewitness but drawing on the testimony of an eyewitness (Peter), and seen as being 'not in order'.

Why did Matthew and Luke follow Mark so closely? In fact, they each follow him in slightly different ways. Matthew uses Mark as a structure within which he inserts large sections of his distinctive teaching. Luke generally fills out Mark's story, section by section, with extra individual stories. Nevertheless, they both use Mark very faithfully, despite the fact that they clearly have many other sources for Jesus' material. This rather suggests that they knew that Mark was from a top authority—a reliable, important witness. That authority can hardly be Mark himself—he wasn't an apostle or even an eyewitness—but the idea would make sense if Mark was known to have been Peter's translator/interpreter, writing down Peter's preaching.

Moving on from here, it might also seem surprising that Mark's Gospel survived at all. Matthew, Luke and John are clearly fuller accounts. Indeed, if almost all of Mark is in Matthew, why keep Mark—particularly as it misses out so much important material, such as Jesus' birth, the Lord's Prayer and the resurrection appearances? (Mark 16:9–20, which is printed in brackets in Bibles, is not actually part of the original Gospel: this is discussed in Chapter 2.) Interestingly, Mark's Gospel is rarely quoted in the early church. When the first Christians wanted to point to what Jesus had done or said, they referred to one of the other three more comprehensive Gospels. Nevertheless, Mark was kept, and was faithfully copied and recopied. Why? Perhaps because it was known to be the voice of Jesus' most important disciple, Peter.

The preservation of the name, 'the Gospel according to Mark', is also intriguing. In the second century AD, there was a great conflict within the growing Christian movement, with different groupings claiming to be faithfully preserving Jesus' teaching. In those conflicts, the apostles were the recognised authorities. Hence, we find that different groups put down their teaching in 'Gospels'—in the name of Thomas or Peter, for example—and people forged letters in the name of Paul. In this battle, 'Mark' would have been a nonentity. Why would anyone take notice of a text that didn't (claim to) come from an apostle? Yet the material from this 'B list celebrity' name was kept. Why? Well, it would certainly make sense if it was known that the Mark in question was Peter's translator/interpreter, meaning that the Gospel 'really' came from Peter. (The same was true of Luke's Gospel: Luke was identified as Paul's travelling companion, so Luke's Gospel was seen as being 'really' Paul's.)

Thus we find that Mark's Gospel was given real importance by the other Gospel writers and was faithfully preserved, despite its having been effectively replaced by Matthew. Furthermore, it was preserved and defended under the 'unimportant' name of Mark. All of this makes sense if Papias is right and Mark's Gospel is Peter's preaching.

Mark: the ebook of his day?

What do you think the original of Mark's Gospel or other books of the Bible actually looked like? What were they made of? Most of us, if we stop and think, bring to mind some distant memory of pictures of Greeks, Egyptians or Romans reading from scrolls. We have books made of paper, but they had scrolls made of papyrus.

It's certainly true that, up to the time of Jesus, all literature from the lands around the Mediterranean was written on scrolls made either of papyrus or of animal skin (vellum). Shopping lists, prayers and notes might be written on scraps of pottery, but, for anything longer, scrolls were used. A scroll—sheets of papyrus or vellum stuck together to make a long roll—was the only way of holding together enough pages. This continued to be the case for a few centuries after Jesus for all types of literature, with one massive exception: Christians did not, on the whole, write on scrolls. They were the 'early adopters' of the latest technology of their day—the book, or codex.

A basic book (called a quire) is like a child's exercise

book—sheets of paper folded over and stitched through the middle (today we might use a staple). This means that there are pages to turn, while a scroll is wound and unwound. If a quire has too many pages, it becomes unwieldy: imagine if the book in your hand now was made up of 100 sheets of A4 paper folded in the middle and fixed with a large staple. Instead, the quires are kept fairly small—maybe 16 pages— and multiple quires are glued or stitched together. If you look down the spine of this book, you will see exactly that—small groups of folded sheets glued to each other.

Books (codices) were just beginning to be used in the first century AD. They are first mentioned by a Roman writer, Martial, and by Paul (in 2 Timothy 4:13). The Romans already had 'note-books' made from stringing together several wax tablets. They were used for all sorts of note-taking by generals, merchants and so on, and examples have been found perfectly preserved in Herculaneum (the Roman city engulfed by lava from the volcano Vesuvius). At some point in the first century AD, it seems that these 'note-books' evolved into the book.

It seems obvious to us that the book is a better technology than the scroll: it is more portable and robust, both sides of the paper can be written on, it can be laid flat for reading, and you can easily flick back and forward. For example, if you wanted to look at something on page 101 in this book, you could do it easily, but it's a very different matter to roll forward to the right place in a scroll to check something and then roll back again. However, humans are often conservative and it takes a long time for new technologies to catch on.

A helpful comparison is with the ebook today. There are many practical reasons why it is a better format for reading the written word, but you are more likely to be reading this book on paper. Why? Well, a key factor is that many people want a book to 'feel' like a book—the look, the touch, even the smell is important to them. We know where we are with a physical book. Times are changing—the new technology is expanding and may soon become dominant—but the change is happening slowly because it's not simply about practicality.

In the same way, although it may seem obvious to us that a book is better than a scroll, the majority of Greek and Roman literature continued to be written in scrolls for another few centuries. The exception to the rule was any kind of Christian literature. Why did the Christians adopt this new technology so enthusiastically?

It is possible to argue that it was just because the codex was more robust than the scroll for people who travelled around a lot, and the early Christian leaders were always on the move. Alternatively, because Christianity was counter-cultural, perhaps the Christians were pleased to distinguish themselves from the rest of the world by using books, not scrolls. These reasons might explain why some Christians abandoned the old ways of writing and adopted the new technology, but why did almost all of them do it? Theodore Skeat, the Keeper of Manuscripts at the British Museum from 1961 to 1972, in his influential book *The Origins of the Codex*, was sure that there had to be a further reason. However convenient the codex was, the Christians would have adopted the new technology so uniformly only if a very early, respected and influential text led the way. So how was the trend for the codex started among Christians?

It was not just the use of the codex rather than the scroll that marked Christians out as different. They also used a system of abbreviations for some words—particularly God, Lord, Jesus and Christ—known to scholars as *nomina sacra* ('sacred names'). For example, rather than writing 'Jesus', which in Greek is IHSOUS, they wrote IHS; rather than Christ (Greek XPISTOS) they wrote XPS (in both cases with a line over the letters). If you are familiar with Christian art, you might recognise the IHS and XP symbols, since they are often used (in XP, the P, which is actually the Greek letter 'r', is normally placed on top of the X). Similarly 'God' and 'son' are shortened.

These abbreviations, again, seem to be a uniquely Christian phenomenon. They are not found in Jewish texts and have no parallel in Greek literature, but they are found almost without exception in every Christian biblical text. Why? Again, scholars have their different views (might it be a sign of respect?) but few escape from the conclusion that, at some point, a hugely influential text invented the abbreviations and set a trend.

So we have two curious hard facts about early Christian literature: it was written in books, not on scrolls, and it used a system of abbreviations. Both of these features suggest that there was an original piece of early Christian literature that set a trend for what 'Christian writing' should physically be like, which was then copied widely.

What was this trendsetting piece of early Christian writing? We don't know for certain, but there is another early Christian 'trend' worth contemplating—the idea of a 'Gospel'. We are used to the idea of a 'Gospel', but, if you ponder for a moment, you will realise that it is a tricky concept.

The word 'gospel' (in Greek, *euangelion*) means 'good news'—in other words, a piece of news which is good. It is not a particularly common word, but we find it being used to refer to announcements of a military victory, success in a court case or the arrival of an emperor. We see the word used thus in the Greek translation of the Old Testament, in 2 Samuel 18:19: 'Now Ahimaaz son of Zadok said, "Let me run and take the *good news* to the king that the Lord has delivered him from the hand of his enemies."' In the New Testament, we see it in Mark 1:15: 'The time has come. The kingdom of God is near. Repent and believe the *good news*!' At times, perhaps it is starting to acquire the sense of 'the particular good news about Jesus': for example, 1 Thessalonians 3:2 says, 'We sent Timothy, our brother and God's colleague in the *good news* of the Messiah.' But in none of these references does 'the gospel' mean a physical book. In fact, nowhere in the New Testament itself is the word 'gospel' used to mean a book, except perhaps in the first verse of Mark's Gospel: 'The beginning of the gospel of Jesus Christ the Son of God.'

How is it, then, that we have four books called 'Gospels' (and, indeed, further Gospel books that were written in the second century and later)? It's not just a matter of the unusual use of the word 'gospel' to refer to a book. The Gospels are a particular sort of book: they are a sort of 'biography with a point'. They combine stories of what Jesus did with blocks of his teaching, stretching from the beginning of Jesus' public ministry in Galilee through to his resurrection (though some have a 'prologue' dealing with his birth). Again, we might think that is obvious, but in the New Testament itself the 'gospel' is a message to be proclaimed, not a life story. So how did all four writers decide that the way of writing the 'gospel' was not to be a theological presentation of the message but an account of Jesus' life?

Finally, we can also note that the titles of the Gospels are distinctive: 'The Gospel according to...'. This use of 'according to' is very unusual when indicating a book's author. An author is usually identified by the word 'of': we have the plays *of* Shakespeare, the letters *of* Paul and so on. We might expect to read 'the Gospel *of* Mark', but instead we have 'the Gospel *according to* Mark'. Presumably the point is that the message is the gospel *of* God: God is the author of the good news. So the use of 'according to' is a mark of humility (effectively, it is 'God's good news, written down by Mark') and a reminder that the 'gospel' is really the message, not the book. At the same time, the source—in this case, Mark—is important (see Luke 1:1–4 for an emphasis on the importance of sources; also John 19:35; 21:24; Hebrews 2:3; 1 John 1:1–3; 1 Corinthians 15:3–8). This may all be very logical, but it would still be rather surprising if all four Gospel writers had the same idea of how to title their work, independently of each other. (It is possible, of course, that the titles were applied slightly later than the Gospels themselves were written, so I wouldn't want to place too much weight on this point on its own.)

How do we piece together this jigsaw? First, let's look at the developments in the idea of a gospel—the progression from 'gospel' meaning the 'good news' to 'Gospel' as the title for a book; the idea that the way to tell the gospel message was by presenting a life story of Jesus; and the use of the phrase 'according to' to indicate the human author or source. There is a fairly obvious reason for all this, if we remember that almost all scholars believe that Mark's Gospel was used by the authors of Matthew and Luke (and was probably known by the author of John). If Matthew and Luke used Mark as a source for some of the words and the order of their Gospels, it seems perfectly reasonable to conclude that they also got the very idea of a 'Gospel book' from Mark's Gospel, together with the sense that a Gospel book should contain

Jesus' life story, and probably that the book should be called 'The Gospel according to...'. This is indeed reasonable but, again, it's striking that this Gospel text had such a wide influence if it was just the work of the relatively unimportant man Mark.

Once we have established that Mark set the trend, copied by Matthew, Luke and John, for the 'Gospel' as a book telling the life story of Jesus according to 'X', then we can look back with new eyes at the two strange 'hard facts' about early Christian writing—the use of the codex and the *nomina sacra* (abbreviated 'sacred names'). They also needed a 'trend starter' to get them going—some hugely influential text, which established the idea that Christian writings 'should' be in a codex, using *nomina sacra*. The obvious conclusion is that this text was also Mark's Gospel—but we can't be sure. Sadly, if doing history is like making a jigsaw, doing ancient history is like making a jigsaw without the picture on the box, and with some pieces missing. However, it's the best explanation available.

So Mark can be seen as the ebook of its day, breaking new ground and creating a distinctive sense of what Christian writing was like, and was copied by all who came afterwards.

Back to Papias

The question still remains, though, as to why people would have followed Mark in this way. Why, in an early Christian world dominated by the apostles, Jesus' brothers and eyewitnesses, would people allow the pattern for Gospels and, indeed, for all Christian literature, to be set by the nonentity Mark?

It all makes sense if we believe what Papias said. If Mark was Peter's translator/interpreter, then Mark's Gospel would have had Peter's authority behind it. Mark's Gospel would have been backed by the authority of the most central, respected figure in the early Christian movement. That would explain why Mark's Gospel played such a trendsetting role.

There are two final pieces of supporting evidence. First, let's go back to the physical processes of writing. According to Papias, Mark's Gospel began as the written record of Peter's preaching. To take dictation or notes from a speaker, secretaries at the time often used the ancient equivalent of a notebook—the strung-together bundle of wax tablets that was the predecessor of the codex. So Mark would initially have taken down Peter's preaching on strung-together wax tablets. He then would have taken it just a step further, writing everything up on the nearest equivalent format, which was papyrus sheets sewn together—the new codex. He may even have felt that the codex set the right tone: it was appropriate for transcribed oral speech or dictation, not properly written literature. We might also find the origins of *nomina sacra* here: it may have been a form of shorthand. Shorthand was used by secretaries in Jesus' day when taking down dictation, so perhaps Mark developed it.

Second, our findings gain further support from a slightly later Christian writer, Justin Martyr, writing about AD155–160. Fifteen times Justin refers to the 'memoirs of the apostles', which might be literally translated as 'what the apostles *remembered*'. Papias used exactly the same word when he said, 'After Mark became Peter's translator, he wrote down accurately, though not in order, everything he *remembered* that the Lord had said or done.' In addition, Justin uses the word 'gospel' to refer to a book just three times, preferring the clearer title 'memoirs of the apostles'. Once, however, he uses the two descriptions in the same sentence, making it clear that they both refer to the same thing ('For the apostles, in the memoirs they produced, which are called Gospels, handed on to us what Jesus commended them': *First Apology*, 66.3).

Justin does not generally mention a particular 'memoir' by name—with one exception:

> *It is said that Jesus changed the name of one of the apostles to Peter. This is written in his own memoir, and also that he changed the names of two other brothers, the sons of Zebedee, to Boanerges, which means sons of thunder.*
>
> JUSTIN MARTYR, *DIALOGUE WITH TRYPHO*, 106

It is only in Mark's Gospel (3:17) that we are told that Jesus renamed the sons of Zebedee 'Boanerges'. So Justin refers to 'Peter's memoir', followed by a reference to something only recorded in Mark's Gospel. This is all the more revealing because Justin is not trying to defend the authority of the Gospels; it merely slips out in passing that he thinks of Mark's Gospel as Peter's memoir.

Peter's preaching

Papias tells us clearly that he heard personally, from people who were there at the time, that Mark's Gospel was Peter's preaching, written down by Peter's translator/interpreter, Mark. It was written down accurately, though not in chronological order and with no attempt to make an 'ordered arrangement' of the Lord's sayings.

What we find in the Gospel itself confirms Papias' words. The Gospel is slightly disjointed, made up of separate stories loosely strung together. The material is grouped by topic or theme, not presented in a strict historical order. It is strikingly honest about the disciples' failings, as only one of the disciples themselves could be, and it contains lots of the sort of details that Peter would have included in his preaching, which later writers edit out.

Papias' statement finds wider confirmation in the way Matthew and Luke bow to Mark's authority, using Mark's words and order as a basis for their Gospels. It makes sense of the fact that the early church kept Mark, despite its being replaced by Matthew and 'improved' by Luke, and that they kept defending it under the unimportant name of 'Mark'.

As we have seen, Papias' statement also makes sense of some of the mysterious 'hard facts' of early Christian writings—the adoption of the codex and *nomina sacra*. Although we can't prove that Mark's Gospel started the trend, this is the best explanation available, particularly as it also looks likely that Mark's Gospel was key in the move to the use of the word 'gospel' to describe a book containing Jesus' life story. Why did people follow the lead of Mark's Gospel in this way? Because it was known to be Peter's preaching, or Peter's memoirs.

What difference does this make? Most importantly, it means that as we read Mark's Gospel, we are hearing Peter's voice. Mark is not just 'a book, drawing on some unknown sources, written by someone unknown, which somehow at some point the church decided should be in the Bible'. If we go back to the question with which this chapter started—'Who told you that?'—we have an answer. It was Peter, one of Jesus' first disciples, who emerged as the leader of the disciples and the central figure in the early church. He was there, all the way through; he heard it all.

This is important for me—to hear the voice, through his translator/interpreter, of Peter himself. I can sit on the bus and read on my phone the message of Jesus' closest disciple, telling me what he saw and heard as he travelled with Jesus. Perhaps, as you ponder this, it may mean that you approach Mark's Gospel with new interest and enthusiasm.

I think it also matters in the wider world. You and I might be happy to accept Mark's Gospel as important because it is 'in the Bible'; for others, this doesn't mean much. But when you explain that it is the written-down testimony of an eyewitness, people are intrigued.

The conclusion that Mark's Gospel is Peter's preaching also explains this book. Obviously it's where the title comes from! But it also explains the content. I have taken at face value Papias' words that Mark didn't intend to write a connected account and didn't write 'in order', and have taken the liberty of approaching the Gospel in a thematic way, rather than chapter by chapter, verse by verse.

We are used to a verse-by-verse approach to studying the Bible, and I certainly don't want to decry it. Nevertheless, freshness helps us see with new eyes, and there are key themes running through 'Peter's preaching' that we miss when we read it in order. If the order is not from Jesus and is not from Peter, we are free to look at it in a different way. Thus, the chapters of this book will focus on different key themes in Mark's Gospel, such as the disciples, who Jesus is and miracles. Each chapter will quote *in full* the parts of Mark's Gospel that are particularly relevant to that theme.

To add further freshness, I have translated the Greek of Mark's Gospel myself, being honest to the sometimes rough style of the original—the voice of Peter, the Galilean fisherman. You will soon notice Mark's somewhat unusual habit of sometimes using a present tense within a story being told generally in past tenses. For example, in Mark 3:13–14, 'He goes [present] up into the hills and calls [present] those he wanted [past], and they went [past] out to him...'. Scholars often talk of this as a 'historic present' tense but have not developed a clear understanding of why Mark uses it in some cases and not in others. Therefore, I have decided to stick literally to Mark's Greek and let you experience the distinctive style.

In the final chapter, we will go back to look at the order in which Mark chose to record events. It might not be from Peter or Jesus, but presumably Mark's order was not just random. For now, though, I invite you to accompany me as we hear and ponder Peter's preaching.

CHAPTER 2

THE DISCIPLES

'What are you doing over the weekend?' Sally asked the others as they got their stuff from the locker room at the end of the shift. As soon as the words had left her mouth, she kicked herself. Next to her, Greg had frozen: this would be the first weekend since his partner had left him.

Julie quickly covered the silence: 'I've got to spend the whole weekend painting. My best friend from school has just got a new flat.'

'You mug,' Pete chipped in, but Julie was having none of it.

'She was my best mate all through school, so of course I'm going to be there for her.'

'Football training all Saturday for me,' added Pete as he pulled on his leathers.

'And you say I'm a mug!' laughed Julie.

'Hey, it's better than sitting on the sofa, and this new coach is great—he has really got us working as a team, and...' But Pete's explanation was lost as Sally and Julie headed into the car park.

'Football mad,' said Sally, 'but a great guy once you get to know him.' Julie smirked. 'I don't mean like that,' Sally laughed. 'After that last one, I'm off men. My friends are what count.'

We all want friends. Some of us just want one or two, some

like to be in a huge network, but Genesis 2:18 hits the nail on the head when it says, 'It's not good for man [or woman] to be alone.' Children quickly learn the 'rules' of friendship. The most important one is that you stick by your friends. That is what marks out a real friend from just 'someone you know'. You put yourself out for them, because that is how it works: you are there for each other in times of need. Sadly, it doesn't always go right. Greg, facing the weekend without his ex, is feeling that terrible pain of being abandoned, being alone—the one he thought he could rely on gone, all those hopes and dreams, all that investment, wasted.

Friendship can often have wider dimensions. For Pete, having a new football coach means that he and his mates are growing in their skills and growing together as a team—even if people on the outside don't understand. Friendships can be inspiring and energising, giving us new confidence. Some of us are fortunate to have had a boss at work who acted as something of a mentor; sadly, in society today we also see the difficulties that some boys face, growing up without good male role models.

Sally was right: some people's true qualities only emerge once you get to know them. Happily, the development is often positive—we appreciate people more as we become better acquainted—but it's also true that sometimes we are just left with the words 'Some friend you turned out to be'.

All of this we will see played out in this chapter, as we look at Jesus and his disciples. 'Disciple' is an unfortunate word, since, although we think of it as an English word, it is not widely used. It generally occurs only in religious contexts or to express some unusually intense devotion—perhaps describing the followers of a particular artist who try to copy his or her style. However, the Greek word normally translated as 'disciple' is *mathetes*, which might be translated more helpfully as 'student', 'learner' or 'apprentice'. Furthermore, although the relationship between Jesus and his apprentices is complex, one important element of it appears to be friendship. When Jesus calls his inner core of followers, Mark describes it thus:

> *He goes up into the hills and calls those he wanted, and they went out to him. He made twelve, whom he called 'messengers', so they would be with him and he could send them out.*
> MARK 3:13–14

The disciples' first calling, then, was to 'be with him'. This is not just about friendship, of course. Nevertheless, we all understand friendship and what it involves—the importance of sticking by your friends, being there for them when you are needed; the pain of being misunderstood, abandoned or alone; the excitement of being part of a team, growing in skills and having a mentor; the testing of friendship by adversity. Therefore, thinking about friendship can give us a valuable perspective as we approach Mark's Gospel and Jesus' relationship with his disciples.

Called to a new type of fishing

Jesus starts to call people to follow him from the first moment of his ministry. In Mark's Gospel we have an introduction linking back to the Old Testament (1:1–3), with an account of Jesus' baptism (vv. 4–13) and an 'executive summary' (vv. 14–15) of his arrival on the scene: he entered Galilee proclaiming the good news that the time had come and

God's reign was near. Then comes the first 'story' from his ministry, which is about the calling of four men to a new form of fishing.

> *As he was going alongside the Sea of Galilee, he saw Simon and his brother Andrew casting nets in the sea. (They were fishermen.) Jesus said to them, 'Follow me, and I will make you fish for people.' Immediately they abandoned their nets and followed him.*
>
> *He went on a little further and saw James, Zebedee's son, and his brother John. They were in a boat repairing nets. Immediately he called them, and they left their father Zebedee behind in the boat with the hired men, and set off behind Jesus.*
>
> MARK 1:16–20

It is significant that this is the opening scene in the main body of the Gospel. The proclamation of the good news—and the relevance and power of God's approaching reign—are demonstrated in the transformation of the lives of these four ordinary men.

The immediacy of their response is striking. Perhaps they already knew Jesus. John's Gospel (1:29–43; 3:22–24) implies that Andrew at least had been baptised by John and heard his commendation of Jesus, and that he and Peter had already had a positive encounter with Jesus. Even so, they seem willing to let Jesus cut across all their own plans and timing. After perhaps many months of waiting, Jesus appears, telling them that now is the moment, and they are happy to respond. The initiative—indeed, the power—lies with him; it is not for them to choose him or even to influence the day or the hour of his call. If we leave to one side John's contribution and read Mark on its own, the disciples' immediate, wholehearted, positive response is even more notable.

The four fishermen leave their nets in response to Jesus' words: 'Follow me.' We need to contemplate this for a moment. Jesus' expectations were incredibly high. What they were being asked to do was enormous. These four had a secure, routine way of life. They had a place within family and community, and work at which they were competent. Fishing wasn't just something they did: they *were* fishermen. Yet all of this was to be left behind.

The simplicity of the call is, in itself, disturbing. If the calling were to a certain programme of action, to fulfil a job description or to join a particular club, then there would be an objectivity about it—a sense of clear shared expectations of what would be involved, and a balance of rights and responsibilities between the two parties. But instead the call is personal—*you* follow *me*—and without limitation; there is no explanation of where 'I' might be going or what might be demanded of 'you'. In this we get a taste of what will come. As the Gospel unfolds, we will find that Jesus' message seems to centre around *him* (see, for example, 8:34–38) rather than the God-given law (see 2:14–17). It also cuts across accepted norms of society, such as the duty that James and John owed to their father (1:20; see also 7:1–15; 14:3–9). It is as if Jesus considers himself more important than anything else.

We are told, though, what will result from their discipleship: they will 'fish for people'. Throughout the rest of the Gospel, more will be said about the role of disciples. Nevertheless, it is striking that in this first scene it is a missionary, evangelistic role that is emphasised. Perhaps there is also a sense that 'if you are going to fish, there are more important things to catch than fishes': in other words, now is the time to be gathering in people. The Old Testament prophets had

37

promised that, at the right moment, God would gather his scattered people (see Jeremiah 32:37–38; Ezekiel 11:17).

This first scene also highlights a key theme for discipleship in the Gospel: the disciples are called to carry out the same work as Jesus himself (we will see this more clearly at 3:13–15). Here he calls/catches them, and tells them that they will call/catch others. We might also note that although these disciples are given a new role, it is in some continuity with their past. 'Fishing for people' is radically new and yet seems to build on who they were, with all their experiences and skills, before they met Jesus.

As we follow the disciples throughout Mark's Gospel, we will watch as they start to misunderstand and fail Jesus. It is easy to start to view them as deeply flawed characters from whose mistakes we can learn. Indeed, as this chapter continues you may well start to conclude that this was Peter's intention in his preaching—to present the disciples as 'people like us', not as 'stained-glass window saints'. Nevertheless, we need to remember the courage and dedication of their first response, as we see it in this opening scene of the Gospel proper. This is where their story starts. It also challenges us to think back to our own response to Jesus—both our original response and our ongoing response day by day. Jesus said, 'Follow me', and Simon, Andrew, James and John did, wholeheartedly.

Called because he wanted them

Over the following few chapters, the main focus of attention is on Jesus' clash with the religious system and authorities. His disciples are part of this scenario: for example, their conduct is criticised and he defends them (2:23–28) and he is criticised for calling the wrong sort of people to follow him (2:14–17). Nevertheless, the main focus is elsewhere. Then, after a summary of the popularity of Jesus' healing and deliverance ministry (3:8–12), Jesus takes the idea of discipleship to a new level.

> He goes up into the hills and calls those he wanted, and they went out to him. He made twelve, whom he called 'messengers', so they would be with him and he could send them out to preach and have authority to drive out the demons.
> He formed the twelve. He gave to Simon the name Peter, and he also gave to James, Zebedee's son, and to John, James' brother, the names Boanerges, which means 'sons of thunder'. And there was also Andrew, Philip, Bartholomew, Matthew, Thomas, James the son of Alphaeus, Thaddaeus, Simon the Zealot and Judas Iscariot, who actually betrayed him.
>
> MARK 3:13–19

The first thing to note is that the initiative clearly lay with Jesus. We have already seen this in the call of Peter, Andrew, James and John: he chose them, and they responded to his call to 'follow me'. It is emphasised here by the phrase 'those he wanted'. In fact, the Greek might better be translated as 'those whom he himself wanted'. This seems clumsy in English but the emphasis is important. It seems to point up a distinction: Jesus welcomes all comers (2:14–17; 3:31–35), yet this inner group, who are, in a sense, going to represent him and take forward his work (see 6:7–13), are his own choice. It's an interesting balance to ponder in our own lives and churches: all are welcome to belong and follow, but we exercise careful choice over who are given key positions of leadership or service.

The emphasis here may also be because of the difference between Jesus and the emerging rabbinical movement. The rabbis (who, around Jesus' time, were emerging from among the 'teachers of the law' and Pharisees) accepted as disciples people who came to them. Jesus was different (compare 1:22): *he* did the choosing. The emphasis also increases the tension of the final words in the passage, that Judas actually betrayed him. Peter does not attempt to lessen the scandal that Jesus was betrayed by one of his own disciples by, for example, implying that Judas always was a shady character or wasn't really Jesus' choice. Jesus chose Judas because he wanted him *and yet* Judas went on to betray him.

'The Twelve' is a complex category. We can easily fall into the idea that Jesus had (just) twelve followers or disciples, but this would be a mistake. This group is mentioned only five more times before Jesus' last hours (4:10; 6:7; 9:35; 10:32; 11:11). Most of the time we hear of 'the disciples', 'those around him' or 'those with him'—a group that seems to involve many others (see 3:31–35; 4:10; 10:32), including important women (see Luke 8:1–3) and others who respond to him (2:14, 5:19). The different Gospels do not even quite agree on the names of the Twelve (compare Luke 6:14–16 with Matthew 10:2–4). Nevertheless, the idea of 'the Twelve' is clearly very important. We see their significance in this passage—these are the ones who are specially chosen, named and listed—and elsewhere, such as Acts 1:15–26, where the one vacancy left by Judas' death *needs* to be filled.

Mark does not explain the importance of the Twelve, but the other Gospels give us a hint. Matthew 19:28 and Luke 22:30 both speak of them as matching, judging and perhaps leading the twelve tribes of Israel. Thus, the calling of 'the Twelve' could be seen as a prophetic action, symbolising the gathering and reforming of God's people. This is particularly striking because most of the twelve tribes had been scattered many centuries earlier and no longer existed in any meaningful sense. Thus, the formation of the Twelve signifies a great new restorative work of God (see Isaiah 49:6), going hand in hand with the proclamation that 'the time has come; God's reign is near' (Mark 1:15).

Strikingly, Jesus gives the Twelve three roles: to be with him, to proclaim the message and to have authority over demons (3:14–15). They are disciples (learners) with him, and apostles (messengers) given a task. Their task is basically the same as Jesus' (1:39: 'Jesus travelled throughout Galilee, preaching in their synagogues and driving out demons'). He is the mentor or coach: by spending time with him, they will be able to learn from him and copy him.

The focus on demons is problematic for many of us today. Even if we believe in their existence, we probably don't put them so high up our agenda, and we might much prefer to see the disciples' purpose as being to preach and to heal. It is perhaps appropriate and helpful, though, to see 'authority over demons' as equivalent to 'authority to release people from whatever binds them'. In the language of the following verses, it means authority to challenge the 'reign of Satan' (3:22–27) in the name of the reign of God, which is now arriving (1:15). We will consider 'God's reign' more fully in Chapter 8 of this book.

Christians from different cultures, times and backgrounds will probably never agree on exactly how to understand the talk about demons. Nevertheless, we can agree that there is much that binds and imprisons people, and God wants to bring release from it all. In Mark 1 and 2 we see Jesus bringing this release to people, and in Mark 3 the disciples are given authority to do the same. They are not just 'learners': they are also sent out.

As disciples of Jesus ourselves, we too have this threefold calling. First and foremost, we are called to be with Jesus— in prayer, through spiritual disciplines, in worship and by dedicating time simply to being with him. Then we are to proclaim Jesus' message and bring out its effects—seeing people released from all that binds them.

Hard-hearted dim-witted cowards?

So far, the story of the disciples—the learners and followers of Jesus—appears to be positive. They have responded whole-heartedly to Jesus' call to 'follow me', and he has chosen them not just to be with him but to be sent out to take forward his work. Mark's arrangement of Peter's preaching gives us this positive picture of the disciples in the first three chapters.

However, the second quarter of Mark's Gospel contains three incidents on boats which tell a very different story. The episodes seem to build on each other, steadily revealing that all is not well. Despite their immediate wholehearted response to Jesus, and Jesus' choosing and commissioning of them, the disciples' faith, courage and understanding soon prove to be limited. This is the other side of friendship— the pain of being misunderstood or let down by those you thought were on your side.

The fact that all three incidents happen on boats presumably reflects Peter's memory that key moments between Jesus and the disciples happened when they were away from the crowds, together in a boat. It also links the stories for the reader: the three 'boat stories' in the Gospel, coming in fairly rapid succession, form a triplet and develop a theme. We will look at them each in turn.

> *That day when evening came, he says to them, 'Let's go across to the other side.' So they leave the crowd and take him with them, just as he was, in the boat (other boats were with it too).*
>
> *Then a ferocious windstorm springs up, and the waves began to crash into the boat. Already it was filling up with water. Yet Jesus was asleep on a cushion at the back of the boat. They wake him up and say to him, 'Teacher, don't you care that we are going to drown?'*
>
> *He got up, rebuked the wind and said to the sea, 'Be quiet! Restrain yourself!' The wind dropped, and it was completely calm. He said to them, 'Why are you such cowards? Don't you yet have any faith?' They were terrified and began to ask each other, 'Who is this? Even the wind and sea obey him!'*
>
> MARK 4:35–41

The final line of this passage makes clear the main significance of this incident, for Peter. It revealed something about who Jesus was. It meant something more than the healings and the conflicts with evil spirits. (We will explore this in Chapter 5.)

The story also reflects on the disciples. These men, chosen by Jesus to be with him and to share his work, are declared to be faithless cowards. We can also understand why Peter remembered the story so vividly: this is the sort of event that we would all remember years afterwards 'as if it were yesterday'.

These disciples were fishermen. The lake was their world: they understood it, and they understood the storms. In the synagogue, Jesus was clearly in charge, but here they were the experts. The boats were not large and were completely open to the elements. (If you travel to Galilee, you can see one from about the time of Jesus, which archaeologists have discovered.) If the fishermen—the ones who knew—were panicking, genuinely believing that the boat might sink and they might all drown, presumably Jesus would accept how serious the situation was. His sleeping almost suggests that their expert judgement about the storm, and their fear, were unimportant to him.

We get a sense of this suggestion in the disciples' words to Jesus: 'Don't you care?' (v. 38). They are words of criticism, almost of challenge. Jesus' response is equally direct: 'Why are you such cowards? Don't you yet have any faith?' (v. 40). 'Yet' seems to be a key word here. Jesus is frustrated, exasperated with them. By now, they should have known better. He had said they were going across to the other side. Did they not trust that he would get them there? After everything that they had seen him do and despite their closeness to him and their commitment, when it came to it, their trust (or faith) in Jesus was lacking.

We should recognise such scenarios ourselves. We don't expect much from a stranger, but we have higher expectations of how a friend should behave, and it is painful and distressing when a friend lets us down. In fact, as is so often true in our friendships, the breakdown is, in a sense, mutual. Behind the disciples' cry of 'Don't you care?' is a sense of hurt and neglect: Jesus doesn't seem to be fulfilling his part of the friendship. When they need him, what is he doing? Sleeping! He seems to be ignoring the most important rule of friendship—that you are there when your friends need you. Something is going wrong.

That night the boat was in the middle of the sea, and he is alone on the land. Just before dawn, he sees them struggling to row because the wind was against them, and he comes towards them walking on the water. It was looking like he was going to pass them by, but when they saw him walking on the sea, they thought it was a ghost and cried out. They all saw him and were terrified. Immediately he spoke with them and said, 'Take courage. It's me. Don't be afraid.'

Then he climbed into the boat to them and the wind stopped. They were completely and utterly amazed, because they had not understood about the bread; rather their hearts were hardened.

MARK 6:47–52

This passage, too, seems to speak about Jesus' identity, so we shall come back to it in Chapter 5. For now, though, our attention is drawn to the final words: 'their hearts were hardened'. It is a direct criticism of the disciples: they are lacking and unresponsive. However, the criticism becomes more pointed when we notice the link with an earlier passage.

Jesus angrily looked around at them, deeply distressed at the hardness of their hearts, and says to the man, 'Stretch out your hand.' He stretched it out and the hand was restored. The Pharisees walked out and immediately began to plot against him with Herod's men about how they might destroy him.

MARK 3:5–6

The disciples now appear to be placed in the same category as Jesus' enemies. Their utter amazement at Jesus' walking on the water only demonstrates how woeful is their lack of understanding and failure to grasp anything about who Jesus is. We expect our friends to understand us: the disciples might as well be his enemies for all the understanding they show. They have just witnessed the feeding of the 5000, which immediately precedes the story of the walking on the water, but they have understood nothing ('they had not understood about the bread', 6:52). Their hearts are hard: they are not so different from those who are plotting his destruction.

The idea of hearts being hardened also links back to the story of the exodus, in which Pharaoh's heart was said to be hard (Exodus 7:13, 7:22, 8:19, 9:35). Pharaoh had opposed God's plan to rescue his people from slavery. Are the disciples really that bad?

> *Jesus left them, got back into the boat and set off towards to the other side of the lake. Now they had forgotten to bring some bread, so they only had one loaf with them in the boat. Then Jesus warned them, 'Watch out: beware the yeast of the Pharisees and the yeast of Herod.' They started to discuss with each other the fact that they had no bread.*
>
> *He realises this and says to them, 'Why are you discussing the fact that you don't have any bread? Have you not yet grasped it, or understood? You have hardened hearts! You have eyes but don't see and ears but you don't listen!*
>
> *'Don't you remember when I broke five loaves for five thousand people? How many baskets full of the pieces did you collect?' They say to him, 'Twelve.' 'When I broke the seven loaves for the four thousand—how many baskets full of the pieces did you collect?' They say to him, 'Seven.' He said to them, 'Do you still not understand?'*
>
> MARK 8:13–21

In the second boat incident, the lack of understanding 'about the bread' was mentioned. Now it is spelt out more forcefully, almost painfully, as Jesus goes through the numbers involved and demands, 'Do you still not understand?' The first time in the boat, the disciples' response to the storm might have been understandable or forgivable because they were so frightened. However, before the second boat incident they had seen Jesus feed 5000 people with just a few loaves, with piles left over, and before the third he had done it again with 4000 people.

But what is it that they are meant to be grasping? The passage doesn't make it clear: we are left as confused as the disciples. We might recognise this situation from our own lives, when we are faced by situations in which we have an underlying confidence that 'God is in control' and yet we just don't understand what is happening around us.

The most obvious thing that they are meant to have 'grasped' from the loaves is about Jesus' power. How could they not have understood by now that Jesus was more than a 'faith-healer' or the sort of miracle worker that was not unknown in the ancient world? He had power not only to heal individuals but also to control the natural world. In addition, when the events of Mark 6 (walking on the water and feeding the 5000) are recounted in John's Gospel (ch. 6), they are followed by a dialogue in which the feeding is connected to the manna that God sent during the exodus (Exodus 16). God's rescue of the people from slavery in Egypt involved their walking across or through the sea and being fed in the desert. It's an intriguing connection, and Mark 6:35 explicitly says that the 5000 were fed in a 'remote place'—the same Greek word as for 'desert'. Were the disciples expected to have seen these connections? Either way, Jesus seems now to regard their lack of understanding as wilful blindness. They are not so much lacking as failing.

Jesus says that they have 'hardened hearts'; they have 'eyes but don't see and ears but don't listen'. As we saw earlier, the word 'hard-hearted' connects the disciples to Jesus' enemies—the very people whose 'yeast' (a hidden, spreading influence) he is warning them against. It's a disturbing phrase, for it reminds us that we, too, while going through the motions of discipleship, can actually grow unresponsive and distant from God. Our hearts become hard.

The images of failing to see and failing to understand also carry resonances from earlier in Mark. At the end of the parable of the sower, we find this:

And Jesus said, 'If you have ears to hear, then listen!' When he was alone, those around him and the twelve asked him about the parables. He said to them, 'To you has been given the secret of God's reign. To those on the outside, everything is in parables so that although they look and look, they don't see, and although they listen and listen, they don't understand; otherwise they might turn and be forgiven!'
MARK 4:9–12

At that point, those around Jesus seemed to be 'insiders' who knew the secret of God's reign. Now they seem to have become like the outsiders.

This sequence of three passages 'in the boat' packs a hard punch. Many of us might have a great deal of sympathy for the disciples. Surely they were doing their best. Was it really their fault they didn't grasp it? After all, the events going on around them were mindblowing. But there is no getting round the meaning given to these incidents by Jesus' words and Peter's telling of the story (indeed, he was one of the people being criticised!). The disciples should have known better. Their friendship with Jesus, and the time he had spent with them, should have resulted in greater faith and understanding. They may have started well but they were moving backwards.

How does the disciples' journey in the first half of Mark's Gospel—from great commitment and response to failure—affect us? In one sense, it is encouraging. Many of us might feel, 'Ah, so I am not so bad after all.' Their weakness makes our frailty seem more acceptable, less worthy of condemnation. They were so foolish, slow to learn and unresponsive, but Jesus stuck with them and they went on to great things. Perhaps there is hope for us!

It is also disturbing, though, for it reminds us forcefully that spiritual highs, commitment and being chosen by God seem to bring no guarantee of continued faith and understanding. It is possible to regress, to turn our backs on our friend—in effect, to betray him. Sometimes biblical language about choosing, insiders and outsiders, disciples and crowds, can suggest that everything is cut and dried; here, things seem less certain.

Half sight

The verses that follow the final boat incident clarify our understanding of the disciples. They are indeed 'with Jesus'. They have not literally become outsiders or just part of the crowd. However, their understanding and faith are lacking: they have so much more to learn.

Mark 8:27—9:7 forms the centre of the Gospel, a hinge on which the action turns. We will come back to it a number of times in this book, so we will not try to plumb its depths in one go. Here, we will look at it from the point of view of what it tells us about the disciples. Before that, though, sandwiched between the hinge passage and the last boat incident (8:14–21), there is a miracle story whose details seem very relevant.

> They come into Bethsaida. And they bring to Jesus a blind man and ask him to touch him. He took the blind man's hand and led him out of the village. Then he spat into his eyes, placed his hands on him and asked him, 'Can you see anything?'
>
> He looked up and said, 'I see people that look to me like walking trees.' Then Jesus placed his hands on his eyes again. He opened his eyes wide and his sight was restored. He could see everything clearly. Jesus sent him home saying, 'Don't go into the village.'
>
> MARK 8:22–26

The blind man does achieve full sight, but not immediately. First, he goes through a stage of partial, distorted sight— no longer blind, but not yet seeing things as he should. Something has been achieved but not enough. We hear about incidents like this today, of people whose sight is medically restored after many years, who have to 'learn to see' once more, as initially the nerve signals from the eyes are overpowering and jumbled. If the patient is someone who has never seen, they need to learn what it is that they are seeing. Such parallels aside, it is clear that Jesus wanted the man to go on to the second stage of full sight. That was the goal.

Is this a picture of the disciples—with a slowly growing understanding but so much still to learn? We might personally identify with that image. We might even see in it an explanation of Jesus' method of teaching his disciples.

Perhaps full sight straight away would have been too much for them. They too needed to 'learn to see'.

> Jesus and his disciples set out towards the villages around Caesarea Philippi. On the way he questioned his disciples, 'Who do people say that I am?' They replied, 'John the Baptist, and others Elijah, and others one of the prophets.' And he asked them, 'And you? Who do you say that I am?' Peter replies, 'You are the Messiah!'
>
> He ordered them not to speak to anyone about him, and began to teach them that it was necessary for the Son of Man to suffer much and be rejected by the elders and chief priests and scribes and to be killed, and after three days to rise again. He was saying this openly to them.
>
> Peter took him to one side and began to rebuke him. But Jesus turned round, looked at his disciples and rebuked Peter: 'Get behind me, Satan! You are not thinking about God's ways, but human ways.'
>
> MARK 8:27–33

Peter, perhaps the most insightful of the disciples, or maybe just the boldest, half got it. *We* heard at the beginning of the Gospel (1:1) that Jesus is the Messiah—God's agent in the world who will bring about a great rescue—yet, so far in the story, no one but the demons has grasped it. Thus, Peter's declaration that Jesus is the Messiah is a real achievement—a true insight. However, Jesus immediately seems to 'correct' it with his teaching about the suffering 'Son of Man' (which we shall explore further in Chapter 5). Then, when Peter objects, Jesus calls him Satan and declares that he is still thinking in the wrong way. Peter's insight seems to be distorted—like seeing people who look like walking trees.

It might have seemed different from Peter's point of view. If your friend has just said he is going to go to his death, surely it is natural to try to dissuade him. This is the action of a compassionate, loyal person. Peter's challenge to Jesus would have come from the best of motives. Yet there is no getting round the strength of Jesus' response: 'Get behind me, Satan!' is not the same as 'I appreciate what you are saying but the way I see it is...' Perhaps Jesus needed to speak so forcefully to get the disciples to start to engage properly with what he was saying. This teaching about his future was so important, yet so unexpected. Maybe we can identify with that as we look back at our lives and realise that we only really listen to God seriously at moments of great crisis or drama.

We can pause the story of the disciples here. In the following chapters, Jesus teaches them more about what true discipleship involves, but, in a sense, the disciples are still at the position of half sight. They have grasped something of Jesus. They have responded with commitment and loyalty. They are with him. They are his friends, even if they are not all they should be. Yet there is so much more they need to grasp.

Betrayal

We pick up the story of the disciples again in Mark 14. Jesus has taught his way to Jerusalem and spoken in words and actions about what he has found there. At the same time, the religious authorities have questioned him, resulting in rising tension (more on this in Chapter 6).

Judas Iscariot, one of the Twelve, left and went to the chief priests in order to betray him. When they heard this, they were overjoyed and promised to give him money. He started to look out for an opportunity to betray him...

The disciples set out and entered the city and found everything just as Jesus had told them, and they prepared the Passover.

When it is evening, he comes with the Twelve. As they are reclining and eating, Jesus says, 'I am telling you the truth. One of you who is eating with me will betray me.' They were upset and began to ask him one by one, 'Surely it's not me?' He replied, 'It's one of the Twelve. Someone who is dipping his bread into the bowl with me. The Son of Man goes just as it is written about him, but woe to that man who betrays the Son of Man. It would be better for him if that man had not been born.'

MARK 14:10–12, 16–21

Betrayal is a terrible thing. It is a violation. Suffering in some way at the hands of a stranger or an enemy is one thing, but betrayal by a friend adds a completely new dimension. Peter leaves us in no doubt that this was betrayal. The word for 'betray' occurs four times in this passage. We are reminded that Judas is 'one of the Twelve'. Then Jesus confirms that the betrayer is 'one of the Twelve'—not just 'one of the disciples', possibly someone on the edge of the group, but one of the core. The reference to dipping the bread only intensifies the focus. It reminds us that the Twelve are not just a chosen group of messengers or community leaders. They are 'with' Jesus; they have shared the common intimacies of a group travelling, eating and sleeping together. There is no getting round the terrible outrage that Judas commits.

But it is just him, isn't it? When a scandal hits an organisation—such as the corruption, racism or abuse claims that seem to be a common part of life today—so often the script is the same. Initially we are told that it is 'just one bad apple', a 'rogue trader'. However, all too often, over the following weeks a different story emerges. We find that the original case is actually just an example of a widespread failure.

In this passage, too, the fact that all the Twelve ask, 'Surely it's not me?' hints that the problem is more widespread. Are they all so close to the edge, wavering in their loyalty to Jesus, that each one can wonder if he might be the betrayer? They do not seem to have progressed from the 'half sight' of Mark 8; indeed, one at least is truly hard-hearted and is working with Jesus' enemies.

When they had sung, they went out to the Mount of Olives. Jesus says to them, 'You will all fall away, because it is written, "I will strike the shepherd and the sheep will be scattered", but after I rise from the dead I will go ahead of you into Galilee.' Peter said to him, 'Even if everyone else falls away, I will not!' Jesus replied, 'I tell you the truth. Today, this very night, before the cock crows twice, you will disown me three times.' Peter insisted, 'Even if I have to die for you, I will never disown you.' Everyone said the same thing.

MARK 14:26–31

'You will all fall away.' Every one of the Twelve, Jesus' chosen friends, those who left everything to follow him—every one of them will abandon him. We are perhaps so used to reading these words that we miss their impact. Jesus is saying that not a single one of his closest friends will stay by him. This is a lot worse than the disciples just misunderstanding.

Jesus and his friends go out to the Mount of Olives, where the disciples fail in their job of keeping watch as Jesus prays. Then the soldiers come and arrest Jesus. Mark tells us, 'They all deserted him and fled. A young man wearing only a tunic had been following Jesus. They grabbed him, but he slipped out of his tunic and fled naked' (Mark 14:50–52).

This snippet about the man fleeing naked has intrigued commentators over the years. It certainly seems to fit the category of eyewitness details that would have spiced up Peter's preaching, and it is noticeable that neither Matthew nor Luke bothers to record it. Indeed, since they seem to be closely following Mark in this story, we might conclude that they have deliberately left it out. Some scholars even speculate that the man might have been Mark himself and this was his moment of glory, although Papias did say that Mark didn't follow Jesus in his lifetime.

It makes a point, though. The disciples started out by abandoning their jobs and livelihood to follow Jesus. Now they are even abandoning their pants to get away from him! (Yes, it was a tunic, but the text seems at pains to tell us that the man was only wearing his tunic, so he really did leave naked.)

So is that it? The journey of the disciples has come to nothing. The promises and devotion have been proved hollow and their discipleship pointless. Perhaps. But what about Peter and his declaration that he would stay with Jesus even if it cost him his life?

Peter followed him at a distance right into the high priest's courtyard, where he sat with the servants warming himself on the fire...

While Peter was down below in the courtyard one of the high priest's servant girls comes and sees Peter warming

*himself. She stared at him and said, 'You were with the
Nazarene, Jesus.' He denied it: 'I don't know or understand
what you are talking about.' He left and went into the
gateway, and the cock crowed.*

*The servant girl noticed him again and began to say to those
who were standing around, 'This man is one of them.' Again
he denied it.*

*A little later again, those standing nearby said to Peter, 'It's
true, you are one of them. You are a Galilean!' He began to
call down curses on himself, swearing, 'I don't know the man
you are talking about.' Immediately the cock crowed a second
time. Peter remembered what Jesus had said, that before the
cock crowed twice you will disown me three times, and he broke
down in tears.*

MARK 14:66–72

At the halfway point in the Gospel, when Peter declared that
Jesus was the Messiah, it looked as if he was in the lead on
the road of discipleship. Yet it has come to this. Repeatedly, he
disowns Jesus. We use the word 'betrayed' about Judas but
the word fits Peter too. If our friends swore blind that they
didn't even know us, we would feel betrayed. Perhaps this is
too harsh, though. Peter followed when the other disciples
fled. You could argue that it would simply have been foolish
for him to throw his life away when questioned in the high
priest's courtyard. Yet that isn't how Peter tells his own story.

Are the women the heroes?

Not everyone fled—or, at least, some who weren't there
that night found Jesus rather than abandoning him. Perhaps

these were the true disciples? Immediately after his account of Jesus' death on the cross, Mark records this:

> There were also some women watching from afar. Among them was Mary Magdalene, Mary the mother of James the small and Justus, and Salome. These women had followed him in Galilee and looked after him. There were also many other women who had accompanied him to Jerusalem.
>
> It was the preparation day before the Sabbath. Therefore, when evening came, Joseph from Arimathaia, a prominent member of the council who was himself waiting for God's reign, was bold enough to go to Pilate and ask for Jesus' body. Pilate was surprised that he was already dead, summoned the centurion, and asked him if Jesus had already died. When he found out that he had, he gave him the body.
>
> Joseph bought a linen sheet. He took down the body, wrapped it in the sheet, and placed it in a tomb cut out from the rock. He then rolled a stone in front of the tomb's entrance. Mary Magdalene and Mary the mother of Justus were watching where the body was put.
>
> MARK 15:40–47

The women were still there; the women were faithful. In a way, this is perhaps not surprising. Throughout Jesus' ministry, he seemed to have a special concern for the 'weak' or the outsider, and also seemed very reluctant to confirm the traditional power structures. Of course, he chose 'the Twelve' as a special group—twelve adult men fitting contemporary ideas of status—yet it somehow isn't so surprising that they were not, in truth, his most loyal followers.

In our own lives and churches, we perhaps see the same tendency. The quiet, unobtrusive, almost unrecognised people perhaps have the strongest faith, which is revealed only when crisis hits. How often do I hear the story of someone's endurance through suffering and realise that their faith is much stronger than mine or the faith of more prominent people? If you are familiar with *The Lord of the Rings*, you might remember how the hobbits are overlooked by so many because they are small and weak, yet, without their superhuman endurance, evil would have prevailed.

So is that it? Is Peter saying that the strong, apparently important disciples fail and those seen as weaker (as women were in his society) are the faithful ones? That would be a challenging message, fitting the 'topsy-turvy' nature of the Gospel—but that isn't what Peter says.

The Gospel continues for a few more verses—though not many more, because almost all scholars agree that 16:9–20 is not part of the original manuscript (you will see the passage marked out as secondary in some way in your Bible). Without going into all the details here, the most reliable copies of Mark either don't include these verses or mark them as dubious. It seems that they were added in the century after Mark was written, drawing on the resurrection appearances in the other Gospels. Presumably this was done to make up for the fact that Mark, finishing at 16:8, didn't include any resurrection appearances. If Mark were the first Gospel written, as most scholars think, there can have been no 'rule' that a Gospel ought to finish with resurrection appearances. Yet once the other Gospels had included them, his would seem 'lacking'. Some scholars argue that Mark originally continued past 16:8 but the ending got lost. It's impossible to argue against this view, but it seems more sensible to assume that Mark intended to finish his book where it did actually finish.

So what happens? Well, the women, faithful still, go to the tomb and find it empty. Then they meet an angel:

When they entered the tomb, they were shocked to see a young man dressed in a white robe sitting on the right-hand side. He said to them, 'Don't be alarmed. You are looking for Jesus the Nazarene who was crucified. He has risen. He is not here. See the place where they put him. But go back and tell his disciples and Peter that he is going ahead of you to Galilee. You will see him there just as he told you.'

They left the tomb and ran away because they were overcome with fear and shock. They told nobody anything, because they were afraid. [THE END]

MARK 16:1–8

The women, faithful almost to the end, are told that Jesus has been raised from the dead and they are to pass on the message, but they are so frightened that they tell nobody anything. This echoes the experience of the disciples in the boat, when Jesus criticises them, saying, 'Why are you such cowards? Don't you yet have any faith?' (6:40), as well as Jesus' prediction, 'You will all fall away... the sheep will be scattered... you will disown me' (14:27–30). Peter followed Jesus into the high priest's courtyard but was overcome with fear when questioned. So, too, for the women: fear undermines them. It's an interesting reflection for our own lives, reminiscent of the American President Roosevelt's famous line, 'The only thing we have to fear is fear itself.'

I am sure it is no coincidence that Mark finishes his Gospel here, and I presume that it is because Peter finished his memoirs at this point, too. Peter invites us—almost compels us—to enter into the darkness he felt at that moment. He, and all of Jesus' followers, had failed. Nobody was capable of standing up to the pressure. The disciples' initial commitment was well-intentioned, yet in their own strength they couldn't make good on it.

Of course, all those hearing Peter's preaching, or reading the Gospel, would have known that the story didn't end there. They knew that the disciples were told about Jesus' resurrection and did meet Jesus, just as he had promised. Nevertheless, to leave the Gospel here, with the failure of the last of Jesus' followers, is far more challenging than to round it off with resurrection appearances and a sense of completion and closure. We have seen the disciples express great commitment and then move through misunderstanding and half sight to failure. We, too, who are listening to Peter or reading Mark's Gospel, have expressed great commitment, but where is our commitment going to end?

Peter knew what he was talking about. He had left everything for Jesus; he had had great spiritual experiences; he had made great assertions and promises. Yet he knew that none of it was a guarantee against complacency, failure or turning away when the pressure got too much.

Of course, in our own weakness and frailty we can take much comfort from this. If even the Twelve, who knew Jesus personally, failed, then our own weaknesses don't seem quite so bad—and, although they failed, they were restored by Jesus and went on to be heroes of faith. Jesus is more forgiving of his friends' betrayal and failure than we could ever be.

There may also be a deeper, more kindly message. Perhaps there is something natural in the story of the disciples. We always set out on a new venture with confidence. If we didn't have that confidence, we wouldn't step out in the first place. When you started reading this book, you must have had some confidence that you would enjoy it, otherwise you wouldn't have even bothered to start. The same is true when we are moving house, getting married or starting a new job. Then reality dawns, whether slowly or dramatically, and we realise that all is not necessarily going to be straightforward. It's not that our initial confidence was misplaced or insincere, or that we simply abandon it later. It's just that reality is often more grimy and messy than our hopes. Perhaps—though this is just speculation—this is why Jesus did not explain things more clearly at the beginning. Perhaps there is something important in the process of moving from initial confidence, through fear, misunderstanding and doubt, to a stronger faith. It is certainly a process that many of us recognise in our own lives.

Nevertheless, as we end this chapter we are reminded of the deal. However committed we are now, whatever 'status' or reputation we have, it is no guarantee that we will not fail in the future. But, however much we fail, our failure does not bar us from becoming true disciples once more. Peter's preaching about the disciples is disturbingly honest and challenging, but it is, in the end, a message of hope. After their failure, the disciples were told that they would meet Jesus again in Galilee, which was the place of their normal life, their workplaces and homes, as opposed to the 'special place' of Jerusalem. Today as you read this, and in the future as you remember it or read Mark's Gospel again, you can hear the same message. You can pick yourself up once more, go back to your normal life, remind yourself of your original commitment to Jesus and meet him again.

CHAPTER 3

FOLLOWING ON THE WAY

'Just 25 more miles to go!' the spectator shouts, thinking it's a clever joke. Most of the marathon runners ignore him, though a few give a half-hearted smile. They are a strange bunch, clad in anything from thin vests and shorts to gorilla outfits, mixed in with a good sprinkling of superhero costumes. Their motives are equally diverse—midlife crisis man alongside the dad running to raise money to beat the disease that took his daughter, the professional fundraiser and the young woman proving she's better off without her ex. As the race grinds on, a strange camaraderie sets in, the unspoken companionship of those who are falling in step with each other. The focus is overpowering. The goal is running the race, keeping going, reaching the end. Then the rain sweeps in.

At the heart of the Gospel, in Mark 8:27–33, Peter makes a great leap of understanding and courage, and proclaims that Jesus is the Messiah. Immediately, to his dismay, Jesus speaks of how his vocation is to include suffering. Then Jesus explains what following him involves.

He called the crowd, along with his disciples, and said, 'If anyone wants to follow behind me, they must deny themselves, pick up their cross and follow me. For whoever wants to save their life will lose it. But whoever loses their life for my sake,

and the gospel's, will save it. For it does you no good to win
the whole world, yet forfeit your life. For what can you give in
exchange for your life?

'Whoever is ashamed of me and my words in this adulterous
and sinful generation, the Son of Man will be ashamed of them
when he comes in his Father's glory, with the holy angels.'
MARK 8:34–38

Following Jesus is like walking behind him 'on the way',
on a journey. Indeed, Mark 8:27—10:52 is set 'on the way'
to Jerusalem (with many references to 'the way' or 'the
road'). The early Christians used the same word to describe
themselves ('those who belonged to the way', Acts 9:2; see
also Acts 18:25–26; 19:9, 23; 22:4; 24:14, 22).

But what sort of journey is this? Jesus' command to pick
up our cross may be familiar but we should not let it lose its
power. People who walked carrying a cross were on their way
to die, for those who were both of low status (a Roman citizen
could not be crucified) and convicted of the worst crimes (in
Roman eyes, rebellion and treason) were condemned to die
in this most horrific of fashions. It was more than just death;
it was public humiliation and shame, displaying the victim's
powerlessness to all, as they were forced to cooperate in their
own execution by walking through the streets, carrying the
cross beam on which they would die. It was designed to be
a slow process, often lasting for days, and in a public place,
normally at a site next to a major road. Jesus' words combine
the idea of 'losing your life' with the idea of 'shame'.

To compare this journey to a marathon might seem
distasteful, although I will leave it to those who have run one
to comment! But there is a similar sense of devotion to the
goal, travelling the road, endurance, the mixture of strange

companions and the range of different motives. It's perhaps not surprising that following Jesus is described in terms of a race in Acts, Paul's letters and the letter to the Hebrews (Acts 20:24; 1 Corinthians 9:24; Galatians 2:2; 5:7; 2 Timothy 4:7; Hebrews 12:1).

There is a danger, though, in picking up on the idea of travelling 'on the way' or of a race to a goal, for Mark 8:34–38 is dominated by the words 'me' and 'my', spoken by Jesus. This is not a journey in pursuit of a philosophical or religious ideal; it is not about sticking to principles or conscience, come what may. It is about following *Jesus*, losing one's life for *Jesus'* sake, being unashamed of *Jesus* and his words, and about *Jesus* returning in the Father's glory. Perhaps the image of a marriage is better: 'Do you take Jesus for better or worse, for richer or poorer, in sickness and in health, forsaking all others until death…?' Jesus' point is that death will not part him from his followers. Indeed, paradoxically, that separation will happen only if we try to avoid death.

For Peter in his preaching, and for us as we read, there is an added layer of meaning, because we know that Jesus did literally take up his cross and die by crucifixion. Given that fact, it's not surprising that Peter remembered these words of Jesus and that he and Mark gave the central place to them. If previous crucifixions had inspired Jesus' original saying, it will definitely have taken on new depths after his own death. Following Jesus 'on his way' becomes far more serious when we remember where Jesus' way took him.

The idea of following Jesus to my death is, thank God, far enough beyond my experience to mean that I have no real way of thinking myself into that situation. Although I know that my fellow disciples of Jesus in other countries do face that possibility, it is not a reality for me. Nevertheless, the idea of facing shame and difficulty, discomfort or a less comfortable life because I follow Jesus is something I can comprehend. Life is full of moments when we choose to follow or choose to avoid shame or discomfort.

The words 'Pick up the cross' can also be understood in a slightly different way, for it was not unusual for a condemned man, after being flogged, to be too weak to carry his own cross. In this case, often someone else would be pulled over to carry it, and we see exactly this happening when Jesus is crucified.

> Simon from Cyrene (the father of Alexander and Rufus) was passing by as he came in from the fields. They force him to carry his cross.
> MARK 15:21

Our calling to 'carry our cross' could be seen in this light. It means sharing in carrying Jesus' cross. It is Jesus who died for us, but we need to share in that work, publicly identifying with the crucified one, even if we do not literally share his death. Without sidestepping Jesus' words about losing our lives for his sake, this idea may help us to connect with the passage. Are we, today, prepared to share in Jesus' work of carrying his cross? Are we prepared to identify with him even as he suffered and faced humiliation and shame? Will we walk with our friend 'on the way'?

You can't choose your family

Much of Jesus' teaching about the nature of discipleship— that is, what 'following him' means—comes in the two chapters that follow this call to 'carry our cross'. As Jesus is 'on the way' to Jerusalem, he talks about what it means to be 'on the way'. It's one of those intriguing structural elements that, remembering Papias' words, might have come from Peter, or Mark, as they brought together in one place material on a similar theme.

However, the discussion of what it means to follow Jesus on the way begins in four passages from earlier in the Gospel. The first two of these involve Jesus' family.

> *Jesus' mother and his brothers come. They stood outside and sent someone in to call him. There was a crowd sitting around him, and they said to him, 'Your mother and your brothers and sisters are outside looking for you.' He replied, 'Who is my mother? My brothers?' Then he looked at the people who were sitting around him in a circle and said, 'See—my mother and my brothers. Whoever does God's will is my brother, sister and mother!'*
>
> MARK 3:31–35

This is a striking passage. In fact, the more I ponder it, the more offensive it seems. It would be all right if Jesus simply said, 'Whoever follows me is my brother or sister.' That would be a striking way of emphasising the close relationship that should mark out his followers. It would speak of the development of a close 'group identity' and of how the 'Christian community' should be a genuinely caring, supportive community. However, this is not what he said.

First, we have to take on board the context of the saying. Jesus made this statement about his followers being his brother, sister and mother in response to a request from his literal mother and brothers (and perhaps sisters) to leave his teaching for a moment and come and talk to them. I don't see how we can read his response other than as a snub to them. At the very least, he is saying that the disciples around him are as important to him as his family, but this is probably too weak an interpretation. Rather, he seems to be saying that the 'family of those who do God's will' have replaced his literal family.

This is shocking in our own age and culture, and would have been more so in the traditional society of that time. However, it is not the only occasion when Jesus apparently contrasts family bonds with our service of God. In Matthew 8:21–22, he even seems to rate following him as more important than burying a dead parent.

We need to be careful not to be sentimental here. Many of us know that 'family' is a double-edged sword. For some, it is a source of support, comfort and positive identity, but for others it is a source of obligation, which imprisons them in a straitjacket of expectations.

Second, Jesus didn't say, 'Whoever follows me...' but 'Whoever does God's will...'. He said, 'See my mother and brothers' while looking not just at the Twelve, but at all those who were sitting around him. Clearly, these were people who had responded to him; nevertheless, there is an openness in Jesus' statement. It undercuts any sense that a small group might be his 'real disciples'. These people did not need to be 'part of the group'; they needed to be doing God's will.

It is intriguing that this passage comes quite soon after Jesus chooses the Twelve; it provides an interesting contrast. Jesus chose a particular small group to be with him and to be his messengers, but at the same time he undercut the idea of a 'special group'. Membership of a group, a church, a ministry team, is not important: what matters is the way we respond to God.

> He left there and goes to his home town; his disciples follow him. When sabbath came, he began to teach in the synagogue and many who heard him were amazed, saying, 'Where does he get this from? What wisdom has he been given? What sort of power is there in his hands? Isn't this the carpenter—Mary's son, the brother of James, Justus, Judah and Simon? Aren't his sisters here with us?' And they took offence at him.
>
> Jesus said to them, 'The only place a prophet is dishonoured is in his home town, and among his relatives and in his own house.' He was not able to do any miracles there, except he put his hands on a few sick people and healed them. He was amazed at their lack of faith.
>
> MARK 6:1–6

Here it is not Jesus' immediate family that is in view, but a wider group who feel that in a sense they 'own him'. A kind response to this passage would be to acknowledge that we all find it genuinely hard to see in a new light someone whom we have known growing up. It would have been difficult for the people of Jesus' home town and his relatives to see him as anything but the local young man they had always known, just like his brothers. However, Jesus' response sounds as if it has quite an edge to it. He seems to be frustrated with them, just as he is with his disciples: they all display a lack of faith, falling short of what might be expected of them.

The marathon runner in the proper sports kit has to accept that she is being matched, pace for pace, by a large man dressed as a banana. The camaraderie of the runners has to be formed in spite of their different backgrounds, abilities, motives and many eccentric costumes. They are bound together by what they are doing, and many of those runners will have encountered surprised or even scornful reactions when they told their colleagues and family that they were going to run a marathon. The people who are closest to us tend to be the most sceptical about our ability to change.

Security

Our family and our neighbourhood are important for many of us because they give us security. This is where we are known, valued and recognised. Even if the community 'keeps us in our place' and, in some sense, limits us, it is a familiar and therefore comfortable place.

However, immediately after this last passage in which Jesus seems to distance himself from the security that might come from being in his home town, he lays out a vision of insecurity for his followers.

He calls the Twelve and began to send them out in pairs, and gave them authority over the unclean spirits. He told them to take nothing on their journey except for one staff—no bread, no bag, no money in their belts—to wear sandals, but not to take any spare clothes. He told them, 'Whenever you enter a house, stay there until you leave that place. If somewhere does not welcome you or listen to you, leave it and shake off the dust from under your feet as a sign against them.'

They went out and preached that people should repent. They drove out many demons and anointed many sick people with oil and healed them.

MARK 6:7–13

69

The disciples are not alone. Each one travels with a partner, and they have Jesus' authority, but that is all the security they are allowed. It's hard to interpret Jesus' instructions as being anything other than a deliberate move to undercut any material security they might have. They are allowed the 'tools for the job'—and for an itinerant preacher this means just a staff and sandals. They are made dependent on the people they meet, with no food or money or spare clothes; they cannot survive on their own.

This is an interesting picture of mutual dependence. Jesus' followers are bringing the message, forgiveness, release from demons and healing, but they need to let other people care for their physical needs. This interdependence would prevent the disciples from developing a 'saviour complex', exalting themselves and reducing other people to dependency on them. It's an important question for those of us who are engaged in Christian ministry: are we too proud to receive as well as to give? At the same time, we might notice that the disciples are sent out in pairs, while we often think of individuals 'having a ministry' or 'heading up' a project.

The instruction 'Whenever you enter a house, stay there until you leave that place' is intriguing. Presumably, a situation is envisaged in which two disciples enter a village and are welcomed by a poor person. Over the next few days, as they perform some miracles, suddenly the wealthy or respectable offer them welcome, but they must now refuse to 'trade up'. They should honour the person who initially welcomed them and stick with the poorer hospitality.

Shaking the dust off their feet as a sign of rejection has its background in the practice of many Jews in Jesus' day. When they re-entered the land of Israel from Gentile territory, they shook off the 'unclean' dust of Gentile lands so that it did not pollute the holy land. The polluting dust of the world was removed: now they were in God's land. Jesus' instructions here, therefore, are shocking. He is telling his disciples to act out a public declaration that towns that do not accept his messengers are no longer part of God's holy land. The sense of judgement is brought out more clearly in the parallel passage in Matthew 10:14–15, and we could also connect the sending out in pairs with the fact that Deuteronomy 19:15 requires at least two witnesses to establish guilt. The boundaries of God's land are being redrawn on the basis of whether or not the people accept Jesus' messengers. When the Twelve were called, Jesus was effectively reforming the people of Israel; now we see that the land of Israel is also being redrawn.

These instructions give a nuanced view of security and status. On the one hand, the disciples are to embrace risk and leave behind any security, going a step further from their original decision to follow Jesus, when they 'left behind' their former lives (Mark 1:16–20). Now they even have to avoid some of the options for security or physical comfort that a wandering holy man might have. Although the shaking of dust from the feet is a powerful symbol, it is only a symbol. The followers are not allowed to 'hit back' in any sense at the places that reject them. They just move on, leaving the situation to God.

On the other hand, they have huge security and status as a result of being Jesus' messengers. Their message is effectively the same as his. 'Proclaiming repentance' presumably should be seen as shorthand for Jesus' message that 'the time is fulfilled, and God's reign is near; repent and believe the good news' (Mark 1:15). Their activity of casting out demons and healing the sick matches his (1:32–34; 3:9–11). They are his apostles ('sent ones', 3:14), carrying his authority. They will be provided for; God will work miracles through them.

This radical reorientation is in keeping with what we see of Jesus himself. He receives the assurance that he is God's favoured Son before he begins his ministry, yet he immediately faces physical danger and deprivation (1:9–13). Jesus himself has become a wandering holy man, with no supportive base in his home town, yet God is obviously with him.

The physical situation may be different for us—few of us are called to an itinerant ministry—yet the challenge remains for us to embrace the same radical reorientation, to see our security and status coming from God and not from our physical situation.

Be bold

It is not just the Twelve who are following Jesus on the way. We have already heard of the crowds around him, whom he calls his new family. Now, we come to one of the most striking passages in the Gospels, when a Gentile (non-Jewish) woman argues with Jesus and appears to win.

> *Jesus left there and went to the region of Tyre, where he entered a house. He wanted nobody to know, but he couldn't escape notice. Immediately a woman who had heard about him and had a daughter with an unclean spirit came and fell down at his feet. She was a Greek—a Syro-Phoenician by birth. She asked him to drive the demon out of her daughter.*
>
> *He said to her, 'Let the children get their fill first. It's not right to take the children's bread and throw it for the dogs.' She*

replied, 'Sir, even the dogs under the table eat the children's crumbs.' He said to her, 'Because of what you have said, go home; the demon has left your daughter.' She went home and found the child thrown on the bed and the demon gone.

MARK 7:24–30

It's a sure sign that a passage is disturbing when much scholarly effort is expended on trying to make it not say what it says! There has certainly been much ink spilt in trying to make Jesus' response to the woman seem less rude. For example, the suggestion has been made that the word 'dog' here really means 'a favourite household pet'. (Of course, this isn't a great improvement: it might make Jesus seem less rude, but it sounds hugely patronising.) Sadly, though, there is no justification for this interpretation, and we should stick with the words we have.

Jesus' reply to the woman seems to match the overall shape of his ministry. His focus is the people of Israel, initially in Galilee and then in Jerusalem. He rarely goes into Gentile lands, and, whenever he does, it seems to be an attempt to retreat from ministry for a time, rather than to engage in ministry there. In Mark, it happens only three times—here in chapter 7, where he tries to hide; in Mark 5, where he briefly goes to the other side of the Sea of Galilee and is approached by a man rather than deliberately engaging in any teaching or ministry; and in Mark 8:27, which sounds like a private trip for the disciples. He does seem to believe that his message is for the 'children of Israel'.

This nameless woman, though, is going to argue. She doesn't take offence at what Jesus says, but she is simply not going to accept it. Her retort is an inspiring combination of humility and boldness. She reminds me of some of the great non-violent protesters of the last century, such as Mohandas Gandhi and Martin Luther King—humble, yet demanding a response. Within the Bible she stands in the tradition of Jacob who 'wrestled with God' (Genesis 32:24–31). In that story, Jacob met with God, physically wrestled with him and would not let him go until God had blessed him. This woman, in her own way, imitates Jacob, who was the 'father of Israel', the man whose sons' descendants formed the twelve tribes. Her example is important in our understanding of what the 'renewed Israel' means—the people following Jesus on the way.

This women seems to have understood more about God than the disciples ever did. They are often fearful and don't understand. She is bold, and seems to have grasped that Jesus is generous and merciful, so that the benefits of his mission will overflow even to people like her. There is going to be so much food on the children's table that the crumbs will cascade down, just as, after the feeding of the 5000, the leftovers themselves could have formed a feast.

We easily assume that the 'true disciple' must be submissive, never questioning God, but this woman challenges that supposition. God, it seems, doesn't mind if we question and wrestle with him. 'Talking back' to God is not bad; humility coupled with boldness is good.

Status

We pick up the narrative now after the revelation on the road to Caesarea Philippi, when Jesus begins to teach clearly that he is on a road marked by suffering and that his followers are to pick up their cross, too. Here we find a fascinating set of stories, loosely linked by the idea of status among those 'following on the way'. The context—just after Jesus has been recognised as the Messiah—is not a coincidence. If Jesus is the Messiah and is bringing in God's reign, presumably his closest followers are going to hold important positions in the new post-revolution world. In any government, business or church, the close followers of the leader might be expected to exercise considerable power. Who is it who 'has the ear' of the leader?

> He went into Capernaum, and in the house he asked them, 'What were you discussing on the way?' They were silent, because on the way they had been discussing with each other who was the greatest. He sat down and called the Twelve and says to them, 'If someone wants to be first, he will be last and servant of all.' He took a child and stood it in their midst, wrapped his arms around him and said to them, 'Whoever welcomes one of these little children in my name welcomes me. Whoever welcomes, does not welcome me but the one who sent me.'
>
> MARK 9:33–37

Notice that it is the Twelve who are having this argument. Those who are closest to Jesus might well feel that they have the best claim to positions of power, but the argument demonstrates that they have not yet understood Jesus' rebuke to Peter (8:33), that he was thinking in earthly ways. The same can easily be observed in our world, where those with most status and power can seem most obsessed with gaining more. This is not how it should be among those 'following on the way'.

Presumably we should take Jesus' words in verse 37 literally and place great importance on welcoming children in his name. In welcoming them, we are welcoming Jesus and God himself. This idea draws on the Jewish tradition of welcoming strangers because they might be God himself, or angels (exemplified in the story of Abraham in Genesis 18; see also Hebrews 13:2). However, Jesus' words are developing the tradition further: God may well be present to us in the weak, not just in the unknown.

There is even more to notice here. Jesus seems to bring the child forward as an example about greatness, not just to make a point about children. Jesus' disciples were given the role of acting as his representatives as they took forward his mission in chapter 6. Those who welcomed them were, in a sense, welcoming Jesus. Now we find that a child has the same status: welcoming the child means welcoming Jesus. Maybe the disciples are not quite as important as they think.

The example of the child is so well known to us that it can lose its force. Furthermore, our culture today tends to have a very high regard for children ('they are our future'). However, in the days of high infant mortality, this was often not the case; sadly, but perhaps understandably, there was less concern for children and less investment in them, either financially or emotionally, when there was a real possibility that they would die before reaching adulthood. Therefore, the little child really did represent the unimportant ones in society, who were expected just to take what they were given.

Despite the great importance that parents place on their own children today, examples of the same attitude can easily be found, whether in public policy or church life. After all, children don't vote and are not given places on the church council. They are half-honoured as the citizens or church of tomorrow, but they are not recognised as equal citizens or members today. It's easy to think of the minister or our leaders 'bringing Christ to us' (and therefore being important) and of the very young, the old, the sick and the mentally ill as people we look after, who are therefore 'less' than us. Clearly, though, status works differently 'on the way'; Christ often speaks 'from the margins' and is present in the marginalised.

> John said to him, 'Teacher, we saw someone casting out demons in your name. We stopped him because he was not following us.' Jesus replied, 'Don't stop him. For nobody who does a miracle in my name can slander me the next moment. Whoever is not against us is with us.'
>
> MARK 9:38–40

The disciples' response to the man driving out demons in Jesus' name is revealing. Demons are a bad thing, so presumably the disciples would have been celebrating to see a demon cast out—especially if it was done in Jesus' name, spreading Jesus' reputation rather than acting in competition to him. But the disciples' reaction is the opposite: they stop the man. Why? Because he is not part of *their* group. They are more concerned about the structures through which the work is being done than the work itself. We will see a similar concern later, when the religious authorities oppose Jesus because he is offering God's presence and forgiveness outside the temple system. Of course, in both cases, the issue is not a disinterested concern about structures; the people concerned are annoyed that what is happening means *they* are no longer the key agents through whom God is working.

Sadly, this pattern can be observed time and time again in

churches. The pastor is disturbed because a group is getting together to study the Bible without his involvement. The Sunday school teachers are frustrated because the children are more interested in playing football with the couple new to the church, who organise a kick-around. The vicar is annoyed by the new, 'more lively' church setting up down the road. People don't support the new community initiative helping older folks and young mums because it is not organised by the church. It can also be true in our families and workplaces. Can we celebrate the good, even if it is bypassing us?

> 'I tell you the truth. Whoever gives you a drink of water in my name because you are the Messiah's will never lose his reward. Whoever causes one of these little ones who believe in me to sin—it would be better for him if a large millstone were tied round his neck and he were thrown into the sea.'
> MARK 9:41–42

Jesus' answer in 9:39 has a dark side, with its reference to people 'slandering' him. The same tone continues here with the notion of rewards and judgement: there will be a reckoning. This rounds off the series of sayings and is very relevant to our discussion of status. The disciples are the Messiah's messengers (and God will reward those who help them), just as those who welcome children are actually welcoming Jesus and, therefore, God. Even if the disciples need to learn that they are only part of God's work and do not define or control it, they are still important and God will care for them. God is also on the side of the 'little ones who believe in me': people will answer for the way they treat them. The obvious way of interpreting this saying is to connect it to the previous verses. In verse 37 we read that welcoming a child is like welcoming God. Now we see the reverse: harm a child and you will answer to God. The phrase 'who believe in me', though, raises the possibility that 'the little ones' is actually (or also) referring to the weak in the Christian community. We will answer to God for the way we treat the weak.

Overall, this series of passages undermines conventional ideas of status. The greatest are the weak, the children, the marginalised. God is 'with them', so welcoming them means welcoming God, and we will answer to God if we harm them. Those 'following on the way' are precious to God and God is on their side. However, they need to resist the temptations of status, recognising that they are only sharing in part of God's work—it isn't theirs to control—and that God's orientation is always to the weak.

True greatness

A chapter later, the argument about greatness re-emerges.

They were on the way up to Jerusalem. Jesus was leading at the front. They were amazed and those following were afraid. Again he took the Twelve aside and began to tell them what would happen to him. 'Look, we are going up to Jerusalem. The Son of Man will be handed over to the chief priests and the scribes. They will condemn him to death and hand him over to the Gentiles. They will mock him and spit on him. They will flog him and kill him, yet three days later he will rise again.'
MARK 10:32–34

Jesus and his followers are now approaching Jerusalem. This prospect seems to be looming large over those 'following in the way'. What will happen when they get there? Revolution? Jesus as God's agent arriving at God's city? We will explore some of these issues further in Chapter 8. For now, though, we can note that revolution involves both danger and the promise of greatness for the victors (presumably).

Jesus, however, paints a different picture. He is willingly going to Jerusalem. Indeed, going there is his choice. Yet he is clear that 'the Son of Man' (a phrase that he keeps using to refer to himself) is going to die there. No wonder the disciples are 'amazed'. This does not sound like the right outcome for the revolution.

> *James and John the sons of Zebedee went up to him and asked, 'Teacher, we want you to do for us whatever we ask you.' He replied, 'What do you want me to do for you?' 'Give us the right to sit one on your right hand and one on your left in your glory,' they said. Jesus told them, 'You don't know what you are asking for. Can you drink the cup which I am going to drink? Or be baptised with the baptism I am going to be baptised with?' They said, 'We can.' Jesus replied, 'The cup which I will drink, you will drink. The baptism with which I will be baptised, you will be baptised. But to sit at my right and my left is not for me to grant—it is for those for whom it has been prepared.'*
>
> MARK 10:35–40

James and John are not put off by Jesus' warnings. Perhaps they choose to ignore his words about the Son of Man: all of us have a surprising ability not to hear what we don't want to hear. They are still thinking about the positions of importance that they expect to receive when Jesus' revolution bears fruit and God's reign arrives. When God rules, who will be his chief ministers?

Their request is particularly manipulative, playing on their closeness to Jesus (after Peter, they were his closest disciples: see 1:16–20; 3:16–17; 5:37; 9:2; 14:33) to get an open-ended promise. Jesus' response is interesting. First, he responds kindly to their 'request', asking them to spell out what they want (just as he does to many who come to him needing healing: for example, 10:51) rather than rebuking their arrogance. Even when their true desire emerges (v. 37), he responds kindly ('You don't know what you are asking for'), seeing, perhaps, the good intentions underneath their ambition.

Whatever their motives, they do have loyalty to Jesus—a willingness to drink his cup and undergo his baptism. (Drinking a cup is a metaphor for destiny, either good or bad: see, for example, Psalm 75:8; Isaiah 51:22; Jeremiah 25:17–18. Baptism means literally 'dipping', as in the submerging of cloth in a tank of dye.)

There is an irony here as well, which will be explored in Chapter 9, for Jesus' 'true glory' will be the very death that he has just spoken about. (This connection is brought out more clearly in John's Gospel, where Jesus is said to be 'glorified' in his death: for example, in John 12:23–24.) There will be people on his left and his right when he dies—but those people will not be James and John because by then they will have abandoned him.

Notice also how, within this controversy about greatness, Jesus avoids slipping into exaggerating his position, stating firmly the limits of his own power (v. 40). How easy it is for leaders to play along with flattery by claiming more influence than they have ('I'll fix it for you')! Jesus and those following on the way all have their place. Loyalty and kindness are important, but so is humility.

> *When the other ten heard, they started to get angry with James and John. Jesus called them all over and says, 'You know that among the Gentiles those who are recognised as rulers lord it over them, and their "great ones" are dictators over them. It is not like this among you. Rather, the one who wishes to be great among you will be your servant. And whoever among you wishes to be first will be slave of all. For the Son of Man did not come to be served but to serve, and to give his life as a ransom for many.'*
>
> MARK 10:41–45

The other ten disciples were not as kind or as understanding as Jesus was. Indeed, the fact that Jesus now makes the point rather more forcefully suggests that they were annoyed with James and John for getting in first, not because they were above such desires themselves.

Jesus' teaching points to the dynamic between rulers and ruled—the dynamic underlying James and John's request. The rulers are those 'recognised' by the ruled, and the rulers then 'lord it over them'.

Rulers are kept in power by those who believe they will receive rewards for their support. This complicity can be seen at a national level, whether the country is a democracy (do members of parliament really share their party leader's views or do they act loyally because loyalty is rewarded?) or a dictatorship (the dictator ensures that it is in his supporters' interests to keep him in power, despite his negative impact on the country as a whole).

It can also be seen within churches, gangs, school cliques and workplaces. The most popular girl in the class has that status only because of the adulation of a wider group; the group members offer that adulation because they gain status from being one of her friends—unlike the others. Both sides are part of the one dynamic. It's commonplace in churches for a minister to deliver what the congregation wants, and for the congregation in return to praise the minister. All is cosy as minister and congregation focus inwards, turning their back on those 'outside'.

Jesus cuts through this dynamic, for, if the 'great' take the role of the servant, what advantage is there in being one of their supporters? There are no positions in glory to be handed out. Sadly, we soon see that once Jesus has adopted the place of a servant—a slave on his way to death—meaning that there is no longer any benefit in being a loyal supporter, his followers fall away. The leader has lost the ability to cultivate his supporters. Nevertheless, it is also at this point that he finds there is no *need* to do so. The cycle of collusion is broken. Both ruler and ruled, leader and follower, are set free. And these are not just empty words. Jesus will not be the servant of 'a few'—his loyal supporters, like James and John. He will be the servant, the slave—indeed, the ransom—of 'many'. If that is true of Jesus, what does it mean for us who are 'following on the way'?

The future

The story moves on. Jesus and his followers do enter Jerusalem. There is celebration but also opposition. The situation is tense. I will discuss the shape of the emerging conflict further in Chapter 6, but for now we pick up one passage within Mark 13 in which Jesus seems to speak directly about the future of those following him on the way.

> *'Watch yourselves! They will hand you over to councils. You will be beaten in synagogues. You will be put in front of kings and rulers for my sake to witness to them. Even to all the nations, the good news must first be preached.*
>
> *'Whenever you are handed over and brought to trial, don't worry in advance about what you will say. But rather, whatever is given to you at that moment, that's what you should say. For it won't be you who is speaking, but the Holy Spirit.*
>
> *'Brother will betray brother to death, and father child. Children will rebel against their parents and have them put to death. You will be hated by everyone because of my name. But whoever endures to the end will be saved.'*
>
> MARK 13:9–13

Of all the material about discipleship, this is perhaps the starkest. It is not framed as 'teaching about discipleship' but, rather, is a prediction of what *will* happen to those following Jesus 'on the way'. You could argue that these words were addressed only to Peter, James, John and Andrew, who are mentioned in 13:3, although the overall tone of this chapter suggests that Jesus is speaking more generally.

Twice in this short passage, Jesus says that the difficulties will arise specifically because they are his followers—'for my sake', 'because of my name'. Their loyalty to him will become a dividing line, leading directly to hatred from others. That loyalty will challenge all other human commitments, even the commitment within families. Fortunately, the betrayal of family members to death is rare (although, sadly, it is not unknown in the history of those following in Jesus' way), but these words certainly make the point clear that, in the end, we can only have one ultimate allegiance. Loyalty to Jesus will call into question all other claims upon us, whether from rulers, culture or family, and this will result in hardship, requiring endurance.

Perhaps my opening comparison with the marathon runners seems slightly bizarre, but it is true that no one finishes a marathon if they are not absolutely focused on running the race. Their reasons for starting may all be about helping other people, and their hopes for its outcome may be to do with the wider community, but while they are running, there is hardship requiring endurance.

There are, however, three elements of comfort within this passage from Mark 13. First, and most simply, the disciples are told that they will face these trials, and hence that they will remain Jesus' disciples. Despite their failures, they will testify to the world about Jesus. This acts as another quiet yet positive prediction of the way the story will work out. Not only will God act to resurrect Jesus (8:31; 9:31; 10:34) and not only will God bring about his reign (9:1), but the disciples will also, in the end, remain loyal. This is particularly important since, as we have already seen, by the end of the Gospel everyone seems to have fallen away.

Second, there is the promise that a positive outcome is assured: 'whoever endures to the end will be saved'. This is the equivalent of a running coach's advice to just keep putting one foot in front of the other, or the bystanders' cry, 'Just keep going!' It might not sound wonderfully hopeful for either the runner or the one following Jesus on the way, but, when the rain lashes down and the way ahead seems impossible, the message that 'you will succeed if you just keep going' is indeed reassuring.

Third, there is the promise of God's presence in the trials. Those following Jesus on the way simply need to be loyal and endure. They do not need to be eloquent, competent or skilful; they just have to be committed. This takes us back to the original calling of Peter, Andrew, James and John, where they did indeed demonstrate commitment. It reminds us of Mary, when faced with the daunting prospect of what would happen to her if she accepted what God was proposing (Luke 1:26–38): 'she was greatly troubled... "How can this happen?"... "Nothing is impossible for God"... "May it happen to me as you have said."' She couldn't understand, and yet she said yes.

Someone understands

In much of Mark's Gospel, the teaching about 'following on the way' seems to be conveyed by means of correction. Inappropriate attitudes emerge and Jesus corrects them. A polite way of putting it would be that the disciples were learning by their mistakes. In our own lives, we all know that this is an important—if slightly depressing—way in which to learn. However, just before Jesus is betrayed, as the opposition to him becomes more focused and deadly, we have a wonderful scene of someone who did 'get it'.

While he was in Simon the leper's house in Bethany, reclining at the table, a woman came in bringing an alabaster jar of extremely expensive perfume made of pure nard. She broke the jar and poured it out over his head.

Some were annoyed and said to themselves, 'Why waste this perfume! This perfume could have been sold for more than a year's wages, and given to the poor.' They rebuked her harshly. But Jesus said, 'Leave her alone. Why are you causing trouble for her? She has done a beautiful thing for me. You will always have the poor with you. Whenever you want, you can do something good for them. You do not always have me. She has done what she could. She has taken the chance to anoint my body in advance for my burial. I tell you the truth. Wherever in the whole world the good news is preached, what she has done will be told in memory of her.'

MARK 14:3–9

Was this woman's action a pointless waste? Many of those following Jesus 'on the way' clearly thought so. The perfume could have been put to good use—being sold and thus providing money to support the poor. What place does extravagant luxury have in God's service?

The grumbling made sense if the purpose of Jesus' mission was to encourage good deeds, such as giving to the poor, or if he had come only to get people to follow 'God's rules' more faithfully. It is natural and understandable to assume that this was Jesus' mission—that he was a messenger from God, come to encourage people to be good. However, if we look back, we see that this wasn't Jesus' agenda. He called people to 'follow *me*'. As we will see in the next chapter, his attitude to the Jewish laws appears rather mixed. His words and actions seem often to focus on himself as God's agent or even God's presence, around which God's purposes revolve and God's people are formed. We are following *Jesus* 'on the way', not merely seeking to follow God.

The unnamed woman understood this. What she did here was an act of pure devotion. Indeed, it was a display of love. Is it a waste to buy an expensive engagement ring or splash out on a silver wedding anniversary present? Most of us would say not. There is more to life than pure logic and dry rationality. Love and relationships, in the broadest sense, are what make life worth living. Of course there is a balance to be struck—spending a fortune on an expensive present and leaving no money to buy food is just silly—but expressing love and devotion in concrete ways is a valuable and natural act. It is a mistake to think that the woman knew she was anointing Jesus in advance for his burial, or even that Jesus was defending her because he knew it: that was an unforeseen consequence. Her gift had value simply as an act of devotion.

It is tempting to see this story as a different telling of the incident reported in Luke 7:36–50, where a 'sinful woman' anointed Jesus' feet with ointment and her own tears, and dried them with her hair. In their details and settings, the stories are quite distinct. Nevertheless, Luke's story makes explicit what is surely implicit here—both women loved Jesus. Theirs were not calculated actions, worked out beforehand to produce the best response; they were the result of overflowing love. The woman at Bethany wanted to give the most precious thing she had to him—not to his cause, not to his agenda, but to him.

There is almost the implication that this was the last straw for Judas, for, immediately after this incident, he offered to betray Jesus (14:10). In less dramatic terms, this passage, or at least its teaching, is the last straw for many, for it demonstrates the idea that has recurred in the last few passages we have considered. Discipleship is not primarily about following good teaching or even being part of the implementation of a just society; it is about commitment, loyalty and devotion to Jesus.

Betrayed

Commitment, loyalty and devotion to Jesus are in short supply in the last scene we will consider in this chapter. Jesus has had his final meal with his friends and, after singing a hymn, they head out into an olive grove on the hillside overlooking the city. It is Passover, so it's a full moon and a night full of wonder and joy—the whole city celebrating how God rescued his people in the past. (Perhaps the closest parallel for us would be Christmas Eve.) Yet Jesus seems to be in a different place: he is filled not with joy but with grief.

They go to a place called Gethsemane and Jesus says to his disciples, 'Sit here while I pray.' He takes Peter and James and John with him and he began to be troubled and distressed. He says to them, 'My soul is so overwhelmed with grief, I could die. Remain here and keep watch.'

Going a little further, he fell to the ground and was praying that, if it were possible, the hour would pass from him. 'Abba, Father, everything is possible for you. Take this cup away from me. But not what I want, but what you want.'

He comes and finds them asleep. He says to Peter, 'Simon, you're asleep! Aren't you able to watch for one hour? Keep watch and pray that you will not come to the point of testing. The spirit is eager, but the flesh is weak.'

Again he left them and was praying, saying the same thing.

Again he came back and found them asleep because their eyes were heavy. They didn't know what to say.

He comes a third time and says to them, 'Are you still sleeping and resting? Enough! The hour has come. See, the Son of Man is betrayed into the hands of sinners. Get up. Let's go. Look, my betrayer has arrived.'

At that moment, while he was still speaking, Judas, one of the Twelve, appeared. With him was a crowd armed with swords and clubs from the chief priests, scribes and elders. Now his betrayer had given them a sign saying, 'Whoever I kiss, that's him. Seize him and take him away securely.' Straight away he comes, and goes up to him and says, 'Teacher!' and he kissed him. They grabbed him and arrested him.

One of those who were standing there drew his sword and struck the high priest's servant, cutting off his ear. But Jesus said to them, 'Why have you come out to arrest me with swords and clubs as if I were a terrorist? Every day I am with you in the temple teaching, and you didn't arrest me. But the scriptures must be fulfilled.' Everyone abandoned him and fled.

MARK 14:32–50

This passage is marked by contrasts. First we can look at the disciples. They were called to 'be with him' (Mark 3:14), yet even this proved too much at the moment of his arrest: 'Everyone abandoned him and fled.' Once, they abandoned their fishing nets and followed him; now it is him they are abandoning. The true measure of their discipleship seems to be demonstrated here: despite all the shared experience, all that they have seen, it proves to be paper-thin.

The scene of Jesus' prayer in Gethsemane seems particularly poignant. Again, all that was asked of Jesus' closest three disciples was that they 'keep watch'. We probably have sympathy with the idea of fleeing in the face of an armed mob, but at least they could have stayed awake when Jesus was in distress, asking simply for some companionship, some solidarity, from this 'inner core'.

I wonder what the closest comparison is for us today. It

is not so easy for us to connect with the idea of the earthly Jesus needing basic human comfort and companionship—but perhaps that is where we are wrong. Perhaps the initial calling of the disciples to be with him is one that we ought to take more seriously. A key aspect of true discipleship, of following Jesus on the way, is being together with him—simple companionship.

Here we can look back again at the unnamed woman in the previous passage, to see the contrast more fully drawn. She understood. She recognised Jesus' need for some simple kindness, for intimacy, for human comfort, and she gave it. She understood that following Jesus on the way is personal. It's not just a matter of common goals, obedience or faith; it's about the connection of two people.

When someone is grieving, which is actually the way Jesus is described here, we all know the accepted wisdom. We might feel we don't know what to say, but that isn't the point. What matters is 'just being there'. Sometimes, even if there is nothing to say, the presence of another human being, the sense that someone is with you, is a great comfort. Jesus looked for a sense of solidarity, or companionship, from his disciples, but found them sleeping.

The next contrast is between Jesus and his disciples. He is facing a trial, just as they are. His words, 'Take this cup away from me', testify that the burden of his situation is bearing down on him. They might be worried about the authorities, but so is he. The difference is that he remains committed to God's will—a commitment shown in his words, 'Not what I want, but what you want', and in his actions, not running away but facing Judas head on. The 'point of testing' does come, and his disciples fail, while he succeeds.

Here we see the good and the bad examples—and we can

learn from both. In the last chapter, we explored how we can learn from the failings of the twelve disciples. As we watched them misunderstand, we gained understanding. Indeed, we have seen in this chapter that James and John's requests for the best seats in God's kingdom led in to some useful teaching. Now, though, we also see a good example—that of Jesus himself. We have a model to follow. This idea might seem a bit contorted: how can Jesus himself be a model for following Jesus? But later reflection, in the letter to the Hebrews, talks of running the race marked out for us with our eyes fixed on Jesus, the beginner and completer of our faith, who has gone ahead of us and who, through suffering, reached perfection, providing a model for our endurance (Hebrews 4:14; 5:7–9; 12:1–3).

Mark 14:32–50 is surrounded by the particular story of Peter. Before the scene in Gethsemane, he asserted, 'Even though all become deserters, I will not' (14:29–30). Afterwards we see that he did indeed show some extra loyalty, because he followed Jesus into the high priest's courtyard, an act that did require courage (v. 54), only to abandon him when questioned by a servant-girl (vv. 66–72). Peter's story dramatises and personalises the general account and makes clear that not only did the disciples in general abandon Jesus, but even the most committed reached the same point. In the end, the differences between them shrink into meaninglessness in the face of the challenge.

The contrast with Jesus could not be clearer. It is not that he is immune to the fear and anxiety; rather, he is willing to follow his calling. 'The Son of Man is betrayed into the hands of sinners' (v. 41) describes the fate he has known about for some time (8:31; 9:31; 10:33), and yet he has continued, for this 'handing over' is the way in which God's redemptive purposes will be fulfilled (see 10:45). Jesus 'endures to the end' (13:13) and is willing to 'lose his life' (8:34–35), a model that his friends refuse to follow.

As we saw in the previous chapter, Mark's Gospel has given enough hints that the disciples will succeed in the end. Jesus himself has said that they will testify in front of kings and rulers, inspired in their words by God's Spirit. Yet Mark leaves us with this negative—or, at least, very challenging— view of discipleship.

Perhaps it speaks to us in our most needy times. Perhaps, like the coach preparing the marathon runners, Peter in his preaching focused on the most difficult times. The coach does not tell his runners how to cope with the first 100 metres. Equally, he doesn't focus their mind on how to endure the last 100. He prepares them for that moment at the 18-mile point when the rain sweeps in. He prepares them for, in Jesus' words, 'the point of testing'. But it is not all pain and endurance. Those on the way have their security in God. They can be bold as well as humble, and they are valued most of all for their companionship.

CHAPTER 4

MIRACLES

The doctor seethes inside when another patient tells him that the surgery is a miracle. 'No, it's just good science,' he wants to shout. The businessman whose turnaround of the company, saving 50 jobs, is described as 'nothing short of miraculous' is less modest. He enjoys the adulation, knowing full well that, when economic downturn comes, all talk of miracles will evaporate. 'If God showed me a miracle, then I'd believe,' explains the shopper to the vicar as she casually throws into her basket ready-chopped mangos, at midnight on Friday night in an English industrial town in January.

We use the word 'miracle' in so many different ways. The businessman is right, of course: a miracle is not just an unexpected, powerful event; it has to be a good thing. A surprising new contract that saves jobs might be a miracle; the surprising loss of one is called something quite different. The doctor and the shopper are united in their reluctance to see miracles—it's just science and the modern capitalist economy—and they are right, of course. Aren't they?

Mark's Gospel is full of what we might call miracles. As well as teaching, Jesus does things—and what he does is surprising, beyond the normal, and good. This has led, particularly in the past two centuries, to no end of arguments. One side tries to 'rationalise' the miracles, explaining that the healings were 'all in the mind', the 5000 were fed by people inspired to share their packed lunches, and Jesus was actually walking not on the water but on a sandbank. Others will argue that the miracles demonstrate that Jesus must be God—because who else can do miracles? (overlooking that there were people like Moses and Elijah and others through whom God worked).

If we are to get to grips with Peter's preaching, we need to examine the miracles. But we should do so with an open mind, not bringing in our own assumptions about what 'miracles' are or what is their purpose. We live in a different age from the time when Peter was preaching, and the differences are most pronounced in the way we understand the world around us. Peter might recognise much about my relationship as a father with my boys, but the computer on which I am writing this book would leave him perplexed. Nevertheless, Peter's preaching has stood the test of time, so let's examine the 'miracles' that Peter recounts and ponder what meaning they might have.

Miraculous words and actions

In Mark's Gospel, Jesus begins his ministry by entering Galilee, proclaiming that 'God's reign is near' (Mark 1:15). Two stories follow, in which Peter features and which must have made a huge impact upon him. It's perhaps not surprising that they had an important place in his preaching. The first is the calling of Peter, Andrew, James and John at the lakeside. We examined this story in Chapter 2, as the starting point of the theme of the disciples and following on the way.

The second passage describes a dramatic sabbath day in

Capernaum when Jesus taught in the synagogue, healed Peter's wife's mother, and performed many more healings and exorcisms.

They go into Capernaum. On the sabbath, he went into the synagogue and immediately began to teach. They were shocked at his teaching, because he didn't teach like the scribes; he taught as if he had authority.

Straight away a man in the grip of an evil spirit appeared in the synagogue and shouted out, 'What do you want with us, Jesus the Nazarene? Have you come to destroy us? I know who you are—God's Holy One.' Jesus rebuked him: 'Shut up, and get out from him.' The evil spirit threw him into a fit, gave a great scream and left him.

Everyone was so amazed that they started asking each other, 'What is this? A new teaching with authority, and he commands the evil spirits and they obey him!' News about him immediately spread everywhere into the whole of the surrounding area of Galilee.

Immediately they left the synagogue and went into Simon and Andrew's house, with James and John. Now Simon's mother-in-law had a fever and was lying down. Straight away they speak to him about her. He went to her, took hold of her arm, and lifted her up. The fever left her, and she started to look after them.

That evening, when the sun had set, they brought to him everyone who was ill or troubled by demons. The whole town was gathered at the door. He healed many who had all sorts of diseases, and cast out many demons. He wouldn't let the demons speak because they knew who he was.

MARK 1:21–34

The teaching, the healing and the casting out of demons are all part of the one activity: this is what it means for God's reign to come near. It's interesting to note that it was the teaching and the casting out of the evil spirit that caused such amazement and led the people to ask who Jesus was. The healings—which, to us, seem like real miracles—apparently provoked less response.

There are many details in this passage that would repay further thought. Notice that it was Simon Peter's mother-in-law who was healed first, and then many in Simon's home town. His decision to follow Jesus with devotion and dedication might appear to have been at the expense of his previous life and his family. Yet, paradoxically, it actually brought good to those around him, and benefited his family and neighbours. The idea that the poor woman immediately waited on them sounds rather harsh to our ears. However, we should probably see it as the 'proof of success', a sign of the person's re-entry into normal society, that we find after almost all of Jesus' healings. You can imagine Peter exclaiming, 'One minute she was laid out with fever, the next she was cooking fish stew!'

The casting out of the evil spirit in the synagogue, then more demons in front of Peter's house, raises many questions, some of which will be considered when we look at the source of Jesus' power. His refusal to let them speak is intriguing and will be discussed in the next chapter of this book, since it touches on the question, 'Who is Jesus?' For now, though, we can note that perhaps demons are not worthy to reveal Jesus' identity. Can we go one step further and suggest that, perhaps, powerful miracles do not reveal Jesus' true nature?

Jesus' teaching was shocking. Indeed, it appears to have

shocked the people almost as much as did the casting out of the evil spirit. It was presented 'with authority', unlike the scribes' teaching. Presumably this says something about his style—perhaps because he gave his own opinions. Scholars believe that, in contrast, the scribes simply articulated what previous authorities had said (see Mark 7:5), although the evidence is patchy.

This passage introduces many of the themes that will continue throughout Peter's preaching. In relation to the theme of miracles, we can start by noting that Jesus' actions were seen as shocking, surprising and good. This isn't a bad definition of a miracle. However, it is just as true of his teaching as of the healings. Furthermore, although it is mentioned that the healings took place on the sabbath, which became an issue later (see Mark 3:1–6), here there is no suggestion that it was a problem. Jesus' activity was simply good news. His words and actions were shocking, surprising and good—a miracle in the wider sense of the word, and a reminder to us today that we are called to bring good news in words and actions.

In league with the devil?

Jesus continued to have this 'miraculous ministry'—surprising the people and bringing good news in his teaching, in his healing and in his victory over the evil spirits. However, from Mark 2 onwards we start to hear of grumbling and opposition. Not everyone welcomed Jesus, but no one could deny that he was performing amazing deeds: presumably there was incontrovertible evidence in front of their eyes. The challenge came in the question 'Is what's happening good?' The onlookers would have called it a miracle only if it had been a good thing, from God, not just something amazing or surprising.

> *Some scribes from Jerusalem were coming down saying,*
> *'He is possessed by Beelzeboul. He is casting demons out by*
> *the power of the ruler of the demons.' He would call them*
> *together and speak to them in parables: 'How can Satan*
> *drive out Satan? If a kingdom is divided against itself, that*
> *kingdom cannot stand. If a household is divided against itself,*
> *that household cannot stand. If Satan has revolted against*
> *himself and is divided, he is not able to stand. His end has*
> *come. But nobody is able to enter a strong man's house and*
> *steal his possessions unless he has first tied up the strong man.*
> *Then he could rob his house.*
> *'I tell you the truth. The sons of men will be forgiven*
> *everything—sins and whatever blasphemies they utter. But*
> *whoever blasphemes against the Holy Spirit will never have*
> *forgiveness—he is guilty of an eternal sin.' (He said this*
> *because they were saying that he had an unclean spirit.)*
> MARK 3:22–30

Demons are at the heart of Mark's Gospel. This can be an inconvenient embarrassment for many of us in the Western world today. At best, we may not think of demons at all; at worst, we may associate talk of exorcisms and demons with unpleasant religious groupings that we want to avoid. However, we cannot ignore the fact that conflict with 'unclean' spirits and demons (the terms seem to be used interchangeably) is a key element in Peter's preaching. Indeed, as we have seen, the first miracle Mark reports is the casting out of a demon, not a healing; and the disciples were sent out to preach and cast out demons (with no mention of healing: see 3:13–15).

What can we say? First, the talk of demons reminds us that the world of the Gospels is not our world. In the previous two chapters of this book, seeing our own experience in the ups and downs of Jesus' followers, we might have felt as if the distance between 'then' and 'now' was nothing at all. The demons remind us, however, that cultures and worldviews profoundly shape our understanding of what we experience. We may prefer our way of understanding the world, but we need humility when encountering other ways, whether they are separated from ours by time or by space. Often, Western academics have declared that the situations described as being caused by demons were 'actually' the result of mental illness, and there may be some truth in this assertion. But we also need to admit that Westerners often assume, as a matter of principle, that everything the Gospel writers put in the category of demons must fit into our category of mental illness. The reality is probably significantly more complicated. There is wisdom, though it requires humility, in accepting one of Shakespeare's famous lines: 'There are more things in heaven and earth, Horatio, than are dreamt of in your philosophy' (*Hamlet*, Act 1, Scene 5, lines 167–68).

If we put to one side our nervousness about this issue, what does the passage reveal? We can see a recognition, even among Jesus' enemies, that in his presence evil was being overturned. There was no doubt that (expressed in their language) 'demons' were being cast out. They didn't doubt that great power was at work. Their accusation, however, was that the power was not good: Jesus was working for Satan and his actions were some form of Satanic trickery.

The image of 'a kingdom divided' reminds us of God's

reign (or God's kingdom), which Jesus proclaimed (1:15). It draws on a way of thinking about the world as being split into two 'kingdoms'—good and evil, God's and Satan's—which Paul displays in his letter to the Colossians (1:13): 'For God rescued us from the power of darkness and transferred us to the kingdom of his loved son.' When Jesus drives out demons, his action is part of the destruction of the powers opposed to God and the establishment of God's reign. This is made explicit in Matthew's and Luke's versions of this story ('If by God's Spirit I drive out the demons, then the kingdom of God is among you': Matthew 12:28; Luke 11:20).

When we think about our world, we recognise that it contains much that oppresses people and destroys life, which cannot be put down simply to the direct action of other people. We might think of institutions, cultures, history and expectations. When the MacPherson Report concluded in 1999 that the (London) Metropolitan Police Service was institutionally racist, it was expressing the belief that the problem extended beyond the individual people involved. It claimed that racism was somehow embedded, that it 'had a grip' on the police service—perhaps similar to the way in which alcoholism gets hold of people, destroying them and their families. Indeed, we still hear people talk about the 'demon drink' in this context.

Counsellors today will talk of 'voices inside our heads', meaning what are technically called 'parental interjects'—the list of 'oughts' and 'ought nots' that we have absorbed from authority figures in the past. Counsellors identify these voices because they hold people back, undermining and condemning them. All too often I meet people whose lives are being similarly held back by words they have heard from mediums. I remember well a conversation with a woman who asked for my help as a priest. She explained at great length that there was the spirit of a little girl inhabiting her house, which was preventing her from selling up and moving. She had asked me to come round because she wanted it stopped—and yet, she insisted, she had been told it was a good spirit. It was doing her harm, but she wanted to call it 'good'. Mark 3 presents a kind of mirror image: Jesus was obviously doing good but his opponents wanted to call him demonic.

However we understand or describe all these things, there is much—beyond the actions of individuals—that needs rolling back if God's reign is to be made real. Jesus did this, and people experienced it as truly miraculous—shocking, surprising and good.

Release

After the calming of the storm, which we studied in Chapter 2, Jesus and his disciples arrived, just as Jesus had said, on the other side of the Sea of Galilee. There Jesus met a troubled man.

They came to the other side of the sea into the land of the Gerasenes. As soon as Jesus got out of the boat, a man with an evil spirit came out from the tombs to meet him. He lived among the tombs. Nobody could restrain him any more, not even with a chain. Often he had been bound with fetters and chains, yet he broke the chains and smashed the fetters. Nobody was able to subdue him. All night and day he would cry out among the tombs and hills and cut himself with stones.

He saw Jesus at a distance and ran and fell down at his feet.

He cried out in a loud voice, 'What do you want with me, Jesus, Son of the Highest God? I beg you in the name of God—do not torment me.' (For Jesus was saying to him, 'Evil spirit, come out from the man.') Jesus asked him, 'What is your name?' He says, 'My name is Legion, for we are many.' The man was frantically begging him not to send them out of the region.

Now, on the hillside a huge herd of pigs was feeding. The man begged him, 'Send us into the pigs so we can enter them.' Jesus allowed them. The evil spirits went out from the man and entered the pigs. The herd—about two thousand of them— rushed down the cliffs into the sea, where they began to drown.

Those who had been looking after the pigs fled and spread the word in the town and the countryside. People came to see what had happened.

They come to Jesus and see the man who had had the legion of demons, sitting, clothed and in his right mind, and they were frightened.

Those who had seen it explained to them what had happened to the demonised man and about the pigs. They began to urge him to leave their region.

As he was getting into the boat, the man who has been demonised asked if he could be with him. Jesus did not allow him to. But he says to him, 'Go back home, to your family, and tell them how much the Lord has done for you, and the mercy he showed you.' He went away and began to preach in the Decapolis how much Jesus did for him, and everyone was amazed.

MARK 5:1–20

This is a wonderfully vivid account, spanning a full 20 verses in Mark's Gospel. By comparison, Matthew manages to squeeze the basis story into just seven verses. The incident clearly made a massive impact on Peter and the other disciples—not surprisingly, perhaps, given the aggression and wildness of the man, the drama of the pigs, and the unwelcoming crowd that surrounded them. I can almost hear, in my head, Peter telling this story to a crowd many years later.

The depiction of the man is terrible and deeply sad. He is literally an outcast, living in the wild. A number of times, a Greek word is used that we might translate literally with the cumbersome phrase 'troubled by demons'. I have translated it as 'demonised' to catch both senses of 'troubled by demons' and 'shunned and rejected by people'. He has been reduced to an animal-like condition. Indeed, the local people value the pigs more than they value him.

The conversation between Jesus and the man/the demons is fascinating. The name 'Legion', which describes the demons, draws on the concept of a Roman legion, which would have been well known to people of the time. It implied great numbers: a legion was the largest single unit in the Roman army, of about 6000 fighting men. However, we also need to catch the emotional sense of the word. A legion was a massive destructive force, ferocious, armed to the teeth and deadly. The whole Roman occupation force in Israel at the time probably numbered just a tenth of a legion, but there were three legions based in Syria to the north. Just one of these, if it had descended on Israel, would have signalled massive destruction.

Some commentators see an anti-Roman sign in this story of the destruction of 'legion'. Perhaps this is right: it is certainly a sign that Jesus is defeating the strongest, more fearsome force imaginable. There seems to be no end to his power. Indeed, there isn't even a battle: as soon as the demons see Jesus, they know they are defeated and start to plead for a way out.

The incident with the pigs is hard to interpret. First, we should note that, in crossing the Sea of Galilee, Jesus had travelled outside the land of Israel to the non-Jewish region called the Decapolis (literally 'ten towns'). These were Greek cities in the area, roughly speaking, of modern-day Jordan. Pigs, of course, were the archetypal 'unclean' animal for Jews. Perhaps this meant that they were the natural place (from a Jewish point of view) for unclean spirits to be sent. Perhaps, too, the destruction of the pigs was seen as a good thing in itself, ridding the world of unclean animals. From a modern perspective, the destruction of so many animals, and the disregard of its impact on the local people, seems wicked and callous.

The response to the miracle is divided. The people of the region are frightened. They can see the good it has done—they can see the man sitting clothed and in his right mind—but this is not the focus of their attention. Perhaps it is the destruction of the pigs that has disturbed them, or perhaps they are simply afraid of the power they have seen at work, which they don't understand.

The man himself, on the other hand, wishes to become a follower of Jesus, like the Twelve. He wishes to 'be with Jesus', like them (5:18; see 3:14), but this is not allowed. Instead, he is told to share his story. Perhaps the logic is that he can do this among his own people, while the twelve Galilean Jews tell the story in Jewish Galilee. It reminds us that, in the Bible, God often tells people to 'go back' to their former situation and make a difference there (for example, Elijah in 1 Kings 19:15).

The message that the man is to give is about the mercy he

has received (5:19). We can also note that when Jesus talks about 'what the Lord has done for you', 'the Lord' would naturally be understood as referring to God, but when the man passes on the message, it is about what 'Jesus' has done for him (v. 20). This reminds us that, from the perspective of someone helped by Jesus, he was God's agent—'God made real' to them.

The miracle did demonstrate God's power, easily overcoming the most destructive and fearsome enemy, but what it was really about was God's mercy for this man. The man asked for help and God helped him.

A tale of two women

Mark 5 continues with a second long account of a miracle. It is similarly full of vivid detail and similarly told much more briefly by Matthew. The account actually covers two miracles, one done on the way to the other. Some scholars argue that these are two separate stories, which have been woven together in the telling, linked perhaps by the fact that both healings affect women and that the number twelve appears in both. However, the linking factors are not particularly strong, and, as we have already discussed, separate stories are usually kept separate and 'strung together' in Peter's preaching.

In the end, it doesn't really matter how we read the stories, although it certainly seems logical to me that here again we have Peter's reminiscences of one particularly striking afternoon.

When Jesus had travelled in the boat back to the other side, a large crowd gathered to him. He was beside the sea.

One of the leaders of the synagogue, called Jairus, comes to him and, seeing him, falls at his feet. He begins to plead with him earnestly: 'My little daughter is dying. Please come and place your hands on her so she will be saved, and live.' Jesus set off with him. The great crowd was following him, pressing into him.

A woman was there who has been bleeding for twelve years. She had suffered greatly at the hands of many doctors, spending all that she had, but it hadn't helped at all but rather she had got worse. She had heard about Jesus and came up behind him in the crowd and touched his cloak. (For she was saying to herself, 'If I even just touch his cloak, I will be saved.')

Immediately the source of the bleeding dried up and she knew in herself that she was healed from her suffering. Straight away Jesus knew in himself that power had gone out from him. He turned in the crowd and asked, 'Who touched my cloak?'

The disciples started to say to him, 'You see the crowd pressing against you, yet you ask, "Who touched me?".' Jesus looked round to see who had done it. Frightened and trembling, the woman, knowing what had happened to her, came and fell down in front of him and told him the whole truth. Jesus told her, 'Daughter, your faith has saved you. Go back in peace, and be healed from your suffering.'

While he was still speaking, messengers from the synagogue leader come saying, 'Your daughter has died. Why still trouble the teacher?' Jesus overheard the message and says to the synagogue leader, 'Don't be afraid, just have faith.'

Jesus didn't allow anyone to come along with him except for Peter, James and John, James' brother. They enter the synagogue leader's house and see the commotion and the women crying and wailing. He goes in and says to them, 'Why *are you making a commotion and crying? The child has not died—she's asleep.' They laughed at him. When he had driven them all out, he takes the child's father and mother and the three who were with him and goes in to where the child was. He takes her by the hand and says to her, 'Talitha koum', which, translated, is, 'Little girl, I say to you, get up.'*

Immediately the little girl got up and began to walk around. (For she was twelve years old.) They were completely astonished. He orders them strictly not to let anyone know about it, and told them to give her something to eat.

MARK 5:21–43

Both of these stories continue to develop the pattern for 'miracles' in the Mark's Gospel. In both cases, the miracle is performed as a result of a direct request, and could be characterised as an act of compassion or mercy. The woman with terrible bleeding does not ask Jesus, in words, to heal her. Nevertheless, because we are told what she was thinking, we are left in no doubt about her intentions.

It is startling, though, that she is healed without Jesus' explicit involvement. There is perhaps a suggestion of a 'two-stage' healing, since, after their interchange, Jesus says, 'Daughter, your faith has saved you. Go back in peace, and be healed from your suffering.' This sounds like a confirmation of the healing, but the text is clear that the healing happened at the moment when she touched Jesus, before Jesus even knew who she was.

It reminds me of the story of the Syro-Phoenician woman in Mark 7, which we considered in Chapter 3. She spoke of crumbs falling from the table, which could benefit people like her, even though they weren't the intended recipients.

God's mercy at work in Jesus was overflowing. So too here, perhaps: healing and salvation overflow from Jesus.

The women's sickness is also significant, for the bleeding was a hidden affliction. It was certainly not something that could be discussed in public with a man. According to the Jewish law, it would have made her 'unclean', thus requiring separation from some elements of normal life and society (if, that is, she chose to admit it). As well as the pain and the financial cost that the passage mentions, it would have been a source of personal shame. Perhaps, therefore, we see an added level of God's mercy here. The woman was able to receive healing without having to face the added indignity of explaining her problem.

The miracle involving the little girl is striking mainly, of course, because she is brought back to life, not just healed. Perhaps the particularly amazing nature of the miracle explains why the command to secrecy is given so strongly (v. 43), but, as we will explore in the next chapter, commands to secrecy are common after Jesus' works of power. The sense of understatement here adds to the effect. Not only has Jesus raised a dead person to life, but the act is treated as if it's 'no big deal'. There seems to be no limit to his power.

The miracle happens as the result of a direct request, though not, of course, from the girl herself. It is not uncommon in the Gospels for people to bring sick friends and relatives for healing (such as the paralysed man in Mark 2:3–4) or to ask on behalf of others (such as Peter's mother-in-law in 1:30–31). In all these cases, there is a sense of a request being met by compassion.

Feeding the thousands

We come now to one of the most famous of Jesus' miracles, known as the feeding of the 5000, although, as we will see, he actually fed more than 5000 people. This is followed, a few chapters later in Mark, by a second feeding miracle—this time of at least 4000 people. The second miracle is rather less well known, reported only in Mark and Matthew, while the feeding of the 5000 is in all four Gospels. In a sense, it doesn't add much to the episode of the 5000. This has led some scholars to presume that the two stories are of the same incident, remembered in slightly different ways. This could be true: it's impossible to identify evidence that would allow us to confirm or reject the suggestion. However, if we accept that Jesus calmed multiple storms, drove out multiple demons and healed multiple numbers of people, I am not sure why multiple feedings should be particularly problematic.

We will look at the feeding of the 4000 at the end of this section. First, though, keeping to the order that Mark gives us, we have the more famous episode.

The 'messengers' reassemble with Jesus and told him all that they had done and taught. He says to them, 'Come privately, just you, to a remote place and rest a little.' (For many people were coming and going, and they weren't even having a chance to eat.)

They set off privately in the boat with him to a remote place. Yet many people saw them going and recognised them. They ran there on foot from all the towns and got there first.

When Jesus got out of the boat, he looked at the crowd and had compassion on them because they were like sheep without a shepherd. He began to teach them many things.

When it was late his disciples came to him and said, 'This is a remote place and it's already late. Send them away so they can go into the surrounding fields and villages and buy themselves something to eat.'

He replied to them, 'You give them something to eat.' They say to him, 'Should we go off and spend eight months of man's wages on bread and give it them to eat?'

He asks them, 'How much bread do you have? Go and see.' They find out and say, 'Five loaves, and two fish.' He told them to get everyone to sit down in groups on the green grass. So they sat down in groups of hundreds and of fifties.

He took the five loaves and the two fish. He looked up to heaven, gave thanks and broke the bread and began to give it to his disciples to hand out to them. He also shared the two fish between them all.

Everyone ate and was satisfied. They picked up twelve basketfuls of broken pieces of bread and fish. There were five thousand men who ate the bread.

MARK 6:30–44

This miracle is presented in such a simple and understated manner. There are no prayers except for a simple word of thanks; no dramatic actions and no mention of God's Spirit or power at work. The people simply sit down and Jesus feeds them. However, the event described is astonishing. (The normal way of translating the final verse is that there were 5000 'men', with women and children extra.)

This miracle, along with the calming of the storm and Jesus' walking on water, falls into a category that we might call the 'nature miracle'. For modern people who are sceptical of the very idea of miracles, miraculous healings can be 'explained' in some way—for example, suggesting that they are 'really' a case of mind over matter or that the disease was psychosomatic. Thus, we could imagine that Jesus gave the person new confidence, acceptance and self-belief, so that they were able to throw of whatever had been holding them back. Outcomes that people once attributed to magic or faith, we now understand in a scientific way. Such explanations risk being rather flippant about the nature of mental illness and run contrary to the clear statements in the text, but they can 'work' at some level. Similarly, rationalistic explanations can be provided for the driving out of evil spirits. However, the nature miracles are rather more difficult to explain in this way. People in Peter's world understood very well (for example) that they could share their packed lunches with each other—this isn't a modern scientific insight that 'primitive people' would have to describe in terms of magic—but that is not what is being described. Thus, in the nature miracles we come unavoidably face to face with the claim that they have occurred by supernatural means.

It is perhaps true that even Mark, and perhaps Peter, saw these miracles in a different light, too. As we will explore further in the next chapter, the nature miracles seem to feed particularly into the question 'Who is Jesus?' (Calming the storm and walking on water makes the disciples ask, 'Who is this?' and, as that is discussed, Jesus mentions 'the loaves', seemingly pointing back to this miracle.)

However, as we have seen, the feeding of the 5000 is described in an understated way: it is not presented as a miracle of such power that people's beliefs about Jesus are overturned. Instead, provision motivated by compassion appears to be the key point throughout. We begin with Jesus recognising the needs of the disciples/'messengers' and making provision for them. They may have been filled with

God's power to work wonders (6:7–13), but they still had natural human needs. It is easy for those caught up in God's purposes to neglect the reality of their own needs, particularly for rest and emotional fulfilment (v. 31).

Then Jesus realises that he needs to provide for the crowd. The description of the people as 'sheep without a shepherd' (v. 34) is full of significance. Ezekiel 34 talks of God's people being like sheep with nobody to care for them because the 'appointed shepherds' (that is, the religious leaders of the day) have misused and neglected their position. As a result, God himself promises to shepherd and provide for his people. The phrase, when used in Mark's Gospel, therefore implies a criticism of the teachers of the law, Pharisees and temple authorities. If the people are like sheep without a shepherd, it must be because the religious leaders are failing in their duties. The phrase also suggests that, through Jesus' ministry, God himself was coming to the people.

The disciples assume that Jesus' response to the crowd will be limited to teaching them (vv. 34–36), but, as we have seen before, Jesus' teaching goes along with action, so he provides for the crowd's physical needs. Indeed, since he provides for them through the disciples (asking the disciples to arrange the people and distribute the food), it is almost as if he is appointing new shepherds to replace the existing, failing ones. The result is overflowing provision—not just enough, but far more than enough (vv. 42–43). Perhaps we ought to stop and ponder who are the 'sheep without a shepherd' today. Are we responding to them with compassion and action, or are we in danger of being replaced?

Another set of connections is developed in John's account (John 6:1–14). First, John says explicitly that the miracle took place during Passover (6:4), which fits with the detail in Mark

6:39 that the grass was green. Second, in Mark, the setting for the miracle is a 'remote place', which could be translated equally well as a 'deserted place' or 'a desert'. This is suggestive of the great feeding miracle in the Old Testament, when God provided manna to the people as they crossed the Sinai desert after the exodus and Passover (Exodus 16). John 6:26–51 then draws on this connection, with Jesus describing himself as the 'bread of life' that 'comes down from heaven'. Finally, returning to Mark's account, the sequence of taking, giving thanks, breaking and giving the bread (Mark 6:41) matches Jesus' actions at the last supper (14:22), commemorated by Christians in Holy Communion or the Eucharist (see 1 Corinthians 11:23–34). It seems reasonable to conclude that, looking back on this miraculous feeding, the early Christians saw connections with the idea of Jesus feeding the people at the new Passover of the Eucharist.

Undoubtedly this feeding is miraculous, but that doesn't seem to be the point. What matters is God's compassion, leading to his provision, and the same motivation—compassion leading to a miraculous provision—is evident in the healing miracles and the casting out of demons.

Since Peter told the story of the 4000 separately, and Mark bothered to record it in his Gospel, we should not overlook it.

Around that time, there was again a great crowd who did not have anything to eat. He calls together his disciples and says to them, 'I have compassion for this crowd. They have already been with me for three days and they don't have anything to eat. If I send them back to their homes hungry, they will collapse on the way—some of them have come a long way.'

His disciples replied, 'In this remote place, where can anyone get enough bread from to satisfy them?' He asked them, 'How much bread do you have?' They said, 'Seven.'

He tells the crowd to sit on the ground. He took the seven loaves, gave thanks and broke them, and began to give them to his disciples to distribute. They distributed it to the crowd.

They also had a few small fish. He gave thanks for them and told them to distribute them as well. They ate and were satisfied and there were seven basketfuls of broken pieces left over. There were 4000 people. Then he sent them away.

MARK 8:1–9

The details in the story are different. Much ink has been spilt in trying to find some significance in the numbers involved—5000 people giving rise to twelve baskets of leftovers; 4000 people and seven baskets full. This debate is perhaps encouraged by Jesus' repetition of the numbers in the subsequent discussion on the boat in Mark 8:19–21. Nevertheless, none of the explanations is very convincing. At least, it is far from clear that Mark or Peter would have expected their audience to understand them immediately.

Overall, though, we see the same pattern—an amazing miracle, motivated by compassion. Moreover, the repetition demonstrates that feeding thousands of people in a 'remote place' was not a feat that Jesus could pull off just once, and it was not the result of particular circumstances. It was comfortably within his power.

In my experience, it can be strangely difficult to move from the idea that once in a blue moon, *in extremis*, God can act supernaturally to help me to the belief that God is regularly involved in my life, shaping events for my good. Maybe that is why Peter and Mark described the feeding of the 4000 as well as the 5000—to remind us that, as amazing as the miracle was, it wasn't unique.

Doing everything well

Then Jesus left the region of Tyre and went through Sidon to
the Sea of Galilee and into the region of the Decapolis.

They bring to him a man who was deaf and could hardly
talk and they beg Jesus to put his hand on him. Jesus took
him away privately away from the crowd. He places his fingers
into his ears, spat and touched his tongue. He looked up to
heaven, sighed deeply and said to him, 'Effatha', which means
'Be opened.'

Immediately his ears were opened, and his tongue was freed
and he began to speak correctly.

Jesus ordered them to say nothing to anyone. But however
much he ordered them, they just proclaimed it even more. They
were completely astounded and said, 'He has done everything
well. He makes the deaf hear and the dumb speak.'

MARK 7:31–37

This miracle is described as a straightforward meeting between
someone needing help and Jesus. We might wonder why, as
a typical healing, it was remembered and used by Peter in
his preaching. There are certainly some distinctive features.
First, we can note that there is no expression of faith or desire
to be healed by the man himself, just by a group of people
introduced as 'they'. Of course, the man's disability may well
have meant that others had to speak for him, but we have to
be careful not to squeeze all such stories into a fixed format, in
which 'faith' is a requirement for healing. This account does
not mention faith; indeed, perhaps there is an encouragement
here for us to act in support of, or on behalf of, those who
cannot help themselves, such as the very young, the very old
and those who are physically or mentally very sick.

Jesus' actions are also intriguing. If the healing took place at Jesus' word, as is normally the case and as seems to be implied here, what was the point of the touching? We will never know. More interesting is the question of why Mark has preserved this detail, with the precise Aramaic word 'Effatha', which would have meant nothing at all to his readers. It certainly gives a vividness and sense of mystery to the account. Perhaps the touching and the use of this word were remembered simply because they were unusual for Jesus, or perhaps this story is just used as a typical example of other healings that are passed over more quickly.

The final two sentences (vv. 36–37) give a particular interpretation to the healing, and Matthew and Luke seem to draw it out more clearly. For example, Matthew, shortly after his account of the miracle in 9:32–33, says:

> *When, in prison, John heard about the works of the Messiah, he sent his disciples to ask him, 'Are you the coming one, or should we look out for someone else?' Jesus replied, 'Go, tell John what you hear and see—the blind see, the lame walk, lepers are clean and the deaf hear. Even the dead are raised and the poor receive good news.'*
>
> MATTHEW 11:2–5

The phrase 'works of the Messiah' here could equally be translated as 'what Christ was doing'. The double meaning is the point. It comes from Old Testament descriptions of what will happen when God acts to save his people, particularly in Isaiah 35. The prophets do not make precise predictions, saying, 'There will be a Messiah and he will do the following signs and wonders: a, b, c...' However, for someone like John the Baptist, who was so familiar with the prophets, the question is reasonable. Jesus' actions closely match the descriptions of what it will be like when God acts to save his people.

This connection is not explicit in Mark, but, to me, the way in which 7:36–37 is phrased seems to point to it. 'He has done everything well' may not mean simply 'He has brought good to this man' but could suggest, 'He is behaving as the Messiah should.' In this case, Jesus' response is important and gives us a taster for the next chapter, which is all about his identity. He seems not to want this kind of praise or to have people concluding from his miracles that he is 'the Messiah' or 'the coming one', so he commands silence. (Indeed, he took the man away privately before doing the healing, so as not to demonstrate his power to the crowd.) We might be amazed by and even long for 'miracles', but for Jesus they were not central to his identity. They were acts of compassion, not proofs of his importance, power or status.

Mark 7:31–37 also raises an important issue with regard to the healing miracles, which has often been overlooked and needs to be faced at some point. What does this kind of miracle say about deaf people today? Indeed, even in my phrasing of that question, am I slipping into a form of paternalism? Perhaps I should ask, what does this kind of miracle say *to* deaf people today? The issue could be raised in relation to any form of disability but it is particularly pronounced in relation to those who are deaf.

For many deaf people, being deaf is a significant part of who they are. British Sign Language is a language. We might think it is just a system in which a sign made with the hands corresponds to an English word, but its grammar is different, its way of thinking about time is different and its 'words' are not English words. No two languages precisely overlap—they have different possibilities, different nuances—and language creates culture.

None of us would think, 'When Jesus returns, he will rescue the poor French people, get rid of their culture and language and miraculously turn them into good English speakers, so that they can partake fully in Englishness.' Nevertheless, that is what some deaf people feel that Christians say about them—that Jesus will change them from being deaf to being hearing people. Hearing people might think it obvious that being deaf is an 'impairment', which should be healed, rather than just a different way of being human. But many deaf people do not see themselves as being in need of healing: they feel that the only healing needed is in the patronising attitudes of hearing people.

It is important to note this issue, although we cannot explore it further here. I think it is right to say that it is a modern issue, however. Most would agree that, for this deaf and dumb man in first-century Israel, his deafness would have been a terrible disability that would have condemned him to poverty and isolation. Thus, for him, his healing was an act of compassion. It also highlights the importance of Jesus' way of operating, which we have already noted. Jesus healed in response to a request. He did not decide for himself what other people needed. His miracles were about compassion, not about displaying his power. Similarly, other people are not to be used by us to demonstrate our power, piety or social activism. Compassion is about love for the other, and love is about *them*, not us.

Faith

Faith is an important concept in many ways within Christianity. The word itself is complicated, for the same Greek noun, *pistis*, can be translated in different contexts as 'faith' or 'trust' or 'belief'. Similarly, the verb *pisteuo* could mean 'I have faith', 'I believe' or 'I trust'.

In relation to miracles, there is a widespread but vague idea that 'faith' can bring healing. There are people who would call themselves faith-healers, and it is fairly common for people to say, 'You have got to have faith' to those who are ill. It is often unclear, though, what this 'faith' is in, and underlying the expression is an idea of self-belief, relating to self-confidence, empowerment and the power of positive thinking. Such things may be valuable but they are different from the 'faith' that sometimes features in Jesus' miracles. When Jesus said to the woman who had been bleeding for twelve years, 'Your faith has saved you' (Mark 5:34), he clearly meant her trust or belief *in Jesus*, not some general sense of self-belief. (We see that trust expressed in her thoughts: 'If I just touch his clothes, I will be healed', v. 28.) At the same time, we have already noted that in some of the stories of healing, faith is not mentioned at all (for example, in 1:40–45).

We cannot arrive at a system describing exactly how and when Jesus healed. However, the issues surrounding faith are drawn out by Mark in a passage describing what happened when Jesus, Peter, James and John returned from the mountain where the transfiguration had happened.

When they approached the disciples, they saw a huge crowd surrounding them and scribes debating with them. When the crowd saw him, they were surprised, ran to him and welcomed him. He asked them, 'What were you debating?' One of the crowd answered, 'Teacher, I have brought my son to you—he has a spirit which makes him dumb. Whenever it seizes him, it throws him down. He foams at the mouth, grinds his teeth and becomes rigid. I asked your disciples to drive it out but they weren't strong enough.'

Jesus said to them, 'Oh, you faithless generation! How long will I be with you? How long will I put up with you? Bring him to me.' They brought the boy to him. When the spirit saw Jesus, it immediately threw the boy into convulsions. He fell to the ground and was rolling round, foaming at the mouth.

Jesus asked his father, 'How long has he been like this?' He answered, 'Since he was a child. Often it has even thrown him into the fire, and into water, so as to kill him. But, if you can do something, take pity on us and help us.'

Jesus said to him, 'What is this "If you are able"? Everything is possible for the one who has faith.' Immediately the father cried out, 'I have faith; help my lack of faith!'

When Jesus saw that the crowd was running towards them, he rebuked the evil spirit: 'Deaf and dumb spirit, I command you, come out from him and go into him no longer!'

The spirit cried out, convulsed him terribly and left. The boy looked so much like a corpse that many people were saying that he had died. Then Jesus took his hand and raised him up, and he stood up.

When he had gone into a house, his disciples asked him privately, 'Why were we not able to drive it out?' He told them, 'The only way this kind can be driven out is through prayer.'

MARK 9:14–29

What does Jesus mean by 'Oh, you faithless generation!' (which could equally be translated as 'unbelieving' or 'with no trust')? He is clearly frustrated with 'them', but whom does he mean? Is it the disciples? In the previous chapter, Peter has been called 'Satan' (8:33) and the disciples described as 'hard-hearted' (v. 17); Jesus has been exasperated that they do not yet understand (v. 21). Did their lack of faith mean they could not drive out the spirit (v. 18)? Alternatively, is Jesus' criticism directed at the father and his son? Jesus certainly picks up on the father's words 'if you are able' as expressing unhelpful doubt.

Perhaps, though, we are falling into the trap of thinking that someone—disciples, father or son—must have had a 'lack of faith', and so that is why the evil spirit couldn't be driven out. After all, when asked for an explanation after the event, Jesus didn't put the disciples' failure down to anything to do with faith at all, merely saying that prayer was needed. So perhaps Jesus' words were a general comment on his times—an outburst similar to those that Luke records, about Capernaum and Jerusalem (Luke 10:15; 19:41–44).

Jesus' exchange with the father has an honesty about it that is memorable and appealing, reminiscent of his conversation with the Syro-Phoenician woman (7:24–30). In both cases, the initial approach to Jesus meets with a rather cold response, but a clever, quick reply transforms the situation. In some ways, this is troubling: were Jesus' actions dependent on smart repartee? Perhaps, though, we should take it as a reminder of the reality of the incarnation. Jesus truly became human, so his actions were shaped by what happened around him. He was not, and is not, an emotionless robot. Who could not be touched by the combination of honesty, desperation and wit in the father's reply?

'I have faith; help my lack of faith!' (or 'I believe; help my unbelief!') expresses the deep mystery of faith, for faith itself is a gift from God (Ephesians 2:8), yet it is also the basis on which we can relate to God. This could seem like a 'catch-22' situation: unless God first gives us faith, we can't have the faith to come to him. However, Jesus' exchange with the father proves otherwise. Faith itself is not required; a desire for faith will do.

Blaise Pascal, the 17th-century French mathematician, scientist and Christian philosopher, suggested that God might say, 'You would not seek me if you had not already found me' (*Pensées*, 553). The logic is that if we are seeking God, it must be because we have already had some experience of him, and that, in turn, must be because God has already come to us. This is reassuring for those who are seeking God but don't feel they experience him: the very fact that they are seeking is itself proof that God is at work in them. On the other hand, it can suggest a sort of fatalism: if someone isn't interested in God, that is because God hasn't come to them, so their lack of interest is God's fault.

This rather philosophical argument does connect with the father's words. However limited his faith in Jesus may have been, the fact that he came to Jesus and, when challenged, asked Jesus to help his lack of faith, shows that he was acting in faith. In his desperation, he was reaching out to God.

Jesus' final comment is intriguing: 'The only way this kind can be driven out is through prayer.' Was this a special kind of evil spirit? Who knows? To someone quite reasonably asking whether the description of the son's affliction suggests the effects of epilepsy, I would give the same response: we don't know. There is no doubt that Mark calls it an evil spirit, but it is impossible to say how we would have described the same situation if we had been there.

What is clear throughout the passage, though, is the importance being given to 'reliance on God' (or faith, belief or trust—whatever word we would like to use), and here we can find an intimate connection to prayer. Prayer is a vehicle for expressing reliance on God and is also the means by which our relationship with God, and thus our ability to rely on him, is built up. Perhaps the challenge for us is not to worry too much about the philosophy of the relationship between 'faith' and 'healing' but to act on the importance of building up our faith.

Healing our blindness

Finally in this chapter on miracles, we come to the healing of blind Bartimaeus in Mark 10. This might be described as the final 'miracle' in Mark's Gospel—though still to come is the cursing of the fig-tree, the tearing of the temple curtain and, of course, the resurrection.

They go into Jericho. Now as Jesus, his disciples, and a large crowd were leaving, there was a beggar, Bartimaeus, the son of Timaeus, sitting near the road. When he heard that it was Jesus the Nazarene, he began to call out, 'Jesus, Son of David, have pity on me.'

Many people were rebuking him, telling him to be quiet. But he was crying out all the more, 'Son of David, have pity on me.'

Jesus stopped and said, 'Call him.' They call the blind man, saying to him, 'Cheer up, he is calling you.' He threw off his cloak, jumped up and went to Jesus.

Jesus said to him, 'What do you want me to do for you?'

The blind man said, 'Rabbouni, I want to see again.' Jesus said to him, 'Go, your faith has saved you.' Immediately he could see again, and he followed Jesus on the way.

MARK 10:46–51

Many of the features of this story are similar to others that Peter preached—the initial approach by the one needing healing, Jesus' welcome for the person, the exchange, the moment of healing, and the proof that the healing had occurred. Interestingly, Mark uses the Aramaic word *'Rabbouni'* in the man's address to Jesus, which means 'my rabbi', or perhaps 'my teacher'. There seems to be no logical reason why the Aramaic is preserved here, while elsewhere—say, in the account of the healing we read previously—we simply have the Greek word for 'teacher'.

The one unusual feature of this healing is that, afterwards, the healed man travels with Jesus 'on the way'. Only once previously has someone tried to follow Jesus after being healed (the man from whom the 'Legion' of demons was cast out, in Mark 5), and he was told to go to his own people instead and tell them what God had done for him. (Of course, it is quite possible that, in travelling up to Jerusalem with Jesus, Bartimaeus was indeed going to his own people.)

At the beginning of the story, Bartimaeus is said to be sitting 'near the way', and by the end he is following 'on the way'. Thus, while it appears to be a story of healing, it is just as much a story of discipleship. Bartimaeus does not just meet Jesus and ask for healing. He has to overcome obstacles in the process—in particular, the opposition of the people around him. Their attitude amplifies his physical difficulties, suggesting an assumption that Jesus would not be interested in someone like him. His place is to sit and receive what people choose to give him, not to cry out and demand attention.

Bartimaeus is having none of it! He is certainly motivated by his desire for healing, but he also shows a great faith in Jesus and confidence in Jesus' concern for the marginalised in society, as he continues to cry out. In his own way, in his own circumstances, he is demonstrating his commitment. Jesus then asks him, 'What do you want me to do for you?' At face value, this seems a bizarre question. We might think, 'Isn't it obvious? He's blind!' But the question demonstrates respect. Jesus does not patronise the sick or disabled, assuming that he knows exactly what they need. He asks them what they want.

For many of us, this story provides a lens through which to view our own discipleship. What barriers keep us from meeting with Jesus? Most of us feel that, for most of the time, Jesus is present, but not really *with* us. He is next door, perhaps, or at the other side of the crowd. What is the barrier? It can be something within us: for Bartimaeus, it was his blindness (an easy metaphor for our own spiritual short-sightedness). Perhaps, though, it is the opinions of those around us, or our own fears about what people will think. Bartimaeus demonstrates single-mindedness and the need for a wholehearted, urgent response to Jesus. Jesus was not going to be walking through Jericho for long: Bartimaeus had to seize the moment.

We can see Jesus' question in the same light. 'What do you want?' is a question that few of us ask of ourselves. We are carried along by expectations and assumptions; life just keeps going. But what is it that we really want? What do we want so much that we would have Bartimaeus' single-minded courage in seeking it?

This chapter on miracles began with the recognition that the word 'miracle' can be used in different ways but tends to denote events that, for those involved, are shocking, surprising and also good. Even in our scientific world, the word is still commonly used and does not necessarily mean 'something beyond scientific explanation' (the birth of a child is often seen as a 'miracle'). This approach fits Peter's preaching well. Jesus' miracles are not really used to point to Jesus' divinity. Indeed, Jesus himself seems to be trying to keep his miracle-working quiet. Instead, the miracles are personal. Jesus' power is immense—even limitless—yet, strangely, it is almost in the background as the story unfolds. Instead, the spotlight is on the relationship between Jesus and the person healed, and sometimes their friends and family.

We will hear Peter's preaching more accurately if we avoid listening to it through the filter of modern arguments between scientific rationalism and religious belief in the supernatural. Not only does an attempt to reread the stories from a 'scientific' point of view quickly descend into mere speculation, but the arguments that ensue distort the message of Peter's preaching. Peter focused not on the amazing power but, rather, on what these miracles said about the people involved—about Jesus' compassion and love, and the ways in which others reacted to him. The healing of Bartimaeus makes a fitting end to this chapter, for the miracles have brought us back somehow to questions about following 'on the way'. Jesus calls. He can deal with whatever barriers there might be. What matters most is our response.

CHAPTER 5

WHO IS JESUS?

'Well, you would never have guessed,' says the neighbour to the news reporter. 'He always seemed such a quiet, hard-working man, kept himself to himself, never any trouble. Who would have guessed that all the time he was...' A spy? A bank robber? The author of the latest blockbuster? The details may be different each time but the script remains the same. Less dramatically, but equally surprisingly, you might find out, when stuck in a traffic-jam with someone you have worked alongside for years, that in their spare time they love to go skydiving or are a Black Belt in judo. A person's identity can be a complicated question.

Jesus' identity—who he is—is at the heart of Mark's Gospel. Many scholars have identified this as the key point that Mark wants his readers to think about—or, indeed, the key question that Peter wished his audience to face. The same question has been at the heart of much evangelism, often in the form made famous by C.S. Lewis and, more recently, in the Alpha course: is Jesus 'Lunatic, Liar or Lord?'

However, as we have seen, someone's identity is a compli-cated question. If we decide that Jesus is God, that doesn't finish the discussion, because it just raises the question, 'But what is God like?' For some people, 'God' means an old man on a distant cloud. For others, 'God' is an angry kill-joy, and for others a loving parent. Peter's preaching does not engage in this kind of wordplay or intellectual games. However, as we will see, he gives us a rich insight into who Jesus is, far deeper than just 'Jesus is God' or something similar. Interestingly, however, he tells us nothing about what Jesus looked like. Perhaps our physical description is the least important aspect of who we are.

God's Son is revealed

We begin our exploration of who Jesus is in the first verse of Mark's Gospel.

> *The good news about Jesus—the Messiah, the Son of God— begins just as it is written in the prophet Isaiah.*
> MARK 1:1

Mark lets us into the secret right at the beginning. It's almost as if he can't help himself. As he sets out how the story of Jesus begins just as the prophet Isaiah said, he adds the information that Jesus is 'the Messiah, the Son of God'.

Of course, this is not an accident. Sometimes a film or book will start with a 'flash forward'—the funeral of the main character or, perhaps, a wedding. This doesn't spoil the ending (since in most cases we already know how the story must end—the hero will survive, the couple will fall in love, and so on). Instead, it focuses our attention. We know how the story ends, so now our attention is drawn into the journey towards that ending.

In the same way, the bare facts about Jesus' identity are revealed to us right at the beginning of the Gospel. He is the Messiah, the Son of God. Most of those hearing the Gospel will know that already, but the way it is stated challenges us to realise that this is only a beginning. It is one thing to call someone 'Messiah' or 'Son of God', but what does this really mean?

As we will see, the whole Gospel is punctuated by reminders of the facts about who Jesus is, even while we watch people struggling to grasp what the facts really mean. As we observe this slow and uncertain development in understanding, we too are challenged to think again about what it means to say that Jesus is 'the Messiah, the Son of God'. Many of us will recognise this process: we, too, might have said long ago that Jesus is the Son of God but we are still working out what it means.

> *The good news about Jesus—the Messiah, the Son of God— begins just as it is written in the prophet Isaiah: 'I will send my messenger ahead of you. He will prepare the way for you.' 'The voice of someone shouting in the desert: "Get the Lord's way ready! Make his paths straight!"' John the Baptiser appeared in the desert, proclaiming a baptism of repentance for the forgiveness of sins.*
>
> MARK 1:1–4

The fact that the Gospel starts with quotations from the Old Testament (first Malachi 3:1 and then Isaiah 40:3) is important. It lays down right at the beginning that Jesus is part of the story of God, Israel and the world described in the Old Testament. This matters because, as we will explore further in the next chapter, throughout much of the rest of the Gospel Jesus seems to be at odds with the religious leadership of Israel. So here, at the beginning, we are shown that Jesus is genuinely in tune with Israel's scriptures. Indeed, he fulfils them.

Mark makes it clear that the quotations apply to John the Baptiser: John is the messenger; his is the voice shouting in the desert, urging people to prepare. However, the quotations also contain important hints about Jesus' status and role. In Malachi 3:1, God actually says, 'I am sending out my messenger. He will prepare the way before *me*. Then the Lord you seek will suddenly come to his temple... Who can endure the day he arrives?' The quotation here in Mark says that the messenger is being sent 'ahead of *you*'. Is John, the messenger, coming ahead of God (as Malachi might imply) or ahead of Jesus (as the 'you' in the quotation here suggests)? Note also that, in the end, *Jesus* does come to the temple and finds it wanting (Mark 11:11–17). The ambiguity is deliberate: Jesus is standing in the place of God.

Isaiah 40:3 ('the voice of someone shouting in the desert...') is a prophecy of the return of the Jewish nation from exile in Babylon. The preceding verse reads, 'Speak to Jerusalem's heart... she has completed her sentence... her sin has been paid for'. The people who returned from exile, because their sins had been paid for, would have come through the desert on their way back to Jerusalem, through the River Jordan—which is exactly where we find John.

John the Baptiser appeared in the desert, proclaiming a baptism of repentance for the forgiveness of sins. The Judean countryside, and everyone in Jerusalem, used to go out to him. As they confessed their sins they would be baptised by him in the River Jordan. (John used to wear camel hair and a leather belt, and eat locusts and wild honey.)

This is what he preached: 'Someone stronger than me is coming after me. I am not even important enough to bend down and untie the strap of his sandals. I baptise you with water, but he is going to baptise you in the Holy Spirit.'

MARK 1:4–8

John—the wild holy man of the desert—could be recognised by his distinctive appearance. The description of his clothing picks up the words of 2 Kings 1:8. When King Ahaziah asked the identity of a certain prophet, he was told that the man wore a hair garment with a leather belt, and he concluded, 'That was Elijah.'

John, as an Elijah figure, fits with the Old Testament quotations, for while Malachi 3:1 says simply that a messenger will come before the Lord, Malachi 4:5 specifies that it is Elijah who will come, preparing the people (see Jesus' discussion in Mark 9:11–13). John's identity points to what is about to happen, and who it is that is coming after him.

John is clear that his baptism is only a symbolic washing. The people are acting out their own return from exile, going into the desert to find forgiveness from their sins, through the Jordan and back to Jerusalem. The one for whom John is making preparations is the one who will actually bring God's rescue to Israel. Indeed, he will bring them God's own Spirit, God's own presence.

> *At that time, Jesus came from Nazareth in Galilee and was baptised in the Jordan by John. Immediately as he came up from the water, he saw heaven being torn open and the Spirit like a dove, coming down into him. And there was a voice from heaven: 'You are my dearly loved son. I delight in you.'*
>
> *Immediately the Spirit drives him out into the desert, where he spent forty days being tested by Satan, surrounded by the wild beasts. Yet the angels were looking after him.*
>
> MARK 1:9–13

Peter now reveals something of Jesus' own struggle over his calling, or even his identity. Before he begins his work, he receives God's Spirit and is assured that he is God's dear Son. Then he has to be tested in the desert. Matthew's and Luke's Gospels make clear that this testing, or temptation, was precisely about his calling and identity: what sort of 'Son of God' was he going to be (see Matthew 4:1–11)? We will see Jesus fighting temptation once more at the end of his ministry, in Gethsemane (Mark 14:32–43), and this confirms the point we discussed earlier. Even for Jesus himself, being 'Son of God' was not the end of the story. It immediately led on to the question, 'What kind of Son of God?'

Identity and calling are closely interrelated. Jesus' ministry begins only once he is secure in God's favour and presence. Even then, he has to face choices about how he will respond to God. If this was important for Jesus, how much more so for us? Our own service of God and neighbour will flourish only when it emerges from the security of knowing God's favour and presence, from a knowledge of who we really are.

A man with authority

We step forward a few verses to Jesus' first public appearance.

They go into Capernaum. On the sabbath, he went into the synagogue and immediately began to teach. They were shocked at his teaching, because he didn't teach like the scribes; he taught as if he had authority.

Straight away a man in the grip of an evil spirit appeared in the synagogue and shouted out, 'What do you want with us, Jesus the Nazarene? Have you come to destroy us? I know who you are—God's Holy One.' Jesus rebuked him: 'Shut up, and get out from him.' The evil spirit threw him into a fit, gave a great scream and left him.

Everyone was so amazed that they started asking each other, 'What is this? A new teaching with authority, and he commands the evil spirits and they obey him!' News about him immediately spread everywhere into the whole of the surrounding area of Galilee.

MARK 1:21–28

Peter leaves us in no doubt: the way Jesus acted surprised people and made them want to know who he was. But Jesus was not just an action man, a protestor, shocking people by his actions. Nor did he just 'talk a good talk' (although he did teach as if he really had something to say, not parroting previous opinion or reinforcing timeworn messages). He did both. He was a man of integrity with actions to match his words.

One reason why many of us are cynical about politics is that we don't see the connection between politicians' words and their actions—although we are probably also well aware that we find it hard to live up to our own intentions and promises. It's easy to protest and denounce something without offering an alternative suggestion. Here, however, right at the beginning of the Gospel, Peter tells of an incident that gets to the heart of Jesus, showing that he both taught and acted with power.

The scribes were not bad teachers. The point is that the whole scribal system—indeed, the whole religious system in Jesus' day—was based on the fact that God had spoken *in the past*. The only authority now lay in those scriptures; the scribes could only seek to explain them clearly. They had no authority to decide for themselves, but Jesus taught as if he did. So this raised the question: who did he think he was? Who can have authority to speak for God?

Many people, of course, claim to have authority to speak for God. Such self-proclaimed prophets and 'messiahs' were well-known in Jesus' day, just as in ours. However, in this incident in Capernaum, the evil spirit's words—and, more to the point, the way the spirit is compelled to obey Jesus' command—seem to imply that Jesus really does have that authority. Word gets round fast: there is something new and powerful going on, but what does it mean? The same is true when we manage to bring together our words and our deeds—when we offer not just talk, and not just good deeds, but words and actions together pointing to something deeper.

Forgiving sins

This first public appearance of Jesus sets the tone: the people are amazed, undeniable good is done, and yet there is an undercurrent of tension with the existing religious system (he is 'not like the scribes'). The next chapter will explore this clash with the religious authorities, but for now we will focus on what the clash says about Jesus' identity.

Some days later, he went back into Capernaum, and people heard that he was at home. So many people gathered that there was no space left, not even by the door, and he began to speak the word to them. Then they come bringing to him a paralysed man, carried by four people, but they couldn't bring him to Jesus because of the crowd, so they ripped up the roof above where he was, and when they broke through they lower the mat on which the paralysed man was lying.

*Jesus saw their faith and says to the paralysed man, 'Child,
your sins are forgiven.'*

*Now some scribes were sitting there thinking to themselves,
'Why does this guy talk like that? It's blasphemy! There is only
one person able to forgive sins—God!'*

*Immediately Jesus knew what they were thinking and
he says to them, 'Why are you thinking these things in your
hearts? Which is harder—to say to a paralysed man, "Your
sins are forgiven", or to say, "Get up and pick up your mat and
walk"? But so that you may know that the son of man has
authority to forgive sins on earth...' he says to the paralysed
man, '... I tell you, get up, pick up your mat and go back
home.'*

*He got up and straight away in front of everyone he picked
up his mat and went out. Everyone was stunned and praised
God, saying, 'We have never seen anything like it!'*

MARK 2:1–12

This is such a vivid story—the desperation of the friends
breaking through the roof, the confrontation with the scribes
and the dramatic healing—but what does the dialogue reveal
about Jesus' identity? The clue is not to take at face value the
scribes' outburst, 'There is only one person able to forgive
sins—God!' In fact, Jesus had not said, 'I forgive your sins',
but rather, 'Your sins are forgiven.' This is not just pedantry,
for, in the law (on which the scribes were supposedly
experts), God had provided for forgiveness to be declared—in
the temple. The whole point of the temple, the centrepoint
of Jewish religion at the time, was that people could find
forgiveness there.

Quite what the scribes were thinking is unclear. Crying
'blasphemy' was certainly a good way to oppose Jesus in a

crowd-catching fashion. It would also imply that Jesus was making himself out to be God, thus labelling him as a religious lunatic. Perhaps the scribes did understand that Jesus had not actually forgiven the sins himself, but, in their mind, it was blasphemy to claim that sins could be forgiven there in a house in Capernaum, rather than in God's temple in Jerusalem. Of course, John the Baptiser had also broken free of the temple system when he preached a baptism in the River Jordan for 'the forgiveness of sins'. The fact that so many went out to John implies that they shared a longing for something more than the scribes and temple were offering.

Jesus does not engage in discussion with the scribes; instead, he claims that he will demonstrate his authority by healing the man—and he does so. In the game of crowd-catching, he has clearly won; but on the theological level, too, what else can the scribes conclude but that God is on Jesus' side? How else could the miracle have happened?

Forgiveness, it seems, is now available in a new way— outside the bounds of the law, away from the temple— through the person of Jesus. But what does this say about who Jesus is?

The scribes had a clear understanding of the system through which God worked. It was a system revealed by God himself; they had not created it. Indeed, that was the point of the crowds' amazement at Jesus' authoritative teaching. The scribes did not have authority to change or develop what had been laid down, but Jesus shattered the system, refusing to be contained by it, claiming that with him everything changed. We, too, tend to have a system, drawn from the Bible and Christian theology, through which we believe God works. We think we know what God does and doesn't do. Indeed, those of us in Christian leadership think we know that God's system involves us, just as the priests in the temple believed that forgiveness came through them. Do we run the risk of shouting 'blasphemy' at Jesus when he chooses to act outside of our 'system'?

So, 57 verses into the Gospel, we seem to have Jesus' identity set out clearly. He is Messiah, Son of God, a teacher with new authority. He can free people from evil spirits and bring healing and forgiveness. He is exactly what we want. Presumably, we will find this identity being proclaimed throughout the rest of the Gospel, won't we? Strangely, we don't.

A hidden identity

Jesus withdrew to the sea with his disciples, and a huge crowd followed, from Galilee, Judea, Jerusalem, Idumea, the region beyond the Jordan and around Tyre and Sidon. A huge crowd who had heard what he was doing came to him.

He was healing many people and everyone who was sick was pushing forward to touch him. So he instructed his disciples to get a boat ready for him so that the crowd didn't crush him. Whenever the evil spirits saw him, they would fall down in front of him and cry out, 'You are the Son of God!' Yet he would rebuke them severely, telling them not to reveal who he was.

MARK 3:7–12

Why did Jesus hide his identity in this way? This is not a one-off, either. The demons are also commanded to silence in 1:34, and many times people are told to remain silent (see 1:44; 5:43; 7:36; 8:30; 9:9). This so-called 'messianic secret' has perplexed scholars for the last 100 years at least.

We think it obvious that Jesus would want people to hear that he was the Son of God. After all, if we were that important, we would want everyone to know! More seriously, surely Jesus' ministry was about 'spreading the word', so why would he command silence? The evil spirits were only saying publicly what God himself had said privately to Jesus at his baptism.

The oddity of this command to silence has led some to suggest that actually Jesus himself didn't issue it. Rather, they speculate, Mark (or Peter) invented the theme as a way of explaining why more people didn't recognise who Jesus was: they would have done, but Jesus himself tried to keep his identity a secret. However, can we really argue that we know instinctively what Jesus must have been like, and if the Gospels don't agree with us they must be wrong? Perhaps—but let's ponder Peter's preaching further before we decide that we know better.

People often surmise that Jesus commanded silence for his own protection. The huge crowds alone would inevitably have been a cause of concern for the authorities. Add in the rumours that he was claiming to be the Son of God (stirred up by his opponents, as we have seen), and perhaps they would have tried to stop him. There may be some truth in this, but Jesus didn't seem to mind generating a lot of public interest. Someone who wants to keep a low profile will probably not be casting out lots of evil spirits in the first place!

Perhaps the point is more that 'Son of God' is actually a vague term. It sounds important, but what does it mean? Jesus himself described all peacemakers as 'sons of God' (Matthew 5:9); Israel is called 'God's son' in Hosea 11:1, and so is David's son in 2 Samuel 7:14. As we noted about the first verse of the Gospel, the words 'Messiah, Son of God' can have no end of different meanings. When evil spirits shouted, 'You are the Son of God' as they were cast out, listeners might have inferred that being 'Son of God' was all about miracles and supernatural power. Perhaps Jesus tried to suppress the view of himself as a divine warrior, destroying all that opposes God, because it was a distortion. It was exactly the version of 'God's Son' that Jesus was tempted with in the desert.

So, a tension has emerged in Jesus' identity. He is Messiah, Son of God. He is a teacher with authority, the one bringing forgiveness and God's presence and rescue from evil. Yet, this is, at best, a distorted picture of who he really is.

Even the wind and the waves obey him

The following chapters of Mark's Gospel do little to dispel the view of Jesus as superhero. Jesus continues to do many miracles, revealing his power even though he also commands silence. Two particular incidents on the Sea of Galilee seem to have made a huge impression on his disciples.

First is the calming of the storm, a story much loved by Christians throughout the ages as a picture of how Jesus remains present in and calms the storms of life. It is also an important milestone in the story of the disciples, for this is the first time that Jesus criticises the limitations of their faith. Our focus now, though, is on what it says about who Jesus is.

That day, when evening came, he says to them, 'Let's go across to the other side.' So they leave the crowd and take him with them, just as he was, in the boat (other boats were with it, too).

Then a ferocious windstorm springs up, and waves began to crash into the boat. Already it was filling up with water. Yet Jesus was asleep on a cushion at the back of the boat. They wake him up and say to him, 'Teacher, don't you care that we are going to drown?'

He got up, rebuked the wind, and said to the sea, 'Be quiet! Restrain yourself!' The wind dropped and it was completely calm. He said to them, 'Why are you such cowards? Don't you yet have any faith?'

They were terrified and began to ask each other, 'Who is this? Even the wind and the sea obey him!'

MARK 4:35–41

There are few places where we would feel more helpless and terrified than in a small open boat during a raging storm, knowing that the boat is losing the battle. Some of the disciples were fishermen, which might have given them more confidence in dealing with the situation, but, on the other hand, they must have known how easily storms could wreck boats. There is also a wider background to be noted here. The Jewish people were not seagoing: the land of Israel had no natural harbours and, in the religious imagination, the sea ('the deep') was a place of chaos, threatening humanity. We see this in Genesis 1:2–10, where the created world is 'carved out' from the deep waters, and in verses such as Psalm 18:16, which talk of God rescuing us from 'mighty waters'.

Many commentators see this miracle as being fundamentally different from the previous ones. It is a 'nature miracle', a miracle on a large scale, not a healing or deliverance from demons, which the sceptical can see as being somehow 'in the mind' (although, of course, it is wrong to think that our minds are more easily healed than our bodies).

The way in which Jesus calms the wind and the waves only increases the impact of the miracle. It sounds as though he is dealing with a petulant child; indeed, the word I have translated as 'restrain' was used to mean putting a muzzle on a barking dog. It's as if Jesus is irritated both with the wind and waves and with the disciples: why bother him about something so trivial? Not only do the wind and waves obey him, but he doesn't even break into a sweat. He can't see what all the fuss is about.

Within the Old Testament, only God can control the waters. Psalm 89:8–9 puts it like this:

Who is like you, Lord God of Heaven's Armies? You, Lord, are strong, and utterly reliable. You rule over the roaring sea; you still the surging waves.

The description in Psalm 107:23–30 is particularly close to the story in Mark:

Some went down on the sea in boats… He stirred up a wind storm that lifted high the waves… In the disaster their courage melted… They cried out to the Lord in their distress, and he brought them out of their calamity. He stilled the storm and the waves were silenced. They were glad when it grew calm, and he guided them to the harbour they wanted.

Similarly, God controlled the waters of the Red Sea when rescuing the people of Israel from the Egyptians (Exodus 14:9—15:21).

We can appreciate the disciples' terror and questioning. The miracle itself would imply that 'Jesus the superhero' has even more power than they have yet seen. But the background in the scriptures and in Jewish thought pushes the point further. Only God can control the waters, so who is this man?

Not a man at all?

The next incident on the Sea of Galilee comes immediately after the feeding of the 5000, which itself speaks of Jesus' great power and echoes God's provision of manna in the desert to the Israelites as they fled Egypt (Exodus 16).

That night the boat was in the middle of the sea, and he is alone on the land. Just before dawn, he sees them struggling to row because the wind was against them, and he comes towards them walking on the water. It was looking as if he was going to pass them by, but when they saw him walking on the sea, they thought it was a ghost and cried out. They all saw him and were terrified. Immediately he spoke with them and said, 'Take courage. It's me. Don't be afraid.'

Then he climbed into the boat to them and the wind stopped. They were completely and utterly amazed, because they had not understood about the bread; rather their hearts were hardened.

MARK 6:47–52

The final verse of this passage is intriguing. It's as if the feeding of the 5000 should have prepared the disciples for what happened next. Perhaps, by now, they should have realised that Jesus' power was incredible and should also have grasped who he really was.

It was obvious to the disciples that no human can walk on water. Nowhere even in the Old Testament do we find

143

such a miracle (although in Job 9:8 we read that God alone 'trampled the waves of the sea'). Therefore, when they saw the figure on the water, they concluded that it could not be a man but must be a ghost, some sort of spiritual being. Then they found it was Jesus. The words translated here 'completely and utterly amazed' are the strongest statement of amazement that we find in the whole Gospel. Why? Perhaps because this miracle, for them, was something beyond a great work of power that a human might *do*; it challenged their ideas of what he *was*. He was acting like a spiritual being (we might say, an angel), not a man.

As we reach the halfway point in Mark's account of Peter's preaching, we have found that Jesus is Messiah, Son of God, more than just a man. He has authority in his teaching, over evil spirits, over sickness and over the natural world. He brings forgiveness and God's presence. And yet, throughout these chapters, we have also found that Jesus is reluctant for people to be told about him on the basis of this power. Then, at the hinge in the middle of the Gospel, it all comes to a head.

So wrong

Jesus and his disciples set out towards the villages around Caesarea Philippi. On the way he questioned his disciples. 'Who do people say that I am?' They replied, 'John the Baptist, and others Elijah, and others one of the prophets.' And he asked them, 'And you? Who do you say that I am?' Peter replies, 'You are the Messiah!'

MARK 8:27–29

Was this just a casual conversation? Did Jesus really want to check up on his popularity? I don't think so. Caesarea Philippi was 25 miles north of Galilee, in Gentile lands, so this journey would have taken Jesus and his disciples away from the crowds. He seems to have been getting some space so that he could try to address the disciples' confusion (8:21: 'Do you still not understand?'). Presumably, Jesus already knew what people were saying about him, but his question was a way of opening up the discussion about his true identity.

Peter's response, 'You are the Messiah!' sounds right. 'Messiah' was a fairly flexible concept at the time—it meant someone anointed by God to bring about God's rescue of his people—but the details of whether the Messiah would be a man or a spiritual being, and how he would bring rescue, were seen differently by different groups. To name him as Messiah is a way of capturing, within a Jewish framework, the sense of Jesus as the focal point of God's authority and activity in the world, bringing forgiveness and longed-for rescue.

Jesus' initial reaction is... mixed.

He ordered them not to speak to anyone about him, and began to teach them that it was necessary for the Son of Man to suffer much and be rejected by the elders and chief priests and scribes and to be killed, and after three days to rise again. He was saying this openly to them.

MARK 8:30–32A

Jesus neither denies nor challenges Peter's conclusion that he is the Messiah. We, of course, have already been told that he is the Messiah in the opening verse of the Gospel, and later, during his trial, Jesus will acknowledge that he is the

Messiah, but that is in the future. At this point, although Jesus does not deny the title, he immediately turns away from it. He forbids the disciples to speak of it (just as he had forbidden the evil spirits to proclaim that he was 'Son of God') and starts to explain some far less appealing teaching about the 'Son of Man'.

'Son of Man' is a complicated phrase. It could mean just 'a human being', in the way that the children in C.S. Lewis's Narnia Chronicles are called 'sons of Adam' and 'daughters of Eve'. It is used with that meaning in Ezekiel (for example, 2:1) and in Psalm 8:4 ('What is man that you remember him, the son of man that you care for him?'). Jesus himself uses it in this way once in Mark's Gospel (3:28: 'all sins will be forgiven to the sons of man except...'). However, the phrase is used differently in Daniel 7:13, where the context is a vision in which God's people are oppressed by evil empires. The empires are represented by beasts, and God's people are represented by 'one looking like a son of man'. The interpretation of the vision in Daniel 7:15–28 makes clear that the 'son of man' represents God's people as they suffer greatly but are finally vindicated by God.

It is right to connect Jesus' use of the phrase 'Son of Man' here with Daniel 7, since Jesus is telling a story of the 'Son of Man' suffering and then being vindicated, matching the story in Daniel 7. (Furthermore, in his trial, in Mark 14:62, he explicitly quotes Daniel 7:13.)

So what is going on? Jesus seems to be sidestepping the title of Messiah, with all its connotations of power and importance, and instead picking up a thread from the Old Testament in which God's faithful people suffer greatly before being vindicated by God. This he is saying 'openly', in contrast to the secrecy surrounding the claims of his Messiahship.

This is not what Peter and, presumably, the other disciples (and, indeed, ourselves if we are honest) want to hear. Peter has seen Jesus' power and authority and has connected them with the promised glorious rescue by God. Why must Jesus pick up this other strand in the scriptures, which talks of suffering? Peter, honest and straightforward as ever, wants to put Jesus right.

> *Peter took him to one side and began to rebuke him. But Jesus turned round, looked at his disciples and rebuked Peter: 'Get behind me, Satan! You are not thinking about God's ways, but human ways.'*
>
> MARK 8:32B–33

Oh dear! Jesus declares that Peter, his closest disciple, is Satan, the power of evil in the world, the one who lies and deceives God's people. It's not surprising that this stuck in Peter's mind and that Mark has placed it as the centrepoint in his account of Peter's preaching.

Peter might have been wrong, but were his words really so terrible? At the beginning of the Gospel, Satan tested, or tempted, Jesus (1:13). Unwittingly, Peter has done exactly the same. Temptation, of course, is only really temptation when it is something persuasive, almost right, and very convenient. I am never tempted to think I am a great footballer, because it would be laughable. But to think that I am a little bit more important than I am, or deserve a bit more respect...? That is tempting.

Here we see that being the Messiah that everyone expects —a figure with authority and power—is a temptation that Jesus is fighting to resist. He is hanging on to a different vision of how God's plan unfolds for God's faithful people.

The 'Son of Man' is eventually vindicated and receives great glory (Daniel 7:14), just as we might expect of the Messiah, but before then he suffers greatly.

Peter is right: Jesus is the Messiah. However, without qualification, the title is deeply misleading and needs to be kept quiet (just like the title 'Son of God'). It implies a 'straight road to glory', while Jesus has in mind a different path. His road to vindication and glory will follow the pattern of the 'Son of Man' in Daniel: it is necessary for him first to suffer much. The title of 'Messiah' is, at best, only the initial step in gaining a true picture of Jesus.

The same is true in many people's development of faith: they begin with a sense of God's powerful rescue, but later, often with great anguish, come to understand that God will not always rescue them from suffering but will go through it with them. It is interesting to note that the passage immediately preceding this one in Mark describes the only 'two-stage' healing in the Gospels: a blind man is healed but, initially, only to a point at which people look to him like 'walking trees' (8:24). Before he achieves full sight, he sees a distortion.

Before we try to assess where this leaves us, we should read on to the beginning of Mark 9, where Jesus takes his disciples up a 'high mountain'. Perhaps Jesus left Galilee (8:27) on purpose to go to this mountain in the region of Caesarea Philippi, and the discussion of who he was, on the road, may have been preparing the disciples for what was about to happen there. These incidents all fit together as a single 'interlude' in Jesus' public ministry—a 'hinge' in the middle of the Gospel—where his true identity and vocation are revealed.

Confirmed

Six days later Jesus takes Peter, James and John and leads them up a high mountain to be completely alone. He was changed in front of their eyes and his clothes became brilliant white, whiter than any bleach on earth could achieve. Then Elijah appeared in front of them with Moses and they were talking with Jesus.

Seeing all this, Peter said to Jesus, 'Master, it is good that we are here. Let's make three shelters, one for you, one for Moses and one for Elijah.' (For he didn't know what to say because they were all frightened.) Then a cloud overshadowed them, and then a voice came from the cloud: 'This is my dear son; listen to him.' Suddenly when they looked around they couldn't see anyone any more, just Jesus alone with them.

MARK 9:2–8

The Gospel is a rollercoaster ride. In the previous passage, Peter proclaimed Jesus' power and authority, only to be rebuked. Now, God himself confirms that same power and authority.

Brilliant white is the standard colour for spiritual beings, such as the angels at the tomb (Matthew 28:3) and even God himself (Daniel 7:9): no bleach *on earth* could match it. Jesus is at one with the greatest Old Testament heroes—Moses, who established the nation and spoke with God face to face, and Elijah, who defeated the powers of evil, was taken up into heaven and was destined to return (Malachi 4:5). Then the voice comes from the cloud, elevating Jesus above even Moses and Elijah. Clearly he is, indeed, 'more than a man'.

However, we are not left just with a vision of his power and importance. God's voice tells the disciples that Jesus is his 'dear son'. This echoes the words spoken at Jesus' baptism, but they were heard only by Jesus, whereas this voice speaks to the three disciples (compare 9:7, '*This* is my son', with 1:11, '*You* are my son'). They are being brought into the secret.

At the beginning of the Gospel, the titles 'Messiah' and 'God's Son' came together. We have the same here, in effect, with Peter proclaiming Jesus as 'Messiah', and God's voice confirming him as 'Son'. In between, Jesus introduces the idea and vocation of the 'Son of Man'. He is Messiah; he is God's Son; but these titles need to be seen through the lens of the 'Son of Man' in Daniel 7. Peter's preaching will not allow us to think of Jesus' power without reminding us that his calling was to suffer first, and only then to reach glory.

While they were going down the mountain, he ordered them not to say anything to anyone until the Son of Man rose from the dead. They seized on to this, discussing among themselves what this 'rising from the dead' might be.

MARK 9:9–10

Once again, here we have the command to silence: what happened on the mountain cannot be spoken about. The fact that Jesus is the 'Son of God' needs to be kept secret until the suffering of the 'Son of Man' has happened. Otherwise, people will get the distorted idea that Jesus' identity is all about power and authority. As Jesus' exchange with Peter ('Satan!') and his prayer in Gethsemane (Mark 14:36) suggest, even he himself needed to keep fighting the temptation to use his power for his own sake. That is not God's way (8:33).

Sadly, the disciples still don't understand—but then, nor do we, most of the time. We constantly find ourselves believing that if we are doing God's will, if we are following Jesus, then everything will work out well and God's power will give us the victory. But Peter tells us that, in fact, power is only half the story. Jesus is Messiah and Son of God, but he is also the Son of Man who suffers before glory.

Confirmation is important. We saw God confirming to Jesus that he was his dear Son and that he was pleased with him, at his baptism, before he started his work. Here, perhaps, his status is being reconfirmed for his benefit, given that he is about to face suffering and death. Perhaps more importantly, it is being confirmed for the disciples' benefit, as they enter a new phase—needing to understand that Jesus is a Messiah who will be rejected in Jerusalem, and will suffer and die. If this was important for Jesus and the disciples, we need not be surprised that it is true for us, too. We need regularly to be reminded of our own status as God's children and of his love for us as we continue our walk.

Surprisingly, perhaps, the question of Jesus' identity takes a back seat in the rest of the Gospel, as other agendas come to the fore. Of course, the Gospel itself is not split into themes quite as neatly as they appear in this book, but on this particular question it seems as if there is nothing more to be said. Jesus' power and authority have been established, as has the fact that he is following a path of suffering.

Confrontation

Finally the question of who Jesus is erupts back on to the stage when he is arrested.

> *They led Jesus to the high priest, and they all gather there—the*
> *most important priests, the elders and the scribes. Peter followed*

him from a distance right into the high priest's courtyard. He was sitting there with the servants, warming himself on the fire.

The important priests and the whole of the council were looking for evidence against Jesus so they could put him to death, but they couldn't find any. For although many were giving false evidence against him, their evidence was contradictory. Then some people stood up and gave false evidence against him, saying, 'We heard him saying, "I will tear down this temple made by human hands, and three days later I will build a temple not touched by human hands."' But even here, their evidence wouldn't agree.

Then the high priest stood up in the centre and asked Jesus, 'Have you no answer to these accusations?' But he remained silent, giving no answer. Again the high priest questioned him: 'Are you the Messiah, the Son of the Blessed One?' Jesus said, 'I am, and you will see the Son of Man sitting on the right side of the Power and coming with the clouds of heaven.'

The high priest tears his robes and says, 'Why do we still need evidence? You heard the blasphemy. What do you think?' They all condemned him as deserving to die.

MARK 14:53–64

The high priest, in a sense, gets it right. (Interestingly, in John 11:49–52 we find the high priest prophesying truthfully, without knowing what he is saying.) The significance of Jesus—what is important about him—is not to be found in individual sayings or particular healings, what he did or didn't say about the temple, or exactly what constitutes blasphemy. What matters is who he is. Is he the Messiah, the Son of God?

This 'trial' is really a clash between two claims to power,

two claims to represent God. The high priest, the Jewish religious leadership and the temple are on one side, and Jesus on the other. In this context, Jesus' quotation from Daniel 7:13, about the Son of Man sitting on the right side of the Power (God) and coming with the clouds of heaven, takes on a particular meaning, because the words 'you will see' are not actually found in Daniel 7:13. To me, this suggests that Jesus is pointing the finger, speaking words of confrontation. 'I am,' he says, 'and *you will see* God prove me right.' After the silence and the cloaking of his identity, finally it seems that the truth is revealed. However, this encounter is not really about truth; it's about confrontation. Despite all the discussion of religious law, the question is personal. Who is God with?

Daniel 7 tells the story of God's people being oppressed by evil, godless empires, suffering but finally being vindicated. Jesus' use of it here effectively claims that the high priest, temple and Jewish religious leadership are a godless empire, and that, despite that empire's apparent power, God will vindicate his true people.

This climax confirms the point that has recurred throughout Mark. His Gospel is personal. It is not about the rights or wrongs of this or that piece of teaching; it is not about the right words or actions; it is not about understanding. It is about responding to Jesus. Which side are you on?

Revealed in his death

So when is it all going to happen? The challenge has been laid down. Who is God with—Jesus or the high priest? When will the high priest 'see'?

Jesus gave a loud cry and died. The curtain of the temple was torn in two from top to bottom. When the centurion who stood facing him saw how he died, he said, 'Truly this man was the Son of God.'

MARK 15:37–39

Jesus' parables, as we will see in Chapter 7, are stories with the wrong endings. Now we find that the whole story of Jesus also appears to have the wrong ending. Jesus has set up a confrontation with the high priest and now... well, he has lost. He has died.

Yet it is at this moment that the Roman soldier who has been responsible for killing him proclaims that he was 'God's Son'. The true impact of this declaration emerges when we notice that this is the first time in the whole Gospel when a human being calls Jesus 'God's Son'. We were told it at the beginning, and the demons have tried to announce it. Indeed, we know that it is Jesus' truest fullest identity, for God has directly confirmed it twice from heaven. Yet it has remained outside human understanding until now—until his death.

Jesus' identity is fully revealed only in his death.

In a sense, of course, we knew this already. When Peter proclaimed that Jesus was the Messiah, Jesus immediately 'corrected' him with talk of his death (8:29–31). Any expressions of his identity that were not based on his death were inadequate. In effect, this means that dying was not something that Jesus *did*, but was, in fact, central to who he *was*. This challenges our tendency to keep Jesus' suffering and death 'in a box'. We know that it happened and we rejoice at the salvation it brings us. Nevertheless, we work on the basis that Jesus was 'really' a powerful, compassionate Saviour. His suffering was just a temporary necessary evil. How uncomfortable it is to see that suffering is integral to Jesus' identity—uncomfortable particularly for us, his followers, who are called to imitate him.

Vindication will come. Indeed, we see a foretaste of it in the tearing of the temple curtain. This is often seen as representing the opening of access to God. Hebrews 10:19–20 certainly suggests that interpretation: 'We have confidence to enter the holy place by the blood of Jesus. He opened up this new and living way for us through the curtain.' However, we can't be sure that this is what Peter had in mind. We are on safer ground to see it first of all as a 'dramatic parable', a divine sign that, in the confrontation between the high priest/temple and Jesus, God was on Jesus' side. Jesus would be vindicated and the whole temple would be destroyed (as Jesus had said in 13:2). In the story in Daniel 7, the 'one like a son of man' does in the end receive authority, glory, power, worship and an everlasting kingdom. (It is also interesting to note that the only other time when Mark uses the word 'tear' is at Jesus' baptism in 1:10, when God tears open the heavens to confirm that Jesus is his Son.)

We know, of course, that the crucifixion was not the end of the story. Jesus rose from the dead. We are told that this will happen at least five times in the Gospel. However, before we rush on to the resurrection, we have to face the fact that the resurrected Jesus is never seen in Mark's Gospel. His account ends at Mark 16:8, without any resurrection appearances. (Mark 16:9–20, as all modern Bibles indicate, is a later addition, dealing with the 'problem' that there are no resurrection appearances by summarising those found in the other Gospels.)

We should keep faith with Peter's preaching and the way

Mark, his interpreter, recorded it. Jesus' true identity is proclaimed not at his glorious resurrection but at his death.

Who is Jesus? He is the Son of God, the Messiah, more than a man. He has authority in teaching, and over nature, sickness and evil spirits. He has compassion and brings God's rescue and forgiveness. He seems to stand in place of God. But most of all, Peter tells us, he is the one who followed God's path through suffering to his own death. If we want to see what Jesus is really like—what 'Son of God' really means—we must look at the man dying on the cross.

CHAPTER 6

THE LAW

'Mum, I'm pregnant.' The words hang in the air, the silence ominous, a storm about to break. 'How could this happen?' is the final reply, as the 17-year-old's mother sinks into a kitchen chair. The daughter wisely stifles a nervous retort about the birds and the bees, as her mum carries on: 'But we brought you up properly; you've been doing well at college. I've worked so hard to make sure this is a proper home, and clean, and you've always had nice clothes.' She lets it all wash over her, not sure what GCSE Maths and her mum's obsession with dusting has to do with anything. Inwardly she is playing out for the hundredth time how her dad will react. Will he really issue those words, 'You are no child of mine', like in some Victorian melodrama?

The next days are grim. She knows what they're saying. She's heard it said about other 'sluts'. 'It's disgusting.' 'Wicked girls like her get pregnant just to get a council flat, while hardworking decent folk are on the waiting list for years.' 'Her brat will soon be running feral around the streets and other people will have to pay for it.'

There are glimmers of hope, though. She almost cries when the woman next door stops her in the street, gives her a hug and whispers, 'Just ignore them—we all have a past, and you'll be a great mum.' And who would have thought

Uncle George, of all people, would tell her, 'If you ever need anything, you just tell me.'

It's her friends' responses that hurt the most. Most of them are sleeping with their boyfriends as well, but that doesn't stop them coming over all moral on her. A few stick with her, but it's as if she has some sort of disease. OK, so their parents are putting pressure on them—using her as an example of what happens if you sleep around—but even so. She feels like an outcast.

This is a scenario played out many times a year in families up and down the land, but it is hugely complex and speaks directly into the question of 'the law' in Jesus' day. The mum's reaction, odd in its way, speaks of the connection at a deep level in the human psyche between moral and physical 'cleanliness', and the importance of keeping up appearances. We see the human tendency to attribute motives, and see ourselves as being harmed by others' actions: it's all a plot to jump the housing waiting list; 'they' will be the ones paying for 'her' actions.

Those who, in fact, are not so different can respond in completely opposite ways. 'We all have a past,' says one kindly, expressing the solidarity of those who have 'been there' themselves. However, for others, the similarity makes them react even more strongly, needing to distance themselves publicly from the offence, precisely because it is so close to their own experience. It's hypocritical, of course, but perfectly logical. For the other young women, their families and the wider community, the 'offender' is a representation of the disaster that is always hovering close by, which needs to be pushed away.

Many of us find it hard to connect with the issues surrounding 'the law' in the Gospels. As soon as we hear the word 'law' or encounter scribes or Pharisees, we think of legalism, petty laws and a lack of forgiveness. We have an image of Jewish people being 'weighed down' by endless laws. But the situation is not so simple. Ask a lawyer today how many laws there are in Britain, and the answer is almost beyond count, certainly tens of thousands, and definitely more than in the Judaism of Jesus' day. Yet most of us don't feel weighed down by them. A law prevents me from putting my child in my own car and driving down the road if he isn't strapped into a car seat. A law prevents me from building my extension if I don't use roof beams of the right thickness. A law prevents me from posting on Twitter what I think of that celebrity in court for shameful crimes. But none of these laws weighs me down, and I am actually pleased that a 'petty law' prevents my neighbours from playing loud music at three in the morning.

Encouraging the good is not straightforward, as my opening story illustrated. Spurning, criticising and 'making an example' of the young woman seems harsh. Yet how else do we encourage good behaviour other than by making sure that life is uncomfortable if you are irresponsible?

Love the Pharisees

What were the Pharisees (and the scribes and others) trying to do? To understand Jesus' clash with them, we need to understand them—and to understand them, we need some history.

Israel was not a contented place in Jesus' day. It was an occupied land, having been conquered by the Romans 100 years before. For the inhabitants, this brought with it the humiliation of being a conquered people, with foreign soldiers controlling their land and Roman governors being in control. It brought poverty, as the Romans demanded taxes, partly to swell the riches of Rome and the Roman ruling classes, partly to pay for the very army that was oppressing them. Roman occupation brought increasing financial burdens, which people could pay only by selling their ancestral lands. Thus, they were reduced to the insecurity of being hired labourers. (Many of Jesus' parables and other teachings are about debt and landless labourers.)

The situation may have felt slightly different in Galilee, as opposed to Jerusalem and Judea. Galilee was ruled by Herod (the son of Herod the Great, who was king of the whole of Israel when Jesus was born). Herod, like his father before him, was a Roman appointee—only a puppet king, put in place to rule as Rome wanted—but his presence meant that Roman soldiers were less visible. It is also true that some in Israel benefited very nicely from Roman conquest. The Romans were happy to rule through local leaders, such as Herod or the high priest. Rulers also need bureaucrats (such as the 'tax collectors' who turn up in the Gospels) and armies need supplies. There was money to be made for a few—but that only added to the sense of division within Israel.

Where was God in all this? It was a question that only added to the sense of discontentment, but it also leads us towards an understanding of the Pharisees. If Israel was God's people in God's land, why had it been conquered by the godless foreigners? That question 'Why?' was not just a cry of desperation. It had been asked for many centuries within Judaism, and many people thought that the answer was clear.

We need to look back briefly to the first time foreign armies conquered Israel. It had been an independent nation for nearly five centuries from the time of David (about 1000BC) through to its defeat by the Babylonians (586BC). There is more detail to be noted, of course; in fact, the nation had split into two kingdoms—Israel in the north, around Galilee, a kingdom that was destroyed in the early 700s BC by the Assyrians, and Judah in the south, around Jerusalem. Nevertheless, if we stick to the big picture, we have 'the Jewish nation' defeated, the temple destroyed and the people taken into exile in Babylon. Why had God allowed this to happen? The Old Testament provides a clear answer:

> *And the nations will know that the people of Israel went into exile because of their sin, because they were unfaithful to me.*
> EZEKIEL 39:23

All was not lost, however. The prophets also gave a promise: God would rescue his people and establish them in peace and prosperity.

> *'Comfort, comfort my people,' says your God. 'Speak to Jerusalem's heart, and proclaim to her that she has completed her sentence, her sin has been paid for, she has received from the Lord's hand double for all her sins.' A voice of someone shouting: 'In the desert prepare the Lord's way; make straight in the desert a highway for our God.'*
> ISAIAH 40:1–3

> *'Get up and shine! For your light has come, and the glory of the Lord has risen upon you… Nations will come to your light, and kings to the brightness of your dawn… The wealth of the sea will be brought to you, the riches of the nations will come to you.'*
> ISAIAH 60:1–5

Had this promise come true? Partly, it had, in as much as the Persian King Cyrus had allowed Jews to return from exile to Jerusalem. The temple had been rebuilt and the Jewish nation was re-established (as told in the biblical books of Nehemiah and Ezra). Yet the nation still wasn't independent. It had been ruled by the Persians, then the Greeks, then the Romans. Periods of great hardship had come, such as the time when the Greek King Antiochus IV had attacked Judaism by sacrificing pigs to the Greek god Zeus in the temple in Jerusalem, burning the scriptures and forbidding circumcision. Moreover, the wealth of the seas and the riches of the nations had certainly not come to Israel. Instead, Israel's wealth and the fruit of its hard labour were draining away to Rome.

This scenario led to different responses. There were armed rebellions, which had some success at times (for example, the Maccabean revolt in 168BC). There was also much compromise, with many Israelites deciding 'If you can't beat them, join them'—backpedalling their Jewish identity and making the best of being part of the Roman empire.

The Pharisees, however, were part of a different, theological response. The prophecies made it clear that the nation had gone into exile for its sin. If the exile had not really ended, it must be because the nation was still sinning. So the answer was to stop sinning—not just as individuals but as a nation. The movement espousing this logic emerged a few hundred years before Jesus, at the time of the Maccabean revolt, when the people refused to compromise, dedicating themselves to their religion, and God gave them victory.

One part of this movement established a community in the desert by the Dead Sea, whose library—the Dead Sea Scrolls—was discovered in 1947. The community applied

Isaiah 40:3 to themselves: they were the voice in the desert calling the people back to God. The same prophecy is applied in Mark's Gospel to John the Baptiser, as we saw in the previous chapter, because John was 'in the desert' commanding people to repent of their sins. Theologians never agree! Nevertheless, there was a broad movement in Jesus' day, which believed that the solution to the Jewish nation's problems was for the nation as a whole to stop sinning. That way, the great prophecies would be fulfilled and God would end the exile.

Enter the Pharisees. They were members of a reform movement within Judaism, aimed at stopping the nation sinning. Three features of their movement are important to us here. First, the Pharisees tried to make the law clear to people, and easy to follow in normal life. Ambiguity or room for personal interpretation would only lead to people making the wrong choices and continuing to sin. For example, the Old Testament says that you should not work on the sabbath (Exodus 20:9–10), but what counts as work? The answer needed to be worked out through theological discussion and then taught to the people. Second, the problem was that 'the nation' was sinning, not just individuals . Therefore the Pharisees spread out across the villages and towns, in Galilee as well as around Jerusalem, trying to teach everyone. Hence their frequent appearances in the Gospels. Third, the fact that the problem was communal (the nation's sin) meant that social pressure needed to be applied—showcasing the good and shaming the bad. 'Each to their own' could not work, because the exile, and the return from exile, were all about the sin of 'the nation'.

So, as we encounter the Pharisees and the scribes (people who helped interpret the law, to make it clearer), we should remember that they were not harsh, pernickety legalists who tried to make life hard for people. They were truly dedicated, seeking to make the law clear and practical, so that God would act to fulfil the prophecies, and peace, prosperity and security would come to the nation.

Teaching with authority

We turn now to the first passage in Mark in which some tension is expressed between Jesus and the religious system of his day. Significantly, this is in response to Jesus' very first piece of public teaching. The clash with religious authorities does not emerge only at the end of Jesus' ministry: Mark establishes it as a theme right from the beginning.

> *They go into Capernaum. On the sabbath, he went into the synagogue and immediately began to teach. They were shocked at his teaching, because he didn't teach like the scribes; he taught as if he had authority.*
>
> *Straight away a man in the grip of an evil spirit appeared in the synagogue and shouted out, 'What do you want with us, Jesus the Nazarene? Have you come to destroy us? I know who you are—God's Holy One.' Jesus rebuked him: 'Shut up, and get out from him.' The evil spirit threw him into a fit, gave a great scream and left him.*
>
> *Everyone was so amazed that they started asking each other, 'What is this? A new teaching, with authority; and he commands the evil spirits and they obey him!' News about him immediately spread everywhere into the whole of the surrounding area of Galilee.*
>
> MARK 1:21–28

We have already considered the miracle of the driving out of the evil spirit (see Chapter 4). Nevertheless, let us think for a moment about the teaching. 'He taught as if he had authority', in contrast to 'the scribes' (v. 22). This idea is repeated in verse 27: 'a new teaching, with authority'. The contrast is drawn because the Pharisees and scribes made it clear that they did not have authority. God's requirements were laid down in the law, which needed clarifying and explaining, perhaps applying to new situations. So the Pharisees and scribes were simply interpreters and teachers of what was already given.

Jesus was different, and this might surprise us. We might think that Jesus was also teaching the Old Testament, telling people how better to follow God's guidance. He certainly seems to have been willing to identify himself with his relative John the Baptiser's movement, by being baptised by him. That baptism 'in the desert' for the forgiveness of sins was definitely part of the belief system into which the Pharisees and most scribes would fit. However, Peter's preaching is clear: the people who heard Jesus thought his teaching was different. Furthermore, what was different was not a particular aspect of its content, but the authority with which Jesus taught.

This passage is only a tantalising glimpse. It doesn't clarify Jesus' relationship to the Jewish law. We could understand it as meaning that he brought new interpretations of the law, which he asserted with great vigour, or that he added to or changed the law, claiming that he personally had authority over God's law. Nevertheless, it establishes right from the start that Jesus cannot comfortably be seen within the religious system of his day. It sets up a tension that will grow.

A testimony of what?

Mark 1 continues with accounts of many more healings and exorcisms. Then we have a particular healing of a leper, which concludes with an intriguing, rather ambiguous phrase, concerning Jesus' relationship with the religious system.

Very early in the morning, while it was still dark, he got up and left. He went off to a remote place and began to pray there. Simon and those with him chased after him and found him. They say to him, 'Everyone is looking for you.' He tells them, 'Let us go elsewhere, to the surrounding villages so I can preach there as well. For this is why I left.' He went into the whole of Galilee preaching in their synagogues and driving out demons.

A leper comes to him, kneeling down and begging, 'If you are willing, you are able to make me clean.' Deeply moved, Jesus stretched out his hand, touched him. 'I am willing,' he says. 'Be clean!' Immediately the leprosy left him and he was clean.

Jesus sent him away with a severe warning: 'Don't say anything to anyone, but go and show yourself to the priest and make the sacrifice for your cleansing which Moses laid down, as a testimony to them.'

But the man went off and began to proclaim and spread the word so vigorously that Jesus was no longer able to enter a town openly, but stayed outside in remote places. They began to come to him from all over.

MARK 1:35–45

Various features of this story echo the themes we have already encountered in this book. We see Jesus' miracle-working motivated by his compassion for the person who comes and asks. We see Jesus attempting to silence those who are healed:

will the miracles give him the wrong sort of reputation? We see the futility of this attempt: the one helped by Jesus spreads his fame. This passage also establishes a sense of Jesus' popularity: Simon and those with him are chasing after him, 'everyone' is seeking him, he is no longer able to enter a town openly, and people come to him from all over the place. Nevertheless, Jesus has a clear sense of purpose, located in an itinerant ministry throughout Galilee: 'Let us go elsewhere...' We can imagine that this movement is necessitated by his popularity—he needs to stay outside in remote places—but it seems to be more than that. John the Baptiser drew huge crowds, who came out into 'the desert' or 'remote places' to see him, but he didn't move around. John stayed put and the people came to him, whereas Jesus seems to want to go to people. He acts out his proclamation that 'God's reign is near' by physically coming near to people.

It's Jesus' command to the man, though, which is of particular interest to us as we explore the theme of the law. 'Don't say anything to anyone' is the intriguing, but normal, command to secrecy. 'Go and show yourself to the priest and make the sacrifice for your cleansing which Moses laid down' refers to the procedures laid out in Leviticus 13 by which priests would examine those with skin diseases, declaring them clean or unclean. 'As a testimony to them', though, is rather more difficult to interpret. As a testimony to whom? And as a testimony of what?

There are two main ways to interpret this phrase. The first is to see it as a conciliatory gesture by Jesus. Yes, the man has been healed by Jesus, but he should still go through the normal procedure for a leper who has become clean, involving the existing religious authorities. Although we might think that healing is the more important element,

Jesus is deliberately accepting the authorities' role, seeking to work alongside, or even within, the existing system. The 'testimony' would presumably be to the people in general and to the priests: they should all note that he is not trying to destroy the established order.

Under the second, more aggressive, interpretation, the man's purpose in going to the priest is to demonstrate to him that God is at work, but not through the temple system. He is, in effect, carrying news of Jesus to the temple, testifying to the authorities that God is at work in a new way in Galilee, beyond them. This interpretation still has Jesus telling the man to carry out what Moses laid down in the law (he is a faithful Jew, after all), but challenging, not working alongside, the religious practices of his day.

Perhaps, though, we should not draw too sharp a line between these interpretations. In both, Jesus is upholding the law as laid down by Moses, and people are getting the message that God is at work powerfully in a new way. This fits the tone of the preceding and following passages. As we have seen, Jesus was thought to have a startling new authority in his teaching and miracle-working, communicating that something new was happening. The passage immediately following is the healing of the paralysed man, which we considered in Chapter 5, in which Jesus proclaims the man's sins forgiven, taking upon himself the role of the temple.

I don't believe we can be certain whether Jesus sent the man to the priests as a conciliatory gesture or a more aggressive one. Nevertheless, this story contributes to the growing picture that, while Jesus may not have been challenging the law of Moses, God was at work in a new way in the person of this Galilean itinerant preacher. This would have been deeply challenging to the religious system and authorities of his day.

The wrong company

When Jesus called Peter, Andrew, James and John (Mark 1:16–20), the call was dramatic and open-ended, and it seemed very personal: 'you follow me'. However, there was no sense that the people being called were inappropriate in any way. It's probably a mistake to romanticise these fishermen as 'the salt of the earth', but they are presented as being normal people. In the middle of Mark 2, though, we find something quite different.

> *He went out again beside the sea. A large crowd would come to him and he would teach them.*
>
> *As he went along he saw Levi, Alphaeus' son, sitting at the tax collector's booth. He says to him, 'Follow me!' Levi stood up and followed him.*
>
> *Later Jesus was eating in his house, and many tax collectors and 'sinners' were eating with Jesus and his disciples, for there were many who followed him. The scribes who were Pharisees saw that he was eating with 'sinners' and tax collectors, and were saying to his disciples, 'Why does he eat with tax collectors and "sinners"?'*
>
> *When Jesus heard this, he says to them, 'It's not the healthy who need a doctor, but the sick. I have not come to call the righteous, but sinners!'*
>
> MARK 2:13–17

At the heart of this short account lies the question of the differences in approach between Jesus and the Pharisees. Although we must be careful when we are turning real people (the Pharisees) into representatives of a particular way of thinking, we see in this story two different approaches to the work of God in the world.

169

Let's take a step back and think about the characters involved. The phrase 'the scribes who were Pharisees' (or 'the scribes of the Pharisees' in some translations) might sound a little contorted, but it is historically accurate. Being a scribe was a job: some Bibles translate 'scribe' as 'teacher of the law', so the scribes were the experts in the law. A Pharisee was someone who held a particular opinion about what was needed to save Israel: the nation as a whole needed to be taught to follow God's law better so that the nation would stop sinning and God would act to bring the exile to a definite end. So 'the scribes who were Pharisees' were experts in the law who shared this opinion. The fact that Mark preserves this technicality (not all scribes were Pharisees and not all Pharisees were scribes) is perhaps another reflection of the detail in Peter's preaching, but we will not lose much if we think of these people as 'Pharisees'.

Who were the tax collectors and the 'sinners'? They were not the poor or those marginalised because of disease, age or gender. This conflict was not about Jesus siding with the poor against the establishment. Nor should we see in the term 'sinners' a reference to all of us: the Pharisees knew that everyone sinned, but this was a particular group.

'Sinners' was a word used to denote those Jews who had chosen to abandon their Jewish heritage, to give up on the covenant. They were not just people who happened to do things wrong, but people who had 'chosen a life of sin', living as if they were no longer Jews. Similarly, the 'tax collectors' were not working to support the Jewish nation, providing funds for schools, defence and infrastructure, as we might think of tax collectors today. They were working for the Romans, extracting money from Jews and passing it over to the oppressive, godless occupying power. The way in which the Romans organised tax collection also meant that the job involved extortion and corruption. Generally, someone would buy the right to be a tax collector, undertaking to pay Rome the tax expected and then using a fair degree of liberty to accumulate as much extra money as they could. Therefore, they were taking money from the people both for personal gain and to hand it over to the hated Romans.

Thus, the tax collectors and sinners together represent Jews who were betraying the Jewish nation—abandoning their own calling as part of God's people and, in the process, watering down the nation or even working for the invaders. This was anathema to the Pharisees in particular. As we have learnt, they were focused on reforming the whole nation, encouraging and steering it to follow the law and to be God's people more faithfully, so that God would rescue the nation. The tax collectors and 'sinners' were, in a sense, the Pharisees' nemesis: they were the ones who were keeping the nation in sin, thus preventing God from rescuing it.

So how does Jesus relate to these people? Presumably it would be acceptable, even praiseworthy, if he was calling the 'sinners' to change their ways. But that is not what is happening. There is no mention of repentance or change. It sounds as if Jesus is simply spending time with them socially. The Pharisees' question, and the information that many tax collectors and 'sinners' followed him, also suggest that the dinner party here was not a one-off incident. This is further supported by Jesus' response: he links his whole purpose with these sorts of people. (In Matthew 11:19 and Luke 7:34, we find him summed up as 'a glutton and a drunkard, a friend of tax collectors and "sinners"'.) Jesus seems to be relaxing with these people and enjoying their company, implying publicly that God likes them. What sort of example does this set?

Jesus' response seems straightforward: he has come to save people like these. However, it begs two questions. First, it might be true, but isn't there the danger that, in the process, he is giving out the wrong message? Isn't he undermining standards in the community and ruining his own reputation as a holy man? I am a vicar and if I spent my time among those seen in our society as notable 'sinners' (maybe loan sharks, benefit cheats and illegal immigrants), telling them to repent, I would be seen as worthy, if a bit misguided. However, if I were known to have spent time with them without telling them to change, that would be seen as a scandal by the wider public and in my own congregations. Jesus doesn't seem to care. Reaching these people is apparently more important to him than maintaining his reputation as a good man.

The second question raised by his actions is: how do you save sinners? Jesus' answer seems to be that it is less about preaching at them and more about living with them; it seems to begin with welcome, not a demand to change. Of course, it is right to note that a doctor treats a sick person so that they will no longer be sick. Jesus does imply that these people are sick and need saving. Nevertheless, it is a mistake to interpret his words as 'I have come to call them to change' and then ignore the tone of the rest of the passage. Something is going on that is causing the Pharisees to question the disciples, and that 'something' is that Jesus is welcoming the tax collectors and 'sinners' as they are, before they have changed. In the process, he seems to be taking upon himself the right to redefine how sinners—and, indeed, how the nation—should be saved, moving in a different direction from the Pharisees.

This sets up a tension for us as followers of Jesus today. Presumably we are called to have Jesus' attitude towards 'sinners'—to follow his programme of acceptance, rather than the Pharisees' approach of encouraging and pressurising people to be good. However, isn't there also a place for publicly upholding standards, supporting those who are trying to be good rather than those who choose wickedness? To put it another way, think back to the story at the beginning of this chapter. Isn't it right to express some disapproval of the pregnant teenager, to dissuade others from following in her footsteps?

This passage highlights the seeds of real animosity between Jesus and the religious system of his day. The 'teaching with authority' and miracle working is one thing. However, in the first story in Mark 2, when healing the paralysed man, Jesus declared his sins to be forgiven, challenging the temple's role as the place where God's forgiveness was obtained. Now, he is undermining the Pharisees' programme for getting Israel to turn from its sins, by offering welcome to the wicked.

New wine

The relationship between Jesus and the law, or at least between Jesus and the religious system of his day, continues to be explored in the next two passages. This is clearly an important issue, which Mark highlights by putting this sequence of passages near the beginning of his Gospel. Indeed, we could see this next passage as two separate pieces, brought together by Mark because they are on the same theme.

Now John's disciples and the Pharisees were fasting. They come and say to him, 'Why are John's disciples and the Pharisees' disciples fasting, but your disciples are not?' Jesus replied, 'The bridegroom's guests can't fast while the bridegroom is with them. For as long as they have the bridegroom with them, they can't fast.' But the days are coming when the bridegroom will be taken from them—then on that day they will fast.

'Nobody sews a patch of unshrunken cloth on to an old cloak. If they do, the patch will pull away from it, the new from the old, and the tear will end up worse. Nobody puts new wine into old wineskins. If they do, the wine will burst the skins and the wine and skins will be lost. No—new wine goes into new skins.'

MARK 2:18–22

The logic of verses 19–20, about the wedding, is clear, though deeply challenging. Jesus asserts that he is a special person (the bridegroom) at a special time ('while he is with them... the days are coming'). The normal structures of life ('fasting') do have their place, but not now, not while he is there.

Who is he, that religious practices should change just because he is there? Jesus seems to be saying that it's not new teaching that changes things; it is he himself. This sense that a personal claim is being made is further heightened by the Old Testament background, in which God is pictured as a bridegroom, with Israel as the bride. Could the image of a bridegroom be used in a religious setting without some hint of this background? If not, then the personal claim becomes even more outrageous: not only are religious rules suspended in Jesus' presence, but he is standing in the place of God.

The reference to the bridegroom being taken away has an ominous tone to it, and can be seen as the first appearance of the 'long shadow of the cross' that occurs throughout Mark. However, it is only a flicker of a shadow; the following saying about the patch has no similar note. Indeed, perhaps this talk of the bridegroom being taken away simply establishes that the current situation is temporary: he is present now, but he won't always be there.

The imagery of the patch on the old garment and the new wine and old skins also makes a clear point. The new cannot be fitted into the old system. This makes sense in the context of the question about fasting. What Jesus is doing is new, so he is not going to conform to patterns of religious observance from the past, such as fasting. His ministry will all go wrong if the old approaches attempt to contain it. Although it is a homely illustration, the implications are huge. Jesus is bringing something new, not just reinvigorating what already exists, and it cannot be contained.

The relationship between old and new in churches is always a matter of tension. It would be wrong to draw great conclusions just from this small saying, which seems to be in the context of things changing during Jesus' ministry or in his presence. However, it is worth pondering further the idea that if the old or existing patterns try to contain the new, it will all end in disaster. It's easy to find ourselves sharing the Pharisees' nervous conservatism when faced with new projects, ministries, leaders and styles of worship in our churches. It's easy in practice, if not intentionally, to be unwilling to let the new flourish in its own way, and to be constantly anxious about how it will 'fit in' with the existing methods. After all, Jesus' mission was not opposed to, or trying to attack, the law and the history of God's covenant with his people. Yet it needed its own space, to be allowed to develop its own integrity.

Taken as a whole, this passage re-emphasises and underpins the conclusions we have been drawing from Jesus' actions. He is not going to fit in and refresh the religious system of his day from within. He is bringing real change.

Furthermore, he as an individual is significant in that change: he is not just a messenger; he is the bridegroom. His presence counts. We might make a connection with his proclamation that God's reign is near, and conclude that God's reign is coming near in Jesus' presence.

Lord of the sabbath

Immediately after the saying about the new wine, we have another incident concluding with a saying that seems to suggest, once again, that the rules are different when Jesus is present.

> One sabbath he was walking through some corn fields, and his disciples began to make their way, plucking ears of corn as they went. The Pharisees were saying, 'Look! Why are they doing what is not allowed on the sabbath?' Jesus says to them, 'Have you never read what David did when he and his companions were needy and hungry? How in the time of high priest Abiathar he went into the House of God and ate the consecrated bread, which it is only lawful for the priests to eat? And he even gave it to his companions!'
>
> Jesus said, 'The sabbath exists for people, not people for the sabbath. Thus the "Son of Man" is lord even of the sabbath.'
>
> MARK 2:23–28

Although this passage seems simple, what it is saying about Jesus and the Jewish law is far from straightforward to work out. First, we need to consider in what way the disciples' actions were forbidden. Presumably, the challenge came because the Pharisees saw plucking corn as 'work' that was forbidden on the sabbath. This interpretation was not necessarily generally accepted: as we have seen, the Pharisees were spreading out throughout Israel to teach their understanding of the law, so that people would not sin. The sabbath rules provide a good example of their concerns. Exodus 20:10 makes it clear that the Israelites should not work on the sabbath, but it does not define what work is, so the Pharisees came up with a list to help people follow the law better. They had no power to enforce their interpretation, but did so by exactly this sort of public challenge. 'Hey, you! Why are you doing that? It's wrong!' from a respected community figure will normally cause self-doubt and shame in those challenged.

It would be reasonable to conclude, then, that this was a disagreement between Jesus and the Pharisees on the correct interpretation of the law. However, this is not how Jesus defends his disciples' actions: his answer is about 'who' is doing it, and why (they are 'needy'). (In contrast, in Mark 7:1–13, we do see Jesus engaging in that sort of argument, claiming that he is sticking to the law but not to the Pharisees' interpretation of it—but that is not what's said here.)

Then we should examine the final sentence about the 'lord of the sabbath'. Is this a statement about Jesus in particular or about all humankind? As Christians, we are used to seeing the phrase 'Son of Man' in reference to Jesus, so this sentence seems to be about Jesus' particular lordship of the Sabbath. However, 'Son of Man' is used elsewhere in the Bible as just another way of saying 'human' (for example, in Psalm 8:6 and Mark 3:28). In addition, the Greek word I have translated as 'people' ('the sabbath exists for people') is the same as the word in 'Son of Man' (it refers to humankind, not just males), and there is no capital letter in either case.

This could well just be an example of repetition or parallelism, which is a common feature of Hebrew poetry—saying the same thing twice with slightly different words, just as in Psalm 8:6. However, we need to recognise that within Mark's Gospel and Peter's preaching, the term 'Son of Man' is generally used to refer to Jesus. Thus, our interpretation of this passage could move in two directions.

On the one hand, this passage seems to speak of the purpose of the sabbath and perhaps more broadly of the nature of God's instructions. Understanding the final sentence as being primarily about 'people' ('the sabbath exists for people, not people for the sabbath'), we find that the law, including high-profile elements such as the sabbath rules, is there for people's benefit. People come first: the law is there to serve them, not the other way around. This principle seems to be further emphasised by the story about David. His hunger overrode the law allowing the consecrated bread to be eaten only by priests. Furthermore, it wasn't just David who ate it, who perhaps could be claimed to be special. The bread was eaten by his companions, too. Human need overrode the law. It might seem logical and appropriate to us that human need overrides the law, when we think about cases such as the story that immediately follows in Mark, about a man being healed on the sabbath (Mark 3:4: 'Is it allowed to do good on the sabbath or evil?'). However, were the disciples really that hungry as they walked through the cornfield? Plucking the ears of corn sounds more like absentminded snacking. Surely, this wasn't really 'need' overriding the law, but just 'desire'. But if human *desire* may override the law, then there can be no law at all.

On the other hand, perhaps the emphasis is on Jesus. While it is true that the story about David shows him giving the consecrated bread to his companions, overall it still seems to be about David as a person: *David* was able to do this. His action included helping his companions, but that was because they were with *him*. Similarly, the final line about the Son of Man seems to be highlighting that Jesus is the lord even of the sabbath. Anyone hearing this passage in the context of the rest of Peter's preaching would have heard 'Son of Man' as a reference to Jesus. Indeed, the previous passage in the Gospel suggests that the rules are different while the bridegroom is present. Thus, this passage may be about how the sabbath rules give way while Jesus, the Son of Man, is there.

So, do the rules bend for Jesus or do they bend in the face of human need? I'm not sure we can decide just on the basis of this passage. Moreover, the gap between the two possibilities starts to shrink if we think of Jesus as the 'representative human'—the one living the true human life as God intended. (Remember, as we have already seen, the 'son of man' in Daniel 7:13 does carry this representative sense.)

Emerging from the detail, we are left with a sense of the contrast between the Pharisees and Jesus. They are making the law clearer so that people can follow it more precisely. Jesus seems to be talking of its purpose—that it is there to benefit people—and suggesting that he (and perhaps everyone) has the power to decide how it should be followed. Is the law about clear boundaries within which we are safe, or about principles that we apply as seems right?

We can easily approach these questions as if they are merely of antiquarian interest, and even with a patronising sense that 'these Jews really did get themselves tied up in knots over the law'. However, the same questions would apply to ethical and religious principles within Christianity.

How flexible should they be? Have we simply created a new set of 'moral laws' that must be followed? Smoking is bad; a glass or two of wine is fine. Borrowing hundreds of thousands to buy a house is good; borrowing a few hundred to buy new clothes is bad. Shouting at someone is bad; talking about them behind their back is normal.

Expanding the law

Fortunately, the next passage we will consider, in Mark 7, is rather more straightforward.

> *The Pharisees and some scribes who had come from Jerusalem gather around Jesus. They saw some of his disciples eating their food with polluted hands, that is, unwashed hands. (For the Pharisees and all Jews will not eat without washing their hands carefully, holding to the tradition of the elders. When they come in from the market, they will not eat if they have not washed. They hold to many other customs which have been passed down—washing cups, pots, kettles and beds.)*
>
> *The Pharisees and scribes asked him, 'Why do your disciples not live according to the tradition of the elders, but eat food with polluted hands?' He replied, 'Isaiah was right when he prophesied about you hypocrites! As it is written, "This people honour me with their lips, but their hearts are far from me. In vain they worship me, teaching mere human rules." You set aside God's commandment and hold to human tradition.' He continued, 'You have a fine way of setting aside God's command so you can uphold your tradition. For Moses said, "Honour your father and your mother" and, "Whoever curses father or mother must die." But you say, "If someone says to father or*

mother, 'Whatever you can expect from me is Corban'" (that is, donation), you no longer allow him to do anything for his father or mother. You set aside the word of God, by the tradition you hand down. You do many other similar things.'

MARK 7:1–13

Notice the first two details. Scribes have come down from Jerusalem: Jesus is gaining some notoriety. And the explanation in the bracket suggests that Mark is writing for (and perhaps Peter was preaching for) a non-Jewish audience.

Once again, we see Jesus challenging the direction in which much of Jewish religious teaching had been moving in the previous couple of centuries, as exemplified by the Pharisees. As we have discussed, there was a movement to clarify in detail what people must do in order to follow God's law correctly. These details were building up into a fixed body of rules, here called the 'tradition of the elders' (more generally called the 'oral law'). It was certainly not 'all about externals', as we might rather dismissively say, and it was motivated by a desire to help the people stop sinning, but it did include more and more burdensome attempts to define God's requirements.

Jesus challenges the tradition here. He attacks the Corban rule because it clashes with the law itself. The question of handwashing is a little different, because the handwashing can't be said to clash with the law; the worst you could say is that it is unnecessary. In fact, Jesus seems more generally to be attacking the increasing 'tradition of the elders'. Perhaps the point is that it is simply unnecessary, or that it obscures what is really from God and therefore important.

It is easy for us simply to categorise these rules as examples of 'silly tradition' ('all this stuff about food laws' and so on) and to feel self-congratulatory that Christianity has 'moved on' from such externals. Protestant Christians, particularly of more evangelical backgrounds, often feel that they have taken to heart a message here about the importance of rejecting human tradition. However, in our world today we have many 'guidelines' or 'principles' about Christian living. We may not formulate them as a 'tradition of the elders' but, in reality, we are doing much the same. The Pharisees had good motives, trying to make clear what God required in practice. I am constantly amazed at how often people both within and outside my congregations want me, as a vicar, to make moral rules for other people and to challenge their behaviour. Has anything changed?

Outputs, not inputs

The passage continues, although we cannot be sure whether this was on the same occasion or whether Peter or Mark are simply bringing together connected pieces of teaching.

Again, he called the crowd and began to say to them, 'Listen to me, all of you, and understand. Nothing going into someone from outside is able to pollute them. But rather it is what comes out from someone that pollutes them.

When he went into a house away from the crowd, his disciples asked him about the parable. He says to them, 'Are you also such fools? Don't you understand that nothing from outside, going into someone, can pollute them? It does not go into the heart but into the stomach and then out into the toilet. (Saying this, Jesus made all food 'clean'.) He said, 'It's what comes out of a person that pollutes them. For from inside, from

people's hearts, come out evil thoughts, sexual immorality,
theft, murder, adultery, greed, malice, deceit, debauchery, envy,
cursing, arrogance, foolishness. All these evils come out from
within and pollute people.'

MARK 7:14–23

This passage goes considerably further than the previous one, for here Jesus seems to be challenging or dismissing parts of the Old Testament law itself. Food laws were not just part of the tradition of the elders, but part of the law itself (see Leviticus 11). To say that nothing that goes into someone from outside can pollute them flatly contradicts Leviticus. (The word translated here as 'pollute' is the technical term for 'making unclean' or 'defiling' that is used in Greek to refer to the concept in Leviticus 11.) Thus, it is hard to argue with the conclusion drawn by Peter (or maybe by Mark) that, in saying this, Jesus was declaring all foods clean. However, Jesus does not say so explicitly, and this fits with the fact that, in the generation after Jesus, there was much argument among his followers as to whether or not the Jewish food laws should be followed.

Jesus' point seems to be more about the importance of what comes out of the heart. In effect, he is saying to the Pharisees that their focus on making the law clear and precise is missing the point. The vices Jesus lists are all about how we treat each other. That is what matters, not the technicalities of religious observances. Jesus is now setting out a very different path from the Pharisees. Not only does he disagree with their interpretations and programme for building up supplementary guidance and traditions in order to make the law clearer and more precise, but he seems to be marginalising the law itself.

Is divorce OK?

Breakdown of marriage is not new. It is certainly true that divorce is more common in our experience now than in our recent past (although, of course, it is very hard to know how divorce figures correlate with the quality of marriages). Nevertheless, marital breakdown has always been a feature of society, and the Jewish society of Jesus' day was no exception. The difficult question is always about how divorce should be regulated and controlled.

> Some Pharisees approached Jesus and asked him as a test whether it was lawful for a man to divorce his wife. He replied, 'What did Moses command you?' They said, 'Moses permitted a man to write out a divorce certificate and to divorce her.' Jesus said to them, 'He wrote this command for you because of the hardness of your hearts. But from the beginning of creation he made them male and female. Because of this, a man will leave his father and mother and be joined to his wife. The two will be one flesh. So there is no longer two but one flesh. Therefore what God has joined together, nobody should separate.'
>
> When they went back into the house, the disciples asked him about this. He says to them, 'Whoever divorces his wife and marries another commits adultery against her. And any woman who divorces her husband and marries another commits adultery.'
>
> MARK 10:2–12

This was a classic situation for the Pharisees' programme of reform. The law described the procedure, as the Pharisees quoted, for a man to divorce his wife by writing out a certificate of divorce (Deuteronomy 24:1). However, the grounds for the divorce are rather vague in Deuteronomy: '... because she does not please him, because he finds something indecent about her'. Vagueness would not do! When could a man divorce his wife, and when couldn't he? If the people were to follow the law properly, they needed to know.

Two camps developed within the Judaism of Jesus' day. One was more permissive, claiming that 'because she does not please him' meant that a husband could divorce his wife simply because he wanted to. The other, more restrictive, camp understood 'something indecent' to mean some identifiable serious fault, such as sexual infidelity. The details need not detain us, though, because Jesus simply didn't enter the discussion at all. Both camps were working on the basis that, once it was clear in what circumstances it was lawful, then a man (and within traditional Judaism, only a man could instigate divorce) was entitled to do it. According to this way of thinking, first we define precisely what God requires us to do and what God forbids us from doing. Then, as long as we follow those definitions to the letter, we are completely justified in doing whatever else we wish. The Pharisees and others would define when it was OK to divorce your wife, and then, well, it was OK to do it.

Jesus sidesteps the question. He does not challenge the fact that the scriptures (Moses) permitted divorce. Instead, he goes back to an earlier part of the scriptures, quoting Genesis 2, which reveals that God's intention is for there to be no divorce.

How is this tension between the two parts of the Old Testament to be resolved? That question has defined the Christian church's approach to divorce across the centuries. It is clear where Jesus is putting the weight: he is emphasising Genesis, which says that God's desire is for marriage to be permanent. He then explains Moses' regulations as a concession, given because of 'the hardness of your hearts'. We might say, '… because people aren't perfect'. Where does that leave us? We still live in the fallen world for which Moses gave his regulations. Presumably, this means that there can be occasions when divorce is a sensible option, given the reality that our hearts are all 'hard' in different ways and for all sorts of reasons. Nevertheless, from Genesis we can see that divorce is always a falling-short of God's desire for us.

It is also, perhaps, significant that Jesus looks back to the time before the fall. Many commentators see this as a suggestion that, in the kingdom brought by Jesus, where God reigns, we will return to a pre-fall state in which the regulations permitting divorce will no longer be needed. Some claim that now, within the church, our 'kingdom ethics' ought to match that pre-fall state, and divorce should not be allowed. But this seems to ignore the fact that the final transformation is still to come; until then, we still live in a world in which human hearts, our own included, are hard. In my experience of working with couples divorcing or remarrying, this makes sense. Almost everyone sees their divorce as a sign that they have fallen short of their own hopes and desires, but, in the circumstances, it seemed the only feasible option.

However, this is not quite the discussion that Jesus is having with the Pharisees. His answer is not to side with one of their interpretative camps or the other, or even to develop a third idea about when it is OK to divorce your wife. His answer is of a completely different kind, deliberately pointing out (not resolving) a tension within the scriptures. His point seems similar to his response to the Corban argument: the Pharisees have been making detailed regulations about when it is OK to divorce a wife, while God makes it clear in Genesis that divorce is never 'OK'. Deuteronomy might make regulations to control it, but that doesn't mean it is ever right. Thus, again, Jesus is rejecting the whole approach by which the Pharisees define precisely what God requires or forbids, and allow freedom to act as we choose in the area in between.

A house for the nations?

Jesus spent most of his time in Galilee, coming to Jerusalem (according to Mark) only at the very end of his life. This is significant for our understanding of his opponents and their power. In Galilee he mainly encountered the Pharisees, or scribes, who were other religious teachers like him and had no material power. Thus, they could argue back and forth. Jerusalem was different. The temple was the heart of Judaism and the high priest was recognised by the Romans as the authority within Judaism. He had physical power, with guards and courts to punish crimes, even though the Romans allowed nobody but themselves to inflict the death penalty. Challenging the temple was a far more dangerous act than debating with the religious teachers in Galilee. We pick up the story on Jesus' second day in Jerusalem.

The next day after he had set out from Bethany, Jesus was hungry. He saw at a distance a fig tree in leaf. He went to it to see if he could find any fruit. When he arrived, he found nothing but leaves (because it was not the season for figs). In response he said to it, 'May nobody ever eat fruit from you ever again!' His disciples were listening.

They come into Jerusalem. When he entered the temple, he began to drive out those who were buying and selling in the

*temple. He overturned the moneychangers' tables and the seats
of those selling doves. He wouldn't let past anyone who was
carrying goods through the temple.*

*He began to teach them: 'Is it not written that my house will
be called a house of prayer for all nations? But you have made
it into a bandits' den.' The chief priests and scribes heard this
and began to look for a way to destroy him, for they were afraid
of him, because the entire crowd was amazed at his teaching.
When evening came, he left the city.*

*The next morning, as they were going along, they saw the
fig tree withered from the root. Peter remembered and said to
him, 'Rabbi, look, the fig tree which you cursed has withered.'*

MARK 11:12–21

The placing of the action in the temple between the two
halves of the incident with the fig tree must be significant.
As we discussed in Chapter 1, we remember events that
are important to us. Peter did not simply tell a story about
a time when Jesus cursed a fig tree and it withered, and
then a separate story about what Jesus did in the temple. He
told them together, presumably because he thought it was
important that they were told together.

As we look for meaning, it emerges fairly easily.

1. Jesus seeks a fig tree and looks for its fruit.
2. He does not find the fruit that he wants, so he curses the
   tree.
3. Later, the curse has taken effect and the tree is withered up.

Similarly:
1. Jesus comes to the temple.
2. Jesus does not like what he finds in the temple, so he
   attacks it.

It seems that we are to draw the conclusion (if another 'step 3' is implied) that the temple is cursed in some way and will 'wither up'. The juxtaposition of the two stories points to the idea that the temple—busy with the supply of the right money and animals for offerings—was as useless as a fig tree with no figs. To put it a different way, the fig tree was making a great show of leaves but producing nothing of value. So, too, the temple was making a great show of religion but to no effect.

Sometimes people call this incident the 'cleansing' of the temple, which might suggest that the problem was simply that the temple was being run in a corrupt fashion. However, the moneychangers and dove sellers were a necessary part of the temple's sacrificial system. Think in terms of a prophet turning up at a church and throwing out all the hymn books and service sheets, saying, 'You have turned this place of worship into a library!' Jesus' words and actions can only be an attack on the temple system itself. That day, Jesus stopped the temple system for a few hours as a symbolic judgement, or even a prophetic prediction that God would stop it permanently (presumably, as is usual with biblical prophets, unless it changed its ways). It is no surprise, then, that this action caused the chief priests to decide to destroy him. They recognised it as an attack on their temple.

A couple of days later, Jesus predicts the temple's destruction privately to his disciples (Mark 13:1–2). A few days after that, he is accused of saying that he will destroy the temple (14:58) and will be condemned to death by the high priest (14:64). As he hangs dying on the cross, the chief priests taunt him for saying that he would destroy the temple (15:21).

This sense of conflict is heightened by Jesus' quotation of the prophets. He brings together two verses:

Has my house, which has my name set upon it, become a bandit's den?
JEREMIAH 7:11

And the foreigners who attach themselves to the Lord... I will lead to my holy mountain, and make them joyful in my house of prayer... for my house shall be called a house of prayer for all nations.
ISAIAH 56:6–7

The context in Jeremiah is that people were saying they were safe because God dwelt in the temple and would protect it and them against their enemies—including foreign armies. But God said that he would only protect them if they repented and changed their ways. Moreover, the word translated as 'bandits' in Jeremiah and in Mark might just as well be translated as 'rebels' in modern English, or 'terrorists' or 'freedom fighters'. It could mean someone who attacks another person and takes their possessions, but it was also the word used to describe the Jewish-nationalistic rebels against Rome, 40 years after Jesus. They had their headquarters in the temple itself—so at that point it certainly was a 'den of rebels'. As a result, the Romans destroyed the temple, hundreds of thousands of Jews died and Judaism was changed for ever.

Thus, in these quotations Jesus is attacking the very fabric of the temple system in his day. People saw it as the *Jewish* temple, because God had chosen Israel alone out of the nations to be his special people. It was their security, the base of their nation, standing over and against the foreigners. Yet Jesus is saying that, in fact, it should be a place for the foreigners, too. God is for all nations, not just for the Jewish nation. Jesus attacked the temple, not because he didn't like animal sacrifices, or because it was too noisy, or even because it was being run in a corrupt manner. No, this was the final symbolic moment when Jesus came to the religious system of his day, found it wanting because of its exclusivity, and proclaimed judgement against it. (We might also point to Malachi 3:1–2, the first part of which was quoted at Mark 1:2, but which goes on, 'Then the Lord you seek will suddenly come to his temple... but who can endure the day he arrives?')

At the same moment in Luke's Gospel (19:41–44), Jesus wept. This must be our own reaction to the way God's people managed to construct a system of worship and religious life that became exclusive and did not produce the fruit that God looked for. Do we do any better?

The more important commandment

The final question asked of Jesus as a teacher was 'Which is the most important commandment?' This is a fitting end to our discussion of Jesus and the law, for so much of the conflict we have seen is really about priorities—what balance to strike between different parts of the law, between precision and flexibility, between recognising effort and focusing on achievement. So what matters most?

One of the scribes approached and listened as they debated.
When he saw that Jesus had answered them well, he asked
him, 'Which is the most important commandment?' Jesus
replied, 'First is: "Israel, listen! The Lord our God is one. You
will love the Lord your God with all your heart, soul, mind

and strength." The second is: "You will love your neighbour as
yourself." There is no other commandment greater than these.'

The scribe said to him, 'Well done, teacher. You are right
to say that he is one, and there is no other beside him. To love
him with all our heart, understanding and strength and to love
our neighbour as ourselves is more important than all burnt
offerings and sacrifices.'

Jesus saw the wisdom in his reply and said, 'You are not far
from God's reign.' Nobody dared to question him any more.
MARK 12:28–34

The first thing to notice is that Jesus praises the Jewish scribe
and declares that he is 'not far from God's reign'. Jesus may
have said very stern things about aspects of religious life in
his day and the religious leaders, but he also approved of
many things.

The two love commands (love for God and love for neighbour) give a direction and pattern for the moral life, which
appeals to many outside the Christian family. We should
rejoice that there is this universal appeal in Jesus' words.

However, this exchange hides a practical problem. In doing
so, it summarises the tension we have seen throughout this
chapter between Jesus and the religious system of his day,
and, in a sense, within the Old Testament law itself.

A necessary feature of human society is that grand principles, like these love commands, need to be encapsulated in
practical rules, customs and guidelines. The enquirer learning
about the faith, when told to 'love God with all their heart,
soul, mind and strength', is likely to ask, 'How?' When
people come to a new faith in Jesus in my congregations,
they want to know what it means for their daily lives. They
are conscious of their current pattern of life and wonder

what should change. These questions are not asked out of a sense of legalism. They are genuine. If our faith is not just mere words, then it must make a different in practice—so how should our practice change? Naturally, then, we have practical rules, customs and guidelines to help us put our faith into practice. The Jews at the time of Jesus had their 'burnt offerings and sacrifices' (v. 33) and other regulations (for example, about the sabbath), as well as religious systems such as the temple. We have our equivalents. But how do grand principles and practical regulations interrelate?

The scribe says that the love commands are 'much more important' than the sacrifices. Does this mean that the sacrifices are still of some importance, or can they be discarded? The same question has emerged from most of the passages in this chapter. We have seen Jesus challenging the customs and institutions of his day, the direction in which the law was being interpreted, and even the Old Testament law itself (when he said, 'Nothing going into someone can pollute them').

Presumably, the answer is that all these practical rules and customs should remain in place only while they actively contribute to the greater goal of loving God and neighbour. But in saying this, we launch ourselves in a small boat on to a stormy sea, for life around us is always changing. This approach would require us to be willing to keep on changing and reassessing the practical rules, customs and guidelines for moral living. Our only guiding star would be love for God and love for neighbour.

This does seem to be what the early church did, reassessing fundamental rules and customs. For example, they re-evaluated circumcision, which was laid down in the scriptures themselves as the essential mark of God's covenant (see

Genesis 17:10–14). They did this in the light of the understanding that the 'one' God would relate to all people in the same way, and that loving neighbours meant no longer treating Gentiles as 'second class' (see Romans 3:27–31; 10:12–13).

Jesus commented on, was in tension with and eventually challenged head-on the religious system of his day. Many of the particular issues involved are not ones we connect with easily—sabbath and food laws, the temple and foreign occupation—although some, such as divorce and nationalism, are still with us. Jesus' challenges came from within the system, drawing on strands in the Old Testament itself. Nevertheless, the result was a definite marginalisation of the Old Testament law. His mission seemed to come from a different starting point. The law and its interpretation were no longer the dominant factors in the relationship between God and people. In his presence, things changed.

It is right that we recognise this original context. However, the truth is that many of Jesus' criticisms would apply to the moral teaching, practice and customs of the church today as well—not because we are particularly wicked (nor were the religious people in Jesus' day) but because they are fundamental criticisms of any religious system of behaviour. When we hear Jesus calling us to reassess our established rules, customs and guidelines of Christian living, in the light of the commandments to love God and love neighbour, we face the same dilemmas.

How flexible should rules be? Should we support those who follow the rules and shame those who don't (remember the story of the pregnant teenager at the start of this chapter)? Or should we support and welcome those who don't follow the rules, in the hope that perhaps, at some unspecified time in the future, they might? Are religious rules, practices and customs important at all? Are they precious to us just because of their history and the security they give us? Do they simply support a sense of exclusiveness? What would it look like if we reassessed everything against the principles of love for God and neighbour? Would it bring freedom or chaos, maturity or immorality? Do we believe that God both forbids and requires certain actions, and that in the areas in between we can do as we please? (We might say, for example, 'I give to charity; I give to the church; I don't support immorality with my spending, so the rest of my money is mine to do with as I want.') Peter's preaching does not raise these questions as clearly as it does the issues surrounding discipleship and the question 'Who is Jesus?' Nevertheless, the questions are as applicable to us as they were to Peter's original hearers. Peter's voice still challenges us.

CHAPTER 7

PARABLES

The following story is attributed to many different sources. Perhaps it never happened, but it's a good story.

A man came to faith in Jesus in a revivalist meeting and went home overjoyed, enthusiastic about his new life. Two months later, however, he had not been seen in church, so the pastor visited him. As they sat in his front room, warmed by a coal fire, the man explained that he could be just as good a Christian outside the church as in it. The pastor said nothing but stepped to the fireplace, picked up a piece of blazing coal with the tongs and put it on the hearth. The two men watched as the flames burnt lower and went out. The pastor left without a word; the man understood.

This story makes the point more powerfully and memorably than a written sentence about how Christian fellowship is important for our continuing journey as disciples. Indeed, I have repeated the action myself, with a youth group—actually lighting a fire and lifting out a piece of burning wood. Words alone may lead to questions and arguments about exactly what is being said, but we connect with an action in a more powerful way.

In 1996, the British Conservative Party released a poster that was recognised by *Campaign*, the weekly journal of the advertising industry, as the year's best advert. It was a picture of the Labour Party leader Tony Blair with his eyes replaced by 'demon eyes', and the slogan 'New Labour. New Danger.' What was the poster saying? That Tony Blair was a demon? That Tony Blair was evil? That the Labour Party was immoral? Not really. It wasn't even saying that Tony Blair was dangerous. The poster worked not by 'saying' anything, but by simply conveying a mood. It was an intentionally vague way of trying to raise nagging doubts about Tony Blair's sincerity. No amount of words could have had the same effect.

I see a mentor every couple of months to talk about church growth. Last year he said, 'Culture eats strategy for breakfast.' He meant that, as far as church growth is concerned, the culture and mood of a church are far more important than its strategies. Therefore, it's more important for me, as vicar, to influence the culture of the church than to bring in carefully designed strategies. If he had explained that to me in a long-winded way, I'd have forgotten it, but the colourful five-word version has stuck with me.

Communication is not just about words, and words are not just about meaning. This needs to be our starting point as we come to consider the parables contained in Peter's preaching. It's perhaps strange that I feel the need to start by saying this. Surely we know it already? Strangely, though, when we study the Bible, we can take on a particular rationalistic and academic approach, as if Jesus was a university philosopher whose focus was on precise intellectual argument. Perhaps it has something to do with the fact that most pastors, preachers and priests are trained today on university courses. But Jesus was a communicator, not an academic.

We have already seen the reaction that Jesus' teaching created.

They were shocked at his teaching, because he didn't teach like the scribes; he taught as if he had authority... 'What is this? A new teaching with authority!'

MARK 1:22, 27

As we explored in the last chapter, the scribes' approach was to seek precision though logical discussion. Jesus was different. Not only was his message different from that of the scribes, but his way of teaching was different—a new medium for a new message. The most distinctive part of his teaching was his telling of parables, for we know of nothing quite like them in his day. Of course, people have always used illustrations, but there is more to Jesus' parables than that.

What is a parable? There is no definitive answer to that question. The best I can do is to explain the conclusion I have reached over the years; then we can study the parables in Peter's preaching together. By the end of the chapter, I hope you will have come to your own conclusion as to whether my understanding of parables is useful or not.

Many people have been taught that a parable is 'an earthly story with a heavenly meaning' or 'theology made simple for the simple'. Jesus could have put his teaching in a few clear, precise sentences of doctrine. However, that approach would not have been very memorable for the village folk he was teaching around Galilee, so instead he 'translated' his point into a story form, to make it more colourful and easier to remember.

I suspect that this is a classic case of making Jesus in our own image, for this is exactly what a preacher does when preparing a sermon. She knows the point she needs to communicate but she wants to make it more colourful and memorable, so she thinks of an illustration. The point comes first;

the illustration is a way of putting it across. Indeed, I have seen 'preaching classes' that work on this basis. The trainee preacher writes down, in two or three bullet points, the message he is trying to bring, and then works out how best to communicate it.

That all sounds good, except that, when we read Jesus' parables, it is often far from clear what simple point they are trying to communicate. What is the point of the parable of the lost sheep? Is it saying that God cares more about one sinner than 99 righteous people? Don't worry about wandering from the faith, because God will rescue you? Vicars should ignore their congregations and focus solely on seeking the lost? Peter recalls a short parable about a man who plants seed, which grows regardless of what the farmer does (Mark 4:26–29). Is the point of this story to encourage laziness and fatalism—as if it doesn't matter what we do?

There is another weakness in approaching the parables as Jesus' way of communicating spiritual truths to uneducated folk. It is clearly patronising, suggesting that they needed simple stories, whereas we don't. Indeed, in my experience it is far from clear that more intellectual people are better at grasping spiritual truths. Perhaps more importantly, this approach allows us to edit Jesus' message to make it more palatable. If we assume that Jesus started with a precise philosophical message, which he turned into a dramatic simple story for simple people, we give ourselves permission to turn the story back into a less dramatic, more balanced doctrinal point. In the process we often tone down the message to make it more acceptable.

The parables seem to me to be deliberately open-ended, ambiguous and challenging. They tell a story that we connect with, but then they leave us intrigued, needing more. They tell a story that seems familiar, but then a twist in the tale leaves us questioning our own assumptions. Like the story of the pastor taking the coal from the fire, or the slogan about culture eating strategy for breakfast, parables are certainly a memorable way of putting a truth across, but they are also something more. There is a power in the format, which is lost if the story is retold as a series of precise points. The 'demon eyes' of Tony Blair suggested something that couldn't be put into words without seeming cheap, tacky or silly. The image worked because it 'got under the skin'.

I don't think it is a coincidence that Jesus taught in parables. As we saw in the last chapter, when we compared Jesus' message with that of the scribes and Pharisees, Jesus deliberately challenged the idea that more precision in defining God's requirements is better. The parables are not straightforward, because God and life are not straightforward. The parables affect us, and change us, rather than communicating a series of doctrinal bullet points. They speak to our hearts. Therefore, as we approach the parables in Peter's preaching, we should be open to the idea that they may defy our attempts to explain them, and yet may challenge our views and assumptions.

The purpose of parables

Where should we begin our study of parables? It seems sensible to start with three verses in the middle of Mark 4, in which Jesus seems to expresses the purpose of his parables.

When they were alone, those who were around him, with the Twelve, asked Jesus about the parables. He said to them,

> *'To you is given the secret of God's reign. But to those outside, everything is in parables, "so that they can look and look, but not see, and hear and hear but not understand, otherwise they might turn and be forgiven".'*
>
> MARK 4:10–12

This must be one of the hardest passages in the Gospels, because it seems contradictory. Surely Jesus taught in parables to make his point clear? Here he seems to be saying that whereas he explains everything clearly to the people around him, those outside his circle just get parables—riddles, to keep them confused. We assume that Jesus must have wanted people to turn and be forgiven. If parables were not going to help them to do so, surely he would have chosen another format for his teaching. Yet he seems to be saying the opposite—that he speaks in parables so that the outsiders will not understand and will not turn and be forgiven. There is also a disturbing note of determinism: what have these people done to be labelled 'outsiders'? Even more confusing is the fact that Jesus has been portrayed as the champion of 'the outsiders'—a friend of sinners. Is this just a show? Does he actually withhold the true message from all except an inner core?

This statement about the purpose of parables, which immediately follows the parable of the sower, seems itself to be a parable—not a homely illustration but a teasing saying that disturbs and intrigues, which centuries of scholarship have not been able to reduce to a simple point.

What can we say, then? Our first step should be to notice who Jesus is speaking to. Which people have been 'given the secret of God's reign'? They are not just the Twelve, the chosen ones. Although the Twelve were selected only a chapter earlier, in Mark 3, since then Jesus has declared that 'whoever does God's will is my brother, sister and mother' (Mark 3:35), and Mark 4:10 places 'those who were around him' alongside the Twelve. If Jesus is speaking to all those who have gathered around him, then the secret of God's reign must be given to them, too.

This turns the saying on its head, for it suggests that anyone who gathers round Jesus gets the secret: receiving it is not dependent on him, but on what we do. We don't have to be part of a special chosen core; we just have to respond to him. This makes particular sense when we realise that the immediately preceding verse, at the end of the parable of the sower, said: 'If you have got ears to hear, then listen!' (4:9). It's all about response. There is no determinism. The secret of God's reign is given to those to respond to Jesus.

Looking from a wider perspective, we can ask, 'What is this secret?' The Greek word translated in Mark 4:11 as 'secret' is sometimes translated 'mystery'. However, it means something that is a mystery until the secret is revealed—something with a hidden meaning, not something that is fundamentally mysterious or spooky. Paul uses the same word in Colossians 2:2, stating that God's 'mystery' or 'secret' is Jesus Christ himself (see also Colossians 1:26–27 and Ephesians 1:9).

The secret of God's reign is Jesus. This makes some sense here: those who respond to Jesus and gather around him are given the secret, which is Jesus himself. Jesus' message, expressed in the parables, is actually about himself. *He* is God's plan that people need to grasp, and this fits with what we have already seen. The sinners gather around Jesus; Jesus is the 'bridegroom'; Jesus redefines the law. Similarly, we have seen Jesus reconstituting Israel around *himself* with his twelve disciples and on the basis of how people respond to *his* messengers.

The world splits in two: those who respond to Jesus (who have the secret of God's reign) and those who don't, who remain on the outside. For them, the parables remain teasing stories: they don't 'get the point'. The parables are not illustrations of doctrine that can be explained clearly to us. Their purpose is not to help us understand 'the faith'. They are stories designed to generate a response to Jesus—to create faith. This is very different from understanding 'the faith': understanding is of the head, and response is of the heart. Without that response, we remain on the outside and are destined not to grasp the 'secret'.

This seems to fit with our life experience. Gaining an understanding of the Christian faith is not the same as becoming a Christian. Many of those who become Jesus' followers start to understand the Christian message, and later, at some distinct point, they decide to 'accept' it, to respond to Jesus. Often they will then say, 'Now it all makes sense', not meaning that every bit of Christian doctrine has become obvious to them but that something fundamental has changed. In the language of this passage, they now have 'the secret'.

We are guilty of thinking that if only a person understood about Jesus, the cross and so on, of course they would become a Christian. We then assume that if someone isn't a Christian, it must be because they don't know the gospel and need it explaining again to them, even more slowly. In fact, though, people can understand without wishing to respond. No amount of further explanation will help them, because understanding is different from responding.

It is also worth remembering that, in Chapter 2, we saw the disciples responding well but then wavering in faith and failing to understand. Response is an ongoing process, and therein lies a challenge for us all. Are we continuing to respond?

Satan's fall

The first time the word 'parable' is used in Mark is not in connection with any of the 'classic' parables, such as the sower or the tenants in the vineyard. Instead, it is in Jesus' response to the accusation that he is not driving out demons by God's power but through the authority of the ruler of the demons.

> *Scribes came down from Jerusalem who were saying that Jesus has Beelzeboul, and that he is casting out demons in the name of the prince of demons.*
>
> *Calling them, he spoke to them in parables. 'How is Satan able to cast out Satan? If a kingdom is divided against itself, that kingdom is not able to survive. And if a house is divided against itself, that family will not be able to survive. And if Satan has revolted against himself and is divided, he cannot survive, but his end has come.*
>
> *'But nobody is able to enter the house of a strong man and steal his possessions, unless he has first tied up the strong man. Then he will steal his house.*
>
> *'I tell you the truth. The sons of men will be forgiven all sins and whatever blasphemies they utter. But whoever blasphemes against the Holy Spirit will never be forgiven. They are guilty of an eternal sin.' (He said this because they were saying that he had an evil spirit.)*
>
> MARK 3:22–30

This first 'parable' is something of a riddle. Jesus takes at face value the scribes' statement that he is casting out demons in the name of (or by the power of) Beelzeboul, the prince of demons, and ponders it aloud. Perhaps the point is that the scribes are not saying to Jesus' face that he is working for Satan. Rather, this is the first-century equivalent of a political dirty-tricks campaign. The scribes are going round spreading the rumour that, in fact, this miracle-worker is in league with the devil. It's a clever attack. Presumably it was impossible to deny that miracles were happening, so they raised doubts over where the power was coming from, claiming that Jesus himself had an evil spirit (v. 30).

So Jesus calls the people together and makes fun of the rumour. In effect, he is saying, 'Let's suppose Satan is driving out Satan. What does that mean? Well, it means that Satan's kingdom is divided, which means that Satan is finished. And that means God's kingdom—God's reign—is here; God is acting to rescue his people.'

What can his opponents say? Jesus has exposed their whispering and slander and made them look stupid. If they are right, and he is working for Satan, then Satan is finished and God's reign is arriving. If they are wrong, then he must be working for God, and therefore God's reign is arriving and Satan is finished. What could be more fun than making the clever and important people from Jerusalem look stupid? The Galilean poor would have loved it.

So this is not a parable in the classic sense, but it does have a meaning that twists and turns as you look at it. It's similar to the old linguistic trick of asking, 'Have you stopped stealing my sweets?' If the answer is 'Yes', you are admitting that you used to steal them; if the answer is 'No', you're admitting that you're still doing it.

Jesus then goes on the offensive, first with a parable about plundering a strong man's house. It's an obviously true statement about real life, but the question is, why Jesus is saying it? Then, in the true style of a parable, the penny drops for the audience. If Satan is the strong man, who could be tying him up? Who is stronger than the prince of demons except God himself? The more the crowds think along those lines, the further from the scribes they move. The rumours about Satan have backfired.

Finally, Jesus starts his own nasty rumour. God is kind and forgiving but—did you know?—there is an 'eternal sin'. The crowd are intrigued, just as the idea of an 'eternal sin' has mesmerised many people for the last 2000 years. What is this terrible crime? 'Blasphemy against the Holy Spirit.'

I don't believe the meaning of this phrase would have been any more obvious to Jesus' hearers than it is to modern commentators. We are told in verse 23 that Jesus spoke to them in parables, and the whole passage is clearly a single piece, with the sentence about the slander that he had an evil spirit (v. 30) bringing us back to verse 22, about Beelzeboul. This is the teaching 'in parables'. However, if it is a parable, it is misguided to try to pin down exactly what 'blasphemy against the Holy Spirit' is. That is as foolish as asking, 'Who are the 99 sheep who are not lost?' Christian theology asserts that no one is beyond God's forgiveness—but the story makes you think.

What impact would this parable have had? Perhaps the crowd would have started to realise that these clever, important scribes from Jerusalem were so caught up in their own world that they couldn't even see that the casting out of demons was a good thing: their learning or their self-importance had obviously gone to their heads. This being the case, no one would be able to take their religious teaching very seriously, and it would become clear that their followers could never find forgiveness.

What about us? Do we sometimes behave like the scribes,

questioning the motives or intentions of people who are clearly doing good but are inconvenient for our own work or threaten our own position? What about the new youth club, which draws people away from our church's existing work; the glamorous new church in town; or the new, very able, member of our team at the office. It's so easy to whisper and raise questions about hidden motives, but we should be careful. Nothing is worse than confusing good with evil— except for *deliberately* confusing good with evil, because it suits us. That is unforgivable.

The sower

Mark 4 brings together a collection of parables, and the first, the sower, takes pride of place. It is told at some length (vv. 3–9), and then, after Jesus has explained the purpose of parables, it is unpacked in detail (vv. 14–20). Many commentators see this as being the 'parable of parables', or the parable about parables, since it is about how we do or don't respond to 'the word' that is sown.

Again he began to teach beside the sea. Such a large crowd gathered that he got into a boat and sat down in it out on the sea. The whole crowd was right up to the water's edge.

He was teaching them many things in parables, and in his teaching he said to them, 'Listen. Imagine a sower went out to sow. As he sowed, some seed fell on the path, and birds came and devoured it. Some fell in the rocky ground where it didn't have much soil. It sprang up immediately because the soil was shallow. Yet when the sun rose, it was scorched because it didn't have roots, and it withered away.

> '*Some fell into the thorns. The thorns sprang up and choked it, and it bore no fruit. Yet some fell into good soil. It produces fruit—coming up, growing and multiplying thirty, sixty, one hundred times!*'
>
> *And he says, 'If you have got ears to hear, then listen!*'

MARK 4:1–9

Immediately we face one of the key issues in interpreting parables. Can we assume that what is being described is normal? Is it a scene from normal life, which points to God? There are two problems with this common approach. First, it seems to be based on an assumption that God is just like us, saying, in effect, 'You know how, in this circumstance, you would do that? Well, God is just the same.' This interpretative approach reduces God to our level. Second, it doesn't fit the parables themselves, for the situation described in each of them soon departs markedly from normal life. They start with a scene from everyday life, drawing us into the story, but then comes a twist. The shepherd abandons 99 sheep in the wilderness to look for one that is lost; the vineyard owner whose servants have been murdered by his tenants sends his defenceless son to speak to them; the Samaritan gives a blank cheque to an innkeeper so that he can look after a Jewish stranger.

My tip for reading parables is to look for the twist—the moment in the story when the parable diverts from normal life. That is where the point lies, because that is the moment highlighting the way God is *not* like us.

The twist comes early in the parable of the sower. Those listening (rural people who understood about sowing) would soon be saying, 'What?' and looking round in confusion. 'A sower goes out to sow.' Yes, we recognise that; it happens each year. But what sort of madman is this sower? Seed is far too precious to be flung around in this manner, with much of it landing among the rocks and thistles. No farmer farms in this way. If he did, he would end up bankrupt and starving. It's also lazy. Of course there is some waste, but you try to minimise it. You don't just throw the seed around and hope for a hundredfold harvest to make up the losses. The listeners would soon have concluded that this carpenter turned preacher knew nothing about farming.

The parable, like all parables, provokes a question. For Jesus, the waste appears not to matter. The farmer will receive his crop in the end—a good crop, growing and multiplying. He need not worry about the wasted seeds falling on the path, in the shallow soil and among thorns. The explanation Jesus gives to his followers (which we will consider further in a moment) makes it clear that this 'sowing of seed' is a way of talking about Jesus' teaching. So what does it mean?

Jesus' teaching seems wasteful. Just as no farmer would throw seed around like this, so, too, no sensible teacher would spend all his time speaking to the crowds of Galilean peasants and low-life miracle-seekers. This teaching method offers no control over what people remember, whether or not they understand, or what they do with what they've learnt. Jesus is just throwing seed into the air, reckless about where it falls—the opposite of what the religious teachers of his day were doing. The Pharisees and scribes were committed to careful, deliberate teaching, passing on a body of material accurately and with the correct meaning.

Furthermore, Jesus' parable seems to throw the responsibility on to the hearers. 'If you have got ears to hear, then listen!' he proclaims. 'I am scattering the seed widely, so make sure you grab some.' The details about the four different types of soil also leads us to ask, 'What kind of soil am I?' The seed is being scattered, and what will make the difference is not the teacher, but me. How responsive will I be?

It's a clever double-edged parable. First, it speaks to us as sowers. When we are thinking about teaching, mission or evangelism, it seems logical to plan carefully and not waste our efforts. However, Jesus seems to cut across that logic, saying, 'Just scatter the seed. What comes of it depends on the soil, not the sower. Don't worry about waste.' But this is a parable, not a manual for church growth. It is not setting out a programme for the way we should 'spread the word'. Rather, it is challenging a habit that we can easily adopt, just as the Pharisees and scribes had done. Under the guise of being rational, strategic and husbanding our resources, we can limit our audience. We focus our attention on those who are most likely to respond, those who seem to be 'almost' there, not the 'sinners and tax collectors'. Perhaps we aim at people who are already community-minded, who have a background in Christianity or live moral lives, as opposed to aggressive people, those whose lives are a mess or whose lifestyles are far from our own. If we have fallen into this way of thinking, the Jesus who preaches widely challenges us. He didn't seem to worry that his words might be wasted on an unlikely audience.

The parable also focuses on our response. We can't hold the teacher responsible for a lack of growth: the farmer sows the same seed in all the different locations. What matters is how we respond, what sort of soil we are proved to be. It's a liberating message, for it means that we are not limited by our past life, background or abilities. All we need to do, in Jesus' words, is 'listen'. On the other hand, it means that everyone is equal and there is nobody else to blame. Our response is up to us. As we saw earlier, the secret of God's reign is given to all those who respond positively to Jesus.

The sower unpacked

Immediately after the parable of the sower, we have the few verses about the purpose of parables and the 'secret of God's reign' that we considered earlier in this chapter. Then we find the parable of the sower unpacked further.

> *He says to them, 'Don't you understand this parable? How then will you grasp all the parables?*
>
> *'The sower sows the word.*
>
> *'These are the ones on the path where the word is sown—people who, when they hear, immediately Satan comes and takes the word which had been sown into them.*
>
> *'These are the ones sown on rocky ground—people who, when they hear the word, immediately receive it with joy. Yet they do not have roots within but are unreliable. When suffering or persecution comes because of the word, they fall away immediately.*
>
> *'Others are the ones sown among the thorns—people who, after they have heard the word, the cares of the age, the deceit of wealth and the desire for all other things come in and choke the word and it is fruitless.*
>
> *'These are the ones sown into good soil—people who hear the word and receive it and bear fruit—thirty, sixty, even a hundred fold.'*
>
> MARK 4:13–20

This passage is often called an explanation of the parable of the sower, but I don't believe it is. It does not explain what the parable means; it simply describes the characters within it. It does not contribute to a discussion of how we should sow, or where the responsibility lies between sower and soil, or why Jesus teaches in this way. All it does is get us started, pointing out that the story is a symbolic one, not really about sowing seed in soil. It gives its hearers the confidence that the parable is not just a strange saying about sowing; it is a piece of teaching about God. However, that no more explains the meaning of the parable than the back cover of this book, together with my biography, tell you what this book means. If you remember the story about the pastor, the convert and the coal fire, it is the equivalent of someone saying, 'The coals are us: we can be on fire for God or go out.' If you haven't yet realised the basic mechanism by which the story is working, this helps you to understand it, but it doesn't spell out what meaning you should take away from the story.

This is fascinating and it supports what we have said so far about parables. If a parable could be reduced to a few bullet points of teaching, then, when explaining it, Jesus would do just that—but he doesn't. He is trying to help his listeners, because, if they don't understand that this story is really about them and God, then they won't understand any of the parables. But he can't actually explain what the parable means without destroying it, just as you can't 'explain' a joke.

What should we conclude from the fact that Jesus deliberately chose to teach by means of parables? How was his purpose strengthened by the fact that he resisted telling people their 'meaning' but merely helped them to get started in understanding the way they worked? It seems logical to conclude that it was important for Jesus that people worked the meaning out for themselves. He saw value in encouraging them to wrestle with ideas of God and ongoing dialogue, to tease out further nuances and ramifications and to see those ideas differently in different contexts, rather than having them presented in black and white, simply to be accepted.

Reinforcing the point

Mark then gives us a number of small sayings that are really quite difficult to understand. They are so short that it is hard to pin them down, and yet they are strangely memorable: they are parables. Some of them occur in different settings in Matthew and Luke, yet we should let their place here in Mark be our guide.

> Jesus said to them, 'A lamp doesn't come to be put under a bucket or under the bed, does it? It comes to be put on a lampstand, doesn't it? Nothing is hidden except to be revealed; nor is anything concealed but so that it might be brought into the open. If you have ears to hear, then listen!'
>
> And he said to them, 'Take care over what you hear. With the measure you use, it will be measured out to you, and more will be added. For whoever has will be given more, and whoever doesn't have, even what they have will be taken from them.'
>
> MARK 4:21–25

The starting point for our interpretation of these sayings is in the sentence 'If you have ears to hear, then listen!' and the warning to 'take care over what you hear'. These words tie the sayings in to the parable of the sower and the earlier saying in Mark 4:10–12 about 'the secret of God's reign' and the purpose of parables. The link is further emphasised by the words in the second paragraph above—'it will be measured out', 'will be given' and 'will be taken'—all of which are a Jewish way of saying, 'God will measure out... give... take' and echo the wording of 'to you the secret of God's reign *will be given*'.

We also need to recognise the strange grammar in the first line, which says, 'A lamp doesn't come to be put under...'. It seems bizarre to talk about a lamp 'coming' to a place—so bizarre that most Bible translations rewrite Mark's words to say something like 'You don't bring a lamp...' However, it's never wise to rewrite a parable so that it sounds more 'normal'. The whole point of a parable is that it contains a twist that makes us think, so, rather than changing Mark for our own convenience, let's stick with the phrase 'A lamp doesn't come...'

'Come' is the sort of word you would use to describe the arrival of a person, not a lamp, and this points us back again to the passage about the 'secret of God's reign', where we recognised that the 'secret' was Jesus himself. Jesus is the secret. Jesus is also the lamp who comes. (We might think of John 1:9: 'The true light, which enlightens everyone, was coming into the world.') We might look for enlightenment but God has come as a person.

So what do we have? We are told that Jesus hasn't come to be hidden away, but to be revealed—and this is followed by the call to listen. Jesus has come as a light: he is here to reveal. But everything depends on whether we listen.

The following sayings (Mark 4:24–25) now make sense. In this context, the words about 'measuring' seem to be saying, 'You get out what you put in', in the sense that if you listen/

respond a little, you will receive a little, and if you listen/respond a lot, you will receive a lot. The phrase 'and will add more' might mean, 'God is generous so he will always add more understanding than our response warrants', or it could just be an intensifier: if you respond a little, you will *definitely* get a little; if you respond a lot, you will *definitely* get a lot. The final saying might then mean, 'If you respond/understand well, God will give you more understanding. If you respond/understand little, you will end up understanding nothing.'

As we have said, trying to pin down the precise meaning of parables is a foolish and unsatisfactory business. However, a general sense emerges here. Jesus has come; what matters is our response to him. The parables provoke and lead us to respond to him. As we do so, we will gain understanding, but without responding to Jesus we won't understand anything.

Growing seed

Finally, we have two more parables about seeds to sit alongside the parable of the sower. What would the Galilean farmers have made of them?

> He said, 'God's reign is like when someone sows seed into the earth. They sleep and wake, night and day, and the seed sprouts and grows, but they don't know how. All on its own the earth produces fruit, first the stalk, then the ear, then the full grain in the ear. When the fruit emerges, then they send in the sickle, because harvest has arrived.'
> He said, 'How should we compare God's reign? Or in what parable should we place it? It's like a mustard seed, which, when sown into the earth, is the smallest of all seeds on earth.

Yet when it is sown it comes up and ends up bigger than all of
the garden plants. It produces branches so big that the birds of
heaven can shelter in their shade.'

In many such parables he would speak the word to them
to them, as much as they could listen. Without a parable he
would not speak to them, but privately to his own disciples he
interpreted everything.

MARK 4:26–34

God's reign is, apparently, like a farmer who scatters seed on
the ground and then ignores it. No weeding, no keeping off
the birds or animals, no irrigation, no work, no anxiety—he
just sleeps and wakes and goes back to sleep. What sort of
crop will such a negligent farmer harvest? A rich one, claims
Jesus, for the earth will produce the grain itself. (The word
for 'earth' here is the same as 'soil' in the parable of the
sower.) The farmer will only need to wield the sickle when
the harvest arrives.

We could draw different conclusions from the parable.
'Laziness is good' might seem to be an overstatement. However, perhaps many of us do need to hear a challenge to
our over-anxiety, overwork and overheightened sense of
responsibility—especially those of us who are church leaders
or heavily involved in Christian ministry.

This fits with our general rule for reading parables, which
is that the key message or challenge lies in the point at which
the parable diverts from normal life. The Galilean farmers
would have been sure that a good harvest couldn't be
produced without stress and toil on their part, and we might
think the same.

As we would expect in a parable, Jesus doesn't answer
the question directly: he doesn't set out a finely tuned anal-

ysis of the balance between laziness (or trusting God) and hard work. Instead, he points out that we don't know how the seed sprouts: the primary relationship is between seed and earth, not between seed and farmer. In that sense, his point is undeniable. God's reign is about seed and soil, not about the farmers. The farmer is given a role—sowing and harvesting—and we have seen Jesus call and send out people to be his messengers. It would be wrong to take this parable to mean that there is no role for us in the development of God's reign. However, it challenges our tendency to overrate our own importance and to see ourselves as key mediators between God and people. No, what really matters is the seed and the soil.

The mustard seed is perhaps a straightforward illustration type of parable; there is no twist. Nevertheless, the point is a very unsettling one, for, if the tiniest seed produces the greatest plant, how are we to make decisions and prioritise our actions? If a chance conversation might produce more fruit than writing this book, how should I make decisions over the way I spend my time and resources? As always, Jesus' parables do not give us answers but leave us with questions to ponder, challenging our standard ways of thinking.

These two parables confront our instincts about control and anxiety, just as the parable of the sower challenges us with the idea that God is a surprisingly indiscriminate sower. If something is important to us, such as our faith and our sharing of that faith, it's hard not to become anxious and controlling about it. Nevertheless, we know that digging up little seedlings to see if they have started to grow is not a way of getting a good crop.

The final verses take us back to where we started, with the 'secret of the parables'. Understanding can only come to 'insiders'. For those 'outside', the way forward is not for them to gain some understanding but to respond to Jesus. Once they respond, understanding will follow. Response has to come first. That is why the parables are as they are: they are not primarily about teaching our heads; they are designed to engage our hearts.

The parable of the sewer

We considered this parable in the previous chapter, since it speaks of Jesus' relationship with the Jewish law. However, it is explicitly labelled as a parable, with the same dynamic of public telling followed by private unpacking, so it is worthwhile touching on it again.

> *Again, he called the crowd and began to say to them, 'Listen to me, all of you, and understand. Nothing going into someone from outside is able to pollute them. But rather it is what comes out from someone that pollutes them.'*
>
> *When he went into a house away from the crowd, his disciples asked him about the parable. He says to them, 'Are you also such fools? Don't you understand that nothing from outside going into someone can pollute them? It does not go into the heart but into the stomach and then out into the toilet.' (Saying this, Jesus made all food 'clean'.) He said, 'It's what comes out of a person that pollutes them. For from inside, from people's hearts, come out evil thoughts, sexual immorality, theft, murder, adultery, greed, malice, deceit, debauchery, envy, cursing, arrogance, foolishness. All these evils come out from within and pollute people.'*

MARK 7:14–23

The force and surprise of this parable can be lost on us, for we live in a culture that doesn't think of certain foods as 'polluting'—but think of Jesus' Jewish hearers. Their reaction would have been something like, 'That's wrong! God's law says that some food does pollute. Does this carpenter-turned-preacher not know anything about the scriptures?' Perhaps the original context made the point, and the shock, even stronger: I can imagine Jesus holding a tasty snack in his hand, pointing across to a foul-smelling latrine or open sewer and saying, 'It's what comes out that is foul, not what goes in.' The point is unarguable, and yet its implications are challenging and disturbing. This parable conveys a similar meaning to Jesus' teaching in Matthew 7:16–20 about recognising a tree and judging its value by what it produces, but it is far more striking.

There is more to the meaning, though, than the words 'Saying this, Jesus made all food "clean"'. Parables are not designed merely to illustrate a rational point of doctrine in a vivid way. This parable undermines the Jewish food laws, but it also challenges all our views of what 'defiles' us. We are not immune to similar thinking. Does Jesus tell the same story to us when we look down on or criticise someone who is extremely overweight from eating too many takeaways, or a heavy drinker or smoker? We have our own views on the morality of 'what goes in'. Our media pour scorn on obese overeaters and yet they indulge in celebrity gossip, as if what goes in matters more than what comes out.

Perhaps we should go further and recognise that 'going into' is a common euphemism in the Bible for sexual inter-course (see Amos 2:7). Would Jesus challenge the obsession of our society and the church with the moralities of sex? 'You are obsessed by what "goes into" whom, but it's what comes out that defiles!' How about the idea of 'what goes in' from the perspective of genetics or upbringing? That is certainly one of our preoccupations: hardly a day goes by without a media story about someone's bad schooling, parenting or genetics. The parable of the sewer challenges us. What has gone into a person—her genes or upbringing—does not make her good or bad; it's what she comes out with that matters.

The tenants in the vineyard

Finally we come to the last of the parables in Peter's preaching as recorded by Mark. It's the only parable that Jesus tells in Jerusalem, and it has the effect of hardening opposition towards him. Parables are all about response, for good or ill.

He began to speak to them in parables. 'A man planted a vineyard, put a wall around it, dug a winepress and built a watchtower. Then he hired it out to tenant-farmers and left the country.

'At harvest-time, he sent a messenger to the tenant-farmers to collect from the tenant-farmers a share of the vineyard's produce. They seize him, beat him and sent him away empty-handed. So he sent back to them another slave. That one they beat round the head and humiliated. He sent another, and that one they killed. And many others, some they beat and some they killed.

'He still had one left—a much-loved son. In the end, he sent him to them, saying to himself, "They will respect my son." But those tenant-farmers said to themselves, "This is the heir. Come, let's kill him and the inheritance will be ours!" They seized him and killed him. Then they threw him out of the vineyard.

'What then will the vineyard owner do? He will come and destroy those tenant-farmers and give the vineyard to others. Haven't you read this scripture? "The stone which the builders rejected has become the cornerstone. The Lord has done this and it is marvellous in our eyes"?'

They realised that he had told this parable against them, and so they began to seek a way to arrest him. Yet they were afraid of the crowd, and so they left him and went away.

MARK 12:1–12

At what point does this parable 'go wrong' and diverge from normal life?

The story begins very reasonably: yes, a rich man would build a vineyard; yes, he would lease it out; yes, he would send a slave to collect the fruit; and yes, sometimes the tenants might refuse to pay. A second slave is sent—yes, that is perhaps reasonable too. Then... the audience will be waiting for the owner to act decisively against the rebellious tenants. Judgement will fall, and rightly so.

But no, the stupid man sends many more slaves, all of whom get the same treatment. Then, to cap it all, he sends his much-loved son, who, not surprisingly, gets killed. Does the carpenter-turned-preacher not know anything about the way the rich handle their tenants?

Finally, when Jesus asks what the owner of the vineyard will do, the crowd will roar with approval. Of course he will come with judgement and destroy the tenants; they most definitely have it coming to them. So we have a story of a stupid master, far too soft, who delays judgement for a ridiculously long time. However, in the end, much to everyone's relief, he does finally act.

What do we make of this? The vineyard was a standard

image for Israel, developed in a similar story in Isaiah 5. Furthermore, it was commonly believed that God was, in some sense, absent from Israel. In Ezekiel 9—11 his glory is said to have departed the temple, and the condition of Israel at the time of Jesus—occupied by a pagan empire—supported the idea that God had not yet returned. However, in Isaiah, God is in dispute with his vineyard and says that he will come and destroy it. In Jesus' 'retelling', the tenants are a new feature. The problem is not the vineyard itself but those who have been in charge of it. God, the master of Israel, has been absent, and others have been doing a bad job of over- seeing Israel on his behalf. They have been acting as if they owned the vineyard themselves, refusing to do God's will.

So far so good, but God does not act like a normal landlord. That is the point of the parable. He is foolishly long-suffering with the tenants, giving them far more chances than any human landlord would. Moreover, he takes personal risks, sending not just expendable slaves but his own precious son. Then, when every possible alternative has been tried, he acts decisively. God is more merciful than we are; God is more long-suffering, but don't be fooled into imagining that he can be taken for a ride for ever. The challenge to the religious authorities is obvious, and they know it. If anyone fits the bill of the 'tenants in God's vineyard', it is them. They stand accused of rejecting God, and their judgement is predicted.

It's worse than that, though. Imagine the crowd's roar of approval when the vineyard owner stops being soft and acts to kick out the tenants. Jesus does not just pronounce judge- ment on the religious authorities. He tells the story in such a way as to get the crowd to think that God has been soft in allowing the authorities to continue so long, and to demand that he acts decisively now. The crowd have not just learnt something; they have grasped the point in their guts, feeling outraged at what the religious authorities have been doing. No wonder the authorities were so afraid of the crowd that they dared not arrest Jesus immediately or in a public place (see 14:1–2, 49) but came for him at night, in a shadowy garden, outside the city, tipped off by one of his so-called friends.

There is a further layer of meaning, which would certainly have struck Jesus' original hearers. The Aramaic words for 'son' and 'stone' are very similar. Hence, the rejected stone in verse 10 is verbally connected with the rejected son. Jesus has told a story about a rejected and murdered son, linked with the idea of a precious cornerstone. So not only will God bring judgement against the tenants, but he will make the rejected one into the 'cornerstone'—the most honoured position.

This idea is not developed here in Peter's preaching—presumably because it relies on the Aramaic pun of 'stone' and 'son', which is lost when the story is told in Greek. However, Peter does develop it at more length in one of his letters (see 1 Peter 2:4–8).

This is a parable with many layers. Nevertheless, we should remember the main point—indicated by the moment when the parable diverts from normal life. God's mercy and patience are astonishing, beyond what we would consider reasonable; we would have acted harshly, with power, much more quickly than God does. In the end, though, judgement will come and justice will be done.

In this chapter, we have engaged with some important teaching of Jesus—about God's mercy, about judgement, about the heart, about the demons, about God's indiscriminate sowing, about our need to put anxiety aside when we 'sow', and about the importance of response. However, we have also seen that to reduce the parables to 'teaching' is to misuse them badly. They challenge rather than teach, in order to engage with us in a way that direct teaching cannot. Their prime purpose is to move the heart, not the head. The parables point to Jesus himself. Jesus really does teach 'not like the scribes'. The scribes point to the law and to God. They think of the 'lamp' as God's written word, but in his parables Jesus points to himself. He is the 'lamp' that has come and will not be hidden.

CHAPTER 8

GOD'S REIGN

'Mum, Mum, is it Christmas today?' shouted the little boy as he ran into his mum's bedroom far too early in the morning. Blurry-eyed, she struggled for comprehension. Christmas? It was still November. 'Not yet,' she said, more kindly than she was feeling. 'Snuggle in here and let's make a plan for today.' There would be many stressful 'todays' before Christmas arrived.

A month earlier, the same mum had been sounding off to her friend Susie. 'I couldn't believe it. I was going through town to find some new shoes for our Luke and all the displays were for Christmas. It was October! All you could see was Father Christmas and tinsel. I could swear it comes earlier every year!' Susie had smiled; all she could remember was Laura sounding off earlier and earlier each year. She liked Christmas. Why not make the shops more jolly? Some bright lights and decorations made the place look better as the autumn gloom set in.

End of term: Susie was sitting in the cramped school hall listening to Charlie from down the street struggling over the line, 'I am Gabriel. I bring you good news. You are going to have a baby.' It took her back to her own school days, when the nativity play had seemed so important. That was when Christmas had really started. But when she said so to her mum that evening, her mum shook her head. 'No, remember what we used to say when you were small. Christmas starts when the tree goes up.'

'Don't be silly,' butted in Susie's sister. 'The works' Christmas do is where it all kicks off.' Her dad was muttering, 'I think we could do with some more Christmas spirit all year round' as he did the washing up on his own again. Susie had to laugh. Dad spent most of his time grumbling—though, to give him his due, when they'd clubbed together in the summer and bought him all that Liverpool Football Club memorabilia, he'd said it was like 'Christmas come early', and for once he'd meant it!

When does Christmas come? On 25 December or before? It's not the most profound of questions, but it is intriguing. We all know that, strictly speaking, Christmas comes on 25 December—but, in many countries, Christmas Eve is the main event. Christingles, school carol services, work parties, shopping, decorating the house—these are all Christmas and signs that Christmas is coming. The question of how a day can be both the event itself and a sign that the event is on its way is a philosophical conundrum that, fortunately, doesn't matter. We all know what we mean. And yes, Susie's dad was right: some Christmas spirit all year round might be nice. We can always do with having a bit more 'peace and goodwill towards all people', relaxing, letting our hair down and thinking about giving rather than getting. Occasionally, if we're lucky, life does feel as if Christmas has come early.

I have never heard anyone saying that God's reign is like Christmas, but it's not a bad comparison, for, as we will soon see, it's hard to pin down when God's reign comes. Theologians often talk of God's reign being 'now and not yet'—which is similar to the idea of Christmas starting on 25 December but also starting at the carol service, or when the lights go up, or whenever. Moreover, if Christmas can 'come early' and we can long for some 'Christmas spirit', it also seems true that there are foretastes of God's reign. There are moments when God's reign seems real or is glimpsed fleetingly. Even if we can't pin it down, we do know what we mean about Christmas coming, and perhaps the same is true of God's reign.

God's reign is near

The theme of God's reign is given huge prominence in Mark's Gospel, occurring right at the beginning, in the summary that introduces Jesus' ministry. He has been baptised and then tempted in the desert. Now is the moment for Jesus to begin his work.

> *After John had been arrested, Jesus went into Galilee proclaiming God's good news: 'The time has come. God's reign is near. Repent and believe the good news.'*
> MARK 1:14–15

'The time' has come—but what time? It can't quite be the time for God's reign to arrive, because the very next words tell us that God's reign is 'near'. Sometimes this word is translated as 'at hand'; we might say 'just around the corner', but it is the time for *something* to happen. It's interesting that John's arrest is the signal that this time has come. Something has come to an end, and a new thing is beginning. Indeed, the phrase 'the time has come' could be translated as 'the time has been fulfilled', the implication being that 'the long-awaited time has come'.

What time has been long promised? As we saw in Chapter 5, John the Baptist is introduced in Mark 1:2–4 by quotations from Isaiah 40:3 and Malachi 3:1. The Isaiah quotation, in context, says this:

> *'Comfort, comfort my people,' says your God. 'Speak to Jerusalem's heart, and proclaim to her that she has completed her sentence, her sin has been paid for, she has received from the Lord's hand double for all her sins.' A voice of someone shouting: 'In the desert prepare the Lord's way; make straight in the desert a highway for our God. Every valley shall be raised up, every mountain and hill made low; the rugged ground shall become flat, the rough place a plain. And the glory of the Lord will be revealed, and all people will see it together.'*
>
> ISAIAH 40:1–5

So the time that has been fulfilled is this time of Israel's 'hard service', during which she has been paying for her sins. The sin has now been paid for. John has done his work of proclaiming in the desert, and now the glory of the Lord will be revealed. Good times are here! This makes sense of the declaration of 'God's good news'. It is good news that the time of hard service and paying for sins is over.

The good news is coupled with the proclamation that 'God's reign is near'. The phrase 'God's reign' is often translated as 'the kingdom of God', but the emphasis is not on a piece of land or a community. We could equally call it 'God's rule', but that could be misunderstood to mean 'God's rules', which is something quite different. Whichever way we translate it, however, it is near.

The term 'God's reign' is not used in the Old Testament in

the way that it appears on Jesus' lips. However, there is a rich background to the phrase. The psalms in particular proclaim that 'God reigns'—for example, 'The Lord has established his throne in the heavens, and his kingdom rules over all' (Psalm 103:19, NRSV; see also 9:7; 47:8; 93:1; 96:10; 97:1; 99:1; 146:10; 1 Chronicles 16:31). Alongside this proclamation is an element of future hope—a promise that God 'will reign'. In some places, this is expressed in the hope for a future king from the line of King David:

> *'When your days are completed and you sleep with your ancestors, I will raise up your offspring after you, who will share your heart, and I will establish his reign. He is the one who will build a house for my name, and I will establish his rule for ever. I will be a father to him; and he shall be a son to me.'*
>
> 2 SAMUEL 7:12–14

We see this hope taken up in Isaiah 9:6–7, with the promise that a child will be born who will reign on God's behalf over David's kingdom. Daniel 7, which we discussed earlier because of the appearance in it of a 'Son of Man', is focused on the arrival of God's kingdom. The climax of the vision is described as follows.

> *As I watched in my vision during the night, I looked and there was one like a son of man coming on the clouds of heaven. He came to the Ancient of Days and was presented before him. He was given authority, glory and reign, and all peoples, nations and language will worship him. His authority is an everlasting authority that will not pass away, and his reign will never be destroyed.*
>
> DANIEL 7:13–14

The vision is interpreted (in 7:16–18, 26–27) as God's inter-vention to give 'the kingdom' back to God's people. The idea that 'God reigns' now, already, but that God's reign also needs to come in the future, is captured in this passage from Isaiah.

> *How beautiful on the mountains are the feet of the one declaring the news of peace, announcing good things, proclaiming salvation, saying to Zion, 'Your God reigns!' The cry of those watching over you rises up—the sound of them rejoicing together—because with their own eyes they see the Lord returning to Zion.*
>
> *Burst into joyful songs together, you ruins of Jerusalem, for the Lord has comforted his people, he has rescued Jerusalem. The Lord has bared his holy arm before the eyes of all the nations, and all the ends of the earth see the salvation of our God.*
>
> ISAIAH 52:7–10

In one sense, this messenger is just announcing what has always been true, that God reigns. However, in his listeners' present reality, it doesn't feel as if God is reigning. It feels as if God is absent. The announcement is that God is returning and will bring salvation to his people.

Jewish writings from around the time of Jesus express a similar imprecise yet somehow very clear message. This is unsurprising, since those writings are, to a large degree, interpretations of the sort of Old Testament passages I have just quoted. There was a huge longing among the Jewish people for God to act. Many, probably most, Jews felt the contradiction between the condition of Israel at the time and the idea that 'God reigns', so there was a widespread hope that God would do something, although people described that 'something' in quite different ways. This isn't the place to delve into the complexities of first-century Judaism, but it was a world in which the announcement of 'God's reign' would have resonated strongly with people's hopes.

However, here in Mark 1:14–15 Jesus does not announce that God's reign has come. The time of waiting, hard service and paying for sins is over, but God's reign is only 'near'. So we are 'in between'.

These two verses succinctly present the crucial chronology of Jesus' ministry. His ministry is in between times: one phase has ended and the next is just around the corner. In his ministry there is a window of opportunity—a chance to 'repent and believe the good news'. Once John has been arrested, Jesus goes into Galilee preaching, 'Now is the moment! Do something!' We can now see how this relates to Jesus' teaching in parables, which was fundamentally a call for a response.

The sense that Jesus stands at the 'final moment' comes out particularly clearly in Luke's Gospel. When speaking about John the Baptist, Jesus says:

> 'He's the one about whom it is written, 'Look! I am sending my messenger before you. He will prepare your way in front of you.' I tell you, nobody born of a woman is greater than John. But the least of those in God's reign is greater than him!'
>
> LUKE 7:27–28

Something big is about to happen. Even the greatest person in the 'world before' is insignificant in the 'world after'. This idea is developed further in a later chapter of Luke's Gospel:

> *'The law and the prophets last until John. But from then the*
> *good news of God's reign is being announced, and everyone is*
> *forcing their way in.'*
>
> LUKE 16:16

'Until… from then', with John as the pivot in between, expresses a theology of 'today'. Luke also shows us Zacchaeus and the penitent thief being told that 'today' salvation has come to them (Luke 19:9; 23:43). However, Luke is simply bringing to the surface an understanding that can be seen throughout the Gospels. For example, in Mark, on their way down from the mount of transfiguration the disciples ask, 'Why do the scribes say that Elijah must come first?' to which Jesus replies, 'Elijah does come first… but I tell you, Elijah has come and they responded to him as they wished' (Mark 9:10–12). Here, Jesus seems to be referring clearly to John (see the connection made in Mark 1:6). There was the 'time of John' and now comes something different.

Thus, we could paraphrase Mark 1:14–15 like this: 'Once John has been arrested, Jesus started to proclaim, "Now is the time. God's reign is about to come! Do something! Respond—repent—and throw your lot in with what God is about to do!"' It is a call to action.

It's very close

In the first half of Mark's Gospel, we have three main references to God's reign. First, in the parable about Satan (3:22–30), there is an implicit contrast between Satan's reign, which is coming to an end, and God's reign, which is arriving in some fashion as Jesus casts out the demons.

However, in terms of the illustration about Christmas from the beginning of this chapter, this arrival could mean it is now 25 December, or it could equally be Christmas Eve, the day of a carol service or nativity play, or even just some equivalent of 'the Christmas spirit'.

Second, there is the discussion after the parable of the sower about 'the secret of God's reign' being given to those who respond to Jesus. God's reign is somehow bound up closely with Jesus and people's response to him.

Third, two of the parables about seeds (the seed growing of its own accord, and the mustard seed) were explicitly said to be about God's reign. We are involved in the coming of his reign but can't bring it about by our efforts, and it seems small but has a huge impact.

Then, immediately before the transfiguration in Mark 9, we have this startling statement.

> Jesus said to them. 'I tell you the truth. Some of those standing here will not taste death before they see that God's reign has come in power.'
> MARK 9:1

This is a tricky verse, so let us proceed carefully. Its basic point seems clear: God's reign will visibly come in power within the lifetime of some of those present. This fits well with what we have already seen. Jesus went into Galilee proclaiming that God's reign was *near*, and here we have a timeframe placed on the word 'near'. (Of course 'near' can have a geographical as well as a chronological reference, but Mark 9:1 seems to be talking about time rather than place.)

The difficulty is that Christians tend to associate 'God's reign come in power' with 'the end of the world'—which manifestly didn't happen within the lifetime any of those present to hear Jesus' words. Of course, one 'answer' might be that Jesus was wrong, and some scholars have taken that line, suggesting that Jesus mistakenly thought God would dramatically intervene to save him from the cross. But there is no need to accept this interpretation; we just need to think a bit more carefully about what 'God's reign come in power' might mean.

When we look back to the hopes expressed in the Old Testament, we find that the idea of God's reign is not connected with the end of the world but with a renewed Israel, safe and secure, like a (rose-tinted) view of the time of the great King David. The watchmen of Jerusalem in Isaiah 52:8 were celebrating not the end of the world but the transformation of Jerusalem's situation in the world. Colloquially, in English, we can use 'end of the world' language when we mean something hugely significant. If we speak of 'earth-shattering events', we mean something very significant but not something that leaves the planet physically broken into pieces. The world can be 'turned upside down' without England and New Zealand changing places.

So what does 'God's reign come in power' mean? We perhaps ought to leave it until the end of the chapter to decide. The obvious answer is that it refers to the events of the crucifixion and resurrection, although some commentators would point to the story of the transfiguration that immediately follows Mark 9:1, where Jesus' glory is revealed, or to events such as Pentecost, or Jesus' miracles, or indeed to Jesus' presence among the people (for he was 'the secret of God's reign', the lamp which has come). Again, though, the comparison with the coming of Christmas might alert us to the dangers of trying to pin down a precise moment.

Lessons from little children

People were bringing infants to him so he would touch them. His disciples rebuked them. When Jesus saw this he was annoyed and said to them, 'Let the infants come to me. Don't hinder them. For God's reign belongs to people like them. I tell you the truth. Whoever does not welcome God's reign like an infant will never enter it.' Then he took them into his arms, laid his hands on them and blessed them.

MARK 10:13–16

In Chapter 3, when we were considering what it means to 'follow on the way', we studied some passages in which Jesus spoke of the importance of welcoming children and caring for them. This passage is slightly different. It starts with the same point, as we see Jesus himself demonstrating the importance of welcoming small children and trying to ensure that his disciples do the same. However, Jesus goes on to use the infants as a visual aid for a message about God's reign.

God's reign, we are told, belongs to people 'such as' these infants. Clearly we need to understand the word 'belongs' in a flexible way. God's reign presumably literally belongs to God, but it is 'for' people such as these. They are the intended beneficiaries, the natural inhabitants or citizens of God's reign.

This is an important statement in itself. Infants—without power or competence—are significant in God's reign. We might be reminded of the parable of the seed growing on its own, which is said to be like God's reign. Its growth doesn't depend on our efforts and labours; therefore, people without power and competence, such as the infants, can be equal citizens under that reign. The statement also points back to

Jesus' response to his disciples when they were arguing over status: he used a child as an example (Mark 9:35–39).

However, Jesus' rebuke to his disciples in Mark 10 is not just a piece of teaching about infants. Jesus speaks of how *we* need to be like infants. In grammatical terms, 'Welcome God's reign like an infant' could mean 'Welcome God's reign as you would welcome an infant'; intriguing as this is, though, it doesn't make much sense. The story has told us that the disciples were not good at welcoming infants, so they should not be welcoming God's reign in such a way. No, presumably the point is that God's reign is 'for' people like the infants, so we need to take on the key characteristic of infants in order to welcome, and enter into, God's reign. But what is the key characteristic? In what way should we try to be 'like' small children?

The passage doesn't tell us, so it's important to be cautious about saying that it 'obviously' means this or that. Continuing the Christmas illustration, I could say that 'receiving God's reign like a small child' means excitedly ripping the paper off but very soon getting bored with the contents and either playing with the packaging or going back to the TV. This is how many infants behave, but presumably it isn't what Jesus means! Many commentators would suggest that a key characteristic of small children is their acceptance of change, gifts and, indeed, all external events, without any desire to control them or even necessarily to understand them. Infants are 'accepting', partly because they don't yet have the sense that an offer of help might be patronising or demeaning. It's certainly true that many adults, in stark contrast to infants, find it very different to 'receive'. We much prefer a trans-action—an exchange. In relation to our religious practice, this tendency leads to the attempt to make bargains—for example, 'Help me, God, and I will do x or stop doing y', or, 'I've worked hard for God, so I deserve x or y'. Jesus hugs and blesses the children. They just need to receive. It sounds easy, but it isn't. Similarly, as we have already seen, Jesus' hearers only need to respond to him and they will get the secret of God's reign, yet many can't or won't respond.

How hard it is to enter

We will return to the question of how we should be 'like children' after we have considered the next part of Peter's preaching, which comes immediately after this passage.

As Jesus was setting out on the road, one man ran up to him and knelt down in front of him and asked him, 'Good teacher, what must I do so that I inherit eternal life?' Jesus said to him, 'Why do you call me good? Nobody is good except for God. You know the commandments—do not murder, do not commit adultery, do not steal, do not give false witness, do not defraud, honour your father and mother.' He replied, 'Teacher, I have kept all these things since I was a boy.'

Jesus stared at him and loved him. He said to him, 'You lack one thing. Go, sell all that you have and give to the poor, and you will have treasure in heaven. Then come follow me.' His face fell at these words and he went away very sad. For he had many possessions.

Jesus looked around and says to his disciples, 'How hard it is for those with possessions to enter God's reign.' The disciples were amazed at his words. Jesus again replied, 'Children, how hard it is to enter God's reign. It is easier for a camel to pass through the eye of a needle than for a rich person to enter into

God's reign.' They were even more astounded, saying to each other, 'Who, then, can be saved?'

Jesus looked around and says, 'For humans it is impossible, but not for God. For everything is possible for God.' Peter began to say to him, 'Look, we have left everything behind and followed you.'

Jesus said, 'I tell you the truth. There is nobody who has left behind house or brothers or sisters or mother or father or children or fields for my sake and for the sake of the good news who will not receive a hundred times as much now, in this age—houses, brothers, sisters, mothers, children and fields, with persecutions—and in the age to come eternal life. Many who are first will be last, and the last first.'

MARK 10:17–31

Let's try to unpick this complicated passage, beginning with the camel and the eye of the needle. There is no justification at all for inventing ways of rewriting the passage so that it doesn't say what it says. Of course, wealthy people throughout the ages have wanted to change its meaning—partly because of our self-interest and partly because we share the disciples' puzzlement. Surely we are the sort of people God wants, and we are the sort of people who can arrange entry into God's reign? So scholars have produced fancies about a 'Needle Gate' in Jerusalem, which a camel could just about pass through, or they have suggested replacing the word 'camel' with 'quite thick string' (thicker than would easily be threaded into a needle). There is no historical justification for any of these alterations, and there is no point to them: why listen to Jesus if we are then going to sidestep the challenge? The disciples clearly recognised that Jesus' image of a camel and the eye of a needle was an image of something impossible. That is why they responded with the question, 'Who then can be saved?'

Is this passage talking about rich people in particular? On the surface, it is: the key characteristic of the man who approached Jesus is his possessions. Jesus tells him to sell them and give to the poor. The command is too hard for the man, and Jesus goes on to talk about the difficulties faced by a rich person. However, the disciples seem to see it as affecting them, too. Their exclamation, 'Who then can be saved?' seems to imply the conclusion, 'If it's that hard for the rich, it's hopeless for us all.' Similarly Peter protests about all that he has left behind, even though he is not rich.

Presumably the logic is that people expected the rich to be at the front of the queue—either because their riches were seen as a sign of God's favour or, more simply, because the rich are adept at making sure they do well out of every new situation. If those at the front of the queue are going to find it difficult to enter, that is not good news for anyone. However, Jesus' final words make clear the mistake. Entering God's reign involves upheaval—the world turned upside down—in which many of the first become last. The implication is that the rich (and, presumably, others who are used to being 'first') will have a particular difficulty, which some others (those who are normally 'last') will not face.

The exchange between Jesus and the young man over the commandments is important. Jesus does not doubt that the man has followed the commandments from his youth. However, something more is required. This is startling: how can something more be required than keeping the covenant that God made with Israel? It connects with our findings in Chapter 6—that, according to Jesus, the law and its interpretation are no longer the dominant factors in the relationship between God and people. Jesus asks the man about his obedience to the commandments—Jesus is not against them—but that is not the whole story.

What more is required? Jesus says that the man only lacks one thing, but then he seems to give two instructions. The man is to sell his possessions and give to the poor, and then he is to follow Jesus. Which is more important? Following Jesus—for that has been at the heart of Jesus' ministry from the start. He calls people to follow him and tells parables urging a response to him. Thus, what the man requires, alongside his obedience to the commandments, is to follow Jesus. Moreover, we saw in the calling of Peter, Andrew, James and John (as Peter reminds us in this passage) that following Jesus means leaving things behind. So possessions are indeed a barrier to following him. Jesus sees that because the man is rich, he will find it difficult to leave his possessions behind. Thus, his wealth will make it hard for him truly to follow Jesus. In this case, it is right to say that wealth is not intrinsically bad, just that, in practice, it can often form a barrier that makes it hard for people to follow Jesus.

Throughout the passage, there is a strand of self-seeking. The way the man runs up, kneels and addresses Jesus as 'good teacher' seems to suggest a bit of flattery—or, at least, Jesus' response implies that he interpreted it that way. Perhaps this sort of polite 'oiling of the wheels' ensures that rich people remain 'the first'. At the same time, though, the disciples are concerned for themselves. Peter points out to Jesus that they have left everything behind—in effect, exactly what Jesus asked the rich man to do. Jesus' response to Peter is intriguing. He agrees with him and assures him and the other disciples that their wholehearted response to him will not be forgotten. At the same time, though, he slips in the word 'persecutions'. An initial dedicated response—which the disciples made but the young man could not make—is important, but there is a need for ongoing dedication, too. The hundredfold reward takes us back to the parable of the sower: the eventual outcome from entering God's reign will be overwhelmingly good.

Finally we come to the key underlying point in this passage—that people need to, and can, 'enter God's reign'. At first sight, this is bizarre, even though the idea might be familiar to us. Surely either God is reigning or he isn't? Tiberius was the Roman emperor at the time of Jesus, and Galileans were under his reign. If Tiberius died, then the reign of another emperor would come—or, indeed, if the Parthians conquered Galilee, then the Galileans would come under the reign of a new ruler. But in no situation could some Galileans, but not others, voluntarily 'enter' into someone else's reign.

The Jewish idea of God's reign or kingdom doesn't help us, either, for the whole point of God's reign, as presented in passages such as Daniel 7, is that it is universal and imposed. God's reign comes and the 'beasts' (the evil empires) are destroyed or put in their place, while the 'son of man' (God's people) is freed from oppression and has a glorious future. The watchmen in Jerusalem are celebrating because the coming of God's reign means that their oppression will end and 'the ends of the earth' will see their salvation.

It is possible to keep hold of a territorial sense of 'kingdom' or 'reign' in this passage—a reign that is universally visible and imposed. We could say that, at a future point, God's reign will be imposed universally. Many will be excluded from it, but those who decide to follow Jesus will, at that point, be able to 'enter' the newly imposed reign of God. However, this would be a strange use of the word 'enter', for it more naturally speaks of a situation in which something (such as a building or a club) already exists. People can then enter into it or not. Furthermore, Jesus' words seem to imply that 'God's reign' is something that the young man could enter into *now*. It almost seems as if entering God's reign is the same as following Jesus. The man needs to get rid of the barrier of his possessions and follow Jesus—but he can't because those possessions make it hard for him to enter God's reign. 'Following Jesus' and 'entering God's reign' seem to be almost synonymous.

Suddenly this makes sense. If following Jesus is the same as entering God's reign, then the passage about the secret of God's reign being given to those who respond to Jesus becomes clear. By responding to Jesus, they have entered God's reign, so they might reasonably be described as possessing its secret. Looking back to the seed parables, the parable of the sower was about responding to Jesus, while the seed growing secretly and the mustard seed were about God's reign. But if responding to Jesus is the same as entering into God's reign, the parables come together as a unity. Furthermore, Jesus' two most distinctive challenges also come together: 'God's reign is near; repent and believe' (in other words, do something) and 'If you have ears to hear, listen! (in other words, respond, or, do something)'. We might say that entering into God's reign means accepting God's reign over our life, which is the same as becoming a follower of Jesus. If this sounds small—individual people entering, not a glorious imposition with universal acclaim—remember the mustard seed and yeast. What starts small ends up having a massive effect.

Is that all there is to it? Is God's reign only a matter of individuals 'entering into it' by following Jesus? The passages we have read so far seem to imply that there is something more, for the seed parables speak not only of growing but of harvest. The mustard seed starts small but the plant ends up so large that the birds of heaven shelter in it. Jesus' words before the transfiguration spoke of 'God's reign come in power' as something that can be seen as a future event. There is still more for us to explore!

Finally, we can cast our minds back to the story of the children. There we were told that we have to 'enter God's reign' like an infant. Now, as it has become clear that 'entering into God's reign' overlaps with 'following Jesus' or 'responding to Jesus', perhaps this helps us to identify the crucial characteristic of an infant. Infants are not proud; they are transparent, they are wholehearted, their lives are not complicated and they are trusting. In contrast, the rich young man was calculating in the way he approached Jesus, and his pride and the complications of his many possessions formed a barrier that prevented him from responding to Jesus' call to follow him and thus from entering into God's reign. He was not able to enter like an infant.

We can also think back to the study of the disciples and those following on the way. The disciples did respond wholeheartedly at first, but their progress was threatened by their attempt to take control (see, for example, Peter's rebuke of Jesus, the disciples' opposition to the one casting out demons in Jesus' name and their attempt to stop the children from coming to Jesus). They were criticised for a lack of faith—that is, a lack of child-like trust. Some of the people whose faith Jesus praised were 'like infants'. For example, the woman who was bleeding was not proud (she did not even want to trouble Jesus by interrupting him); her desire was transparent and wholehearted and she had great trust.

What are the barriers that prevent a wholehearted response to Jesus from us? One might be our many possessions, as it was for the young man. In the parable of the sower, though, it wasn't just the 'deceit of wealth' that could choke the seed but also 'the cares of the age' and 'the desire for all other things'. Ambition, fear, stress, desire, pride—there are many possible barriers.

The king arrives

Finally Jesus arrives at Jerusalem. It's worth remembering that, in Peter's preaching, this is the first and only time that Jesus goes there. Jesus' ministry is in Galilee, around the fields and towns, around the sea, and into Syria and the Decapolis to the north and east of Galilee. Then he goes up to Jerusalem. On his way, he predicts three times that he will die there (Mark 8:31; 9:31; 10:33). The tension is high.

The religious background adds to that tension. In the passage from Isaiah 52 that we considered earlier, the watchmen were crying out because the Lord (God) was returning to Jerusalem (Zion). Prophecies of a future king like David would naturally have been connected with David's city, Jerusalem. Mark's Gospel opens by connecting Isaiah 40 (the voice crying out in the desert, 'Prepare the way for the Lord') with Malachi 3 (the messenger sent ahead to prepare the way), but Malachi 3 says more:

I am sending out my messenger. He will prepare the way before me. Then the Lord you seek will suddenly come to his temple; the messenger of the covenant you delight in—look, he

is coming, says the Lord Almighty. But who can endure the day
he arrives? Who can stand when he appears? For he is like a
refiner's fire and like cleansing soap.

MALACHI 3:1–2

Yes, there is a messenger (or was: see Mark 9:13), and after
his arrival the long-expected Lord will come to the temple in
Jerusalem. However, this will not necessarily be good: 'who
can endure the day of his coming?' What is going to happen?

When they get near to Jerusalem, to Bethphage and Bethany
at the Mount of Olives, Jesus sends two of his disciples, saying
to them, 'Go into the village opposite and as soon as you go into
it you will find, tied up, a donkey which nobody has ridden
yet. Untie it and bring it. If anyone asks you, "Why are you
doing this?" say, "Its master needs it and he will send it back
here straight away."' They went and found the donkey tied
at a doorway outside in the street and they untie it. Some
bystanders began to say to them, 'What are you doing, untying
the donkey?' They replied just as Jesus had said, and they let
them carry on.

They bring the donkey to Jesus and throw their cloaks on to
it, and he sat on it. Many people spread their cloaks on the road,
and others branches they had cut from the fields. Those leading
the way and those following on were shouting out, 'Hosanna!
Blessed is the one who comes in the Lord's name! Blessed is the
coming reign of our father David. Hosanna in the highest!'

Jesus entered Jerusalem, into the temple, and looked around
at it all. Then, because it was already late, he went out to
Bethany with the Twelve.

MARK 11:1–11

The story about the donkey is fascinating. Matthew 21:4–5 makes explicit the link with Zechariah, which, presumably, is intended here in Peter's preaching, too.

> *Rejoice greatly, O Daughter of Zion! Shout, Daughter of Jerusalem! See, your king comes to you, righteous and bringing salvation, gentle and riding on a donkey, on a colt, the foal of a donkey.*
> ZECHARIAH 9:9

The donkey conveyed the important message that Jesus was a king, but a particular sort of king—one who was righteous and humble, bringing salvation and fulfilling God's plan. The crowd's response—the spreading of cloaks and branches, and the shouts—suggests that they got the point.

Told from the perspective of the disciples (after all, this is Peter's preaching), the story about fetching the donkey is somewhat mysterious. How did Jesus know the donkey was there? Why did the bystanders let them take it? Presumably Jesus had carefully planned it—and that is important, for it means that Jesus had decided and planned to enter Jerusalem in this way. It was, in effect, a publicity stunt. He wanted people to bring to mind these prophecies about God returning to Jerusalem.

The prophecy of Malachi quoted above is not straightforwardly fulfilled, though. Jesus may be acting as 'the Lord' coming to the temple, but judgement doesn't immediately follow his arrival. He looks round and then goes home for the night. The next day he curses a fig tree, symbolically attacking the temple, and at his death the curtain of the temple is torn in two (Mark 15:38), but these events do not happen on the 'day' of his arrival. Perhaps, though, we are taking the word 'day' too literally, or perhaps the delay is an expression of God's mercy: judgement, even now, is held back.

The crowd's shouts do directly connect Jesus' arrival in Jerusalem with the theme of God's reign. The 'coming reign' of David must be a reference (via passages such as 2 Samuel 7) to the hope that God will send them a new glorious king, like David, who will establish his reign. The parallelism between 'Blessed is the one who comes in the Lord's name' and 'Blessed is the coming reign of our father David' seems to imply an intimate connection between the one coming in the Lord's name and the coming reign. It implies that Jesus is the one coming in God's name and with him comes God's long-expected reign. Indeed, from what we have seen earlier, in fact Jesus is the secret of God's reign: his arrival (whether in Jerusalem or in people's lives) is the arrival of God's reign.

Launch the rebellion!

Jesus produces a simmering tension in Jerusalem. That first day, the shouts of the crowd welcoming him will have raised tensions. Then, the next day, he causes commotion in the temple, symbolically attacking it. That is enough for the chief priests and scribes, who start to plot to kill him. But it goes on. Jesus refuses to acknowledge the authority of a delegation of the chief priests, scribes and elders (who together made up the highest religious authority in Judaism), and then he tells a parable attacking the religious authorities for rebelling against God, predicting that God will destroy them (Mark 11:12—12:11).

There is a problem for the religious authorities, though. The crowds like Jesus, and somehow he has avoided doing anything obviously wrong, anything that could justify his arrest. Furthermore, Jerusalem was always tense at Passover time. The Roman governor, with his troops, would come from his usual base down on the coast to ensure that order was kept. The Jewish historian Josephus records various riots and disturbances at Passover time. What can the authorities do?

Their answer, it seems, is to try to trap Jesus into making clear revolutionary statements, or to force him to disappoint his followers with the realisation that he is speaking empty words.

> *They send to him some Pharisees and Herodians to trap him with his words. They came and say to him, 'Teacher, we know that you have integrity and you show no favour to anyone. For you do not seek for people's response but rather in truth you teach God's way. Is it right to pay tax to Caesar or not? Should we pay, or should we not?'*
>
> *Jesus was well aware of their hypocrisy and said to them, 'Why are you testing me? Bring me a denarius so I can have a look.' They brought one. And he says to them, 'Whose image is this, and whose inscription?' They said to him, 'Caesar's.' Jesus told them, 'Give Caesar's things back to Caesar and God's things back to God.' They were amazed at him.*
>
> MARK 12:13–17

The trap is simple but effective. There are only two possible answers to the question about the tax: either they should pay it or they shouldn't. If Jesus says they shouldn't, that will be a clear attack on the Roman state, a crime that the governor will have to take seriously. No Roman governor could allow a charismatic man with a following to be going around telling people not to pay their taxes. This will be the 'best' answer from the point of view of the Jewish religious authorities. If, on the other hand, Jesus says that they should pay their taxes, it will mean that he is acknowledging the Roman emperor's reign over Israel. It will mean disappointing all the followers who have been whispering about how Jesus is going to bring God's reign. It will turn him effectively into an advocate for the hated tax collectors.

The flattering build-up to the question intensifies the difficulty. The Pharisees and Herodians are not leaving Jesus any room to duck the issue or treat it lightly. Of course it is an important question, but, as Peter in his preaching says, it is hypocritical, for the people asking it (the ruling religious authorities) keep their power only because they compromise with Roman rule.

It is interesting that the authorities have sent Pharisees and Herodians—religious teachers and supporters of Herod, a Roman puppet-king—to ask the question. You could say that they represent the two sides—God and Roman power—or, indeed, the compromise that the religious authorities have made between the two.

Jesus' response has sometimes been taken to justify a division of the world into two spheres—the religious and the political. This division has tended to be advocated by those wishing to keep religion 'in its box'—powerful people who wish to silence the church when it speaks up for the poor or powerless. Generally it is quoted with the stress on the first part of Jesus' statement, 'Give to Caesar what is Caesar's', with the implication 'I am "Caesar" so give me what I want.' At times the church has played into this division, using the statement as a justification for creating its own 'religious empire', within which its rule should be absolute. All of that, though, is a misunderstanding of Jesus.

Jesus' answer mocks his questioners and exposes their hypocrisy. It is similar to a parable: it doesn't really answer the question but instead offers a challenge. The religious authorities are the ones who are concerned about money and taxes, and, more to the point, they are the ones with Roman coins in their possession (thus breaking the second commandment, because the coins bear the image of the emperor). By contrast, Jesus makes a point of examining the denarius as if he hasn't come across one before. His response is then cleverly flippant: 'If it's got his name written on it and his picture, I would give it him back.'

We could complain that Jesus is dodging the question. The coin itself is, in a sense, immaterial; the point is that Jewish farmers are having to pay taxes (for example, a share of their crops) to the Romans. Nevertheless, his response communicates disdain for the religious authorities' concern about wealth and possessions.

The second part of Jesus' statement, 'Give God's things back to God', is a direct challenge. The word 'give back' is important here. Jesus isn't saying, 'Allocate these sorts of matters to Caesar, and those to God.' He isn't saying, 'The world is divided into two spheres.' The command 'Give back' implies, 'You have someone else's possessions. Now give them back!' Are Jesus' listeners holding God's possessions, which he is demanding back? We only need to think of the parable of the tenants in the vineyard. The challenge of that parable was that the religious authorities were behaving as rebellious tenants who had seized possession of God's vineyard, Israel. They needed to give it back to him.

The religious authorities are being challenged to recognise that all the status and power that they have is God's, not theirs, and they are accountable to God. In effect, it echoes the prophecy of Malachi 3:1–2. Jesus has come to test, to put on trial, what he finds in the temple. Similarly, when Jesus saw the fig tree, he went to find out if it had borne any fruit, but it hadn't. It was producing showy leaves but nothing of value, so it was condemned. (Mark 11:13–14, 20–21). Jesus challenges the authorities: give God's things—the temple, the law, the leadership of God's people—back to him. Their question was designed to make Jesus declare himself as either a rebel against Caesar's reign or a supporter of it, but he has turned the focus to the impending arrival of God's reign, the one that really matters. Are they rebels against *that* reign, or are they its supporters?

The same question comes to us. For those of us in Christian ministry or leadership, the question is posed directly, for we have 'God's things' in temporary custodianship. I look out of my window and see a church building for which I am legally responsible, but of course it really belongs to God. More significantly, I am seen in the community as 'speaking for God', representing him. Do I turn those responsibilities into my possessions or am I ready to give them back to God? Do I need to hear Jesus' disdain for my anxiety about money and his challenge to give God's things back to God?

More broadly, Psalm 24:1 says, 'The earth is the Lord's and everything in it: the world, and all who live in it.' Therefore, all that we have, and all our talents and abilities, might be reasonably identified as 'God's things'. Jesus' challenge, therefore, is to accept that we must 'give them back', in the sense of recognising his lordship over them, and that we must give an account of how we have used them. While we are concerned with our wealth and possessions, Jesus challenges us to act in line with the truth that all is God's, and thus to live in accordance with God's reign.

Not business as usual

Some Sadducees come to him (these are people who say that there is no resurrection). They asked him, 'Teacher, Moses wrote for us that if a man's brother dies and leaves a wife but no children, then the brother should take his wife and raise up offspring for his brother.

'Now, there were seven brothers. The first one took a wife and died without offspring. The second took her and died without leaving any offspring. And the third similarly. In fact, all seven did not have offspring. Last of all, the woman also died. At the resurrection, when they are raised, whose wife will she be? For all seven had had her as their wife.'

Jesus said to them, 'Is this not why you are wrong? Because you know neither the scriptures nor the power of God. For when they rise from the dead, they will not marry or be given in marriage but they are like the heavenly angels. As for the resurrection of dead—haven't you read in the book of Moses in the passage about the burning bush, how God said to him, "I am the God of Abraham, and the God of Isaac, and the God of Jacob"? He is not the God of the dead, but of the living. You are badly wrong.'

MARK 12:18–27

The Sadducees held to a different strand of Jewish opinion, also represented in the ruling council and the temple. They were associated with more conservative, wealthy people, and had a significant following among important priests. They focused on the written law, disagreeing with the Pharisees' programme of clarifying the law by expanding it, and in general seem to have been more accepting of the status quo in Israel. Their beliefs are depicted here by the statement that they didn't believe in the resurrection from the death. Much of the Old Testament doesn't speak of resurrection: the dead are seen as descending to Sheol, a shadowy underworld of non-existence (there are 65 references to Sheol in the Old Testament, including Genesis 37:35; Psalm 6:5). However, in some later books there is a hope for resurrection, most clearly in Daniel, where an angel says:

> 'Many of those sleeping in the dust of the earth shall awake, some to everlasting life, and some to shame and everlasting contempt. Those who are wise shall shine as brightly as the heavens, and those who lead many to righteousness, like the stars for ever and ever.'
>
> DANIEL 12:2–3

This hope was developed in some parts of Judaism around the time of Jesus as a way of understanding how God would put right the terrible injustices done to his people, including the execution of some for their loyalty to the covenant. Precisely why the Sadducees did not accept it is not known to us, although it is easy to see that the idea of God turning the tables and putting right the wrongs suffered in this life would have been less attractive to those who were generally in a higher place in Jewish society.

There is no particular reason to interpret the Sadducees' question as a trap. Indeed, it looks as if they are putting to Jesus a standard point of disagreement between themselves and the Pharisees. Perhaps they were checking to see if Jesus was really on their side, or they may have simply been interested in what this new teacher had to say. We could see it as a standard 'tricky question' that they used to embarrass the Pharisees and tie them in knots. Why not ask it of Jesus, too?

Their argument is that the idea of a resurrection contradicts the instructions in Deuteronomy 25:5–6 regarding marriage to a brother's widow. Of course, the point would be the same in any case of remarriage to a second partner: which would be the person's spouse at the resurrection? Nevertheless, turning the question into a story of seven brothers certainly makes it entertaining.

We might have little sympathy with this kind of rule-based argument, but woe betide any vicar at a funeral who dares to suggest that the deceased will not now be united with the spouse who died a few years earlier! At a wedding we might say that the marriage lasts 'until death us do part', but in popular consciousness couples are 'reunited in heaven'. That idea still leads to confusion and awkwardness if a person has been married twice, so the Sadducees' question is not alien to our concerns today.

Jesus answers them in their own terms with a technicality from another part of the scriptures. On its own, this doesn't particularly satisfy us either: it feels like an argument from a different world. However, there is a broader underlying point. Jesus doesn't claim only that they don't know the scriptures, but also that they don't know the 'power of God'. In part, this is an assertion that God is quite capable of dealing with the sort of legal conundrums that the Sadducees produced. It is similar to Jesus' response to the Pharisees over healing on the sabbath (Mark 3:1–6), where he appealed to a wider sense of 'doing good' over details from the law. We have already seen that although Jesus doesn't seem to attack the law, he does seem to marginalise it. Other things are more important to him, in the relationship between God and people.

Jesus' response also asserts that after the resurrection it will not just be 'business as usual': there will be no marriage in heaven. Things will be so different that this sort of question simply will not be relevant. Strictly speaking, Jesus is speaking about the resurrection, not God's reign. However, it seems right to add this passage to our study of God's reign, for it brings depth to the point that God's reign is going to be very different, not simply a matter of a pious Jewish king ruling an independent Israel.

Indeed, the reference to the heavenly angels might suggest that God's reign will have the characteristics of heaven, an idea that occurs also in the Lord's Prayer: 'May your reign come. May your will be done—as in heaven, also on earth' (Matthew 6:10). Although we have studied passages which seem to imply that people 'enter' God's reign now, this part of the Lord's Prayer connects with other passages, such as Mark 9:1, with its talk of 'God's reign come in power', and the ideas elsewhere of not just growing seeds but reaping the harvest.

When will this happen?

We now come to a chapter that is often seen as the most difficult in Mark's Gospel—chapter 13. It's a very different sort of passage. It occurs after all of Jesus' disputes with others in and around the temple, but before the night on which he is betrayed. It is set 'opposite the temple' and is presented as a block of private teaching to the disciples, all on the same theme.

As Jesus was leaving the temple, one of his disciples says to him, 'Teacher! Look, what massive stones! What amazing buildings!' Jesus said to him, 'You see these huge buildings?

Not one stone here will be left upon another. Every one will be thrown down.'

As he sat at the Mount of Olives, opposite the temple, Peter, James, John and Andrew asked him privately, 'Tell us, when will these things happen? What will be the sign that all of this is about to be fulfilled?' Jesus began to say to them, 'Watch out that nobody deceives you. For many will come in my name saying, "I'm the one", and they will deceive many.

'Whenever you hear of wars and rumours of wars, don't be alarmed. These must happen, but it is not yet the end. For nation will rise up against nation and kingdom against kingdom; there will be earthquakes in various places; there will be famines. These are the beginnings of the labour pains.'

MARK 13:1–8

We can imagine that Peter well remembered Jesus' response to the disciples' praise of the temple's grandeur. The disciples were not from Jerusalem. For them, the temple was a place to which people travelled occasionally on pilgrimage. It truly was a magnificent building, all the more so for pilgrims and those of humble backgrounds. But Jesus was having none of it.

In part, his condemnation of the temple could simply be a challenge to any sense of false security. This is a theme in parts of the Old Testament, such as Jeremiah (see 7:4), where we find a warning that the existence of God's temple in Jerusalem does not mean that God will protect the people of Jerusalem if they disobey him. This could lie behind Jesus' response. The disciples are so admiring of the temple, praising its grandeur, that they must be warned not to put their trust in it.

There is more, though. Jesus clashed with the temple. We saw this early in his ministry, when he declared forgiveness of sins, which was a function of the temple itself (Mark 2:1–12).

More dramatically, when he entered Jerusalem he symbolically attacked the temple, temporarily closing down the activity of the temple courts (11:12–18). When he is eventually put on trial, he is accused of threatening the temple (14:58; 15:29). The temple was considered as a sign of God's presence among his people. Jesus claimed something similar for himself—that in his ministry God's reign was coming close. This clear competition is dramatised in Jesus' trial, which is a confrontation between Jesus and the high priest.

The search for 'signs of the end' is not new. Around Jesus' day, in some strands of Judaism, there were schemes of history laid out, which aimed to demonstrate that, however bad it seemed, everything was working out according to God's preordained plan. These schemes set out signs by which people might see 'the end' coming. Today there is no less interest, as a quick internet search will tell you. It's a heady combination of our longing for change and our desire to be 'in the know'.

Jesus does not commend this interest, though. He starts by stressing the need for his followers not to be deceived. Then it might seem as if he is giving some signs—the labour pains of the new age. However, the 'signs' he mentions—earthquakes, wars and famines—have always been with us. They do not signal that 'the end' is close. They simply signal the need for the new age and assure us that one will come. Jesus gives us security but not a chronology.

How dreadful it will be

The next part of Mark 13 we considered in Chapter 3, since it related to those 'following on the way'. It gives a description of terrible events that must be endured, and the theme is further developed in what follows.

'When you see the devastating horror established where it should not be (the reader should understand), then those in Judea should flee into the hills. Anyone on the roof of their house should not go down and go in to get anything from his house. Anyone in the fields should not turn back to get their cloak. How terrible it will be for those who are pregnant or nursing infants in those days. Pray it does not happen in winter. For the suffering in those days will be worse than anything since the beginning of creation—which God created—right up to now, and will not be again. If the Lord has not cut short those days, no one would have survived. But because of the chosen ones, whom he has chosen, he has cut the days short. At that time, if anyone says to you, "Look! Here is the Christ! Look there!" do not believe them. For false christs will arise, and false prophets, and they will give signs and wonders in order to deceive the chosen ones, if that is possible. You must watch out. I have told it all to you in advance.'

MARK 13:14–23

In general, this passage seems to be continuing the theme from the first verses of the chapter. Jesus is describing terrible times, in which people will keep on claiming that the end is here, or that God's anointed one has come, but it will all be deception. The details of the passage are more specific, though. It seems as if a particular 'devastating horror' is being described.

However, the additional words, 'the reader should understand', points out that this phrase has history: it occurs in three times in Daniel (9:27; 11:31; 12:11) and also in 1

Maccabees, a Jewish text describing the revolution in 168BC against the Syrian-Greek ruler of Jerusalem, Antiochus IV, who set up an altar to the Greek god Zeus in the temple at Jerusalem. The advice to flee to the hills, along with the sense of horrendous death and destruction, also fits the events of AD70, about 40 years after Jesus, when the Romans destroyed Jerusalem and the temple—though there was no obvious 'devastating horror' set up in advance of that siege.

It is probably wisest to see the phrase as pointing to a type of event rather than a particular event that will happen only once in the whole of history. Jesus is saying, when you see the ultimate horror, get out, but still don't be deceived by people claiming, 'This is it.' Even in times of horrendous evil (and, sadly, the past century has provided too many examples), God is at work to lessen the evil—shortening its days—though not preventing it, despite all our hopes and longings. Still, these are just the beginnings of the labour pains, which have gone on since creation and which point out that re-creation is necessary.

The Son of Man

'But in those days, after that suffering, the sun will be darkened, and the moon will not give her light, and the stars will be falling from heaven, and the powers in the heavens will be shaken. And then you will see the Son of Man coming on the clouds with great power and glory. Then he will send the angels and they will gather his chosen ones from the four winds, from the end of the earth to the end of heaven.'

MARK 13:24–27

Here we face the challenge of biblical language. It is understandable that some readers will suppose that this passage is describing a literal 'end of the world'. However, each of the phrases 'the sun will be darkened', 'the moon will not give her light', 'the stars will be falling from heaven' and 'the powers in the heavens will be shaken' are found in the Old Testament. There they describe what we would call 'earth-shattering events' but they are not events that literally leave the earth shattered.

For example, look at Isaiah 13:

Wail, for the day of the Lord is near; like devastation from the Almighty it will come. Because of this, every hand will go limp; every heart will melt. They will be dismayed, pain and anguish will seize them; they will writhe like a woman in labour. They will look aghast at each other, their faces aflame. See, the day of the Lord comes—cruel, with wrath and burning anger—to make the land a waste and exterminate the sinners from it. The stars of heaven and their constellations will not shine their light. The sun will rise dark and the moon will not give its light... Therefore I will make the heavens shudder; and the earth will shake from its place at the wrath of the Lord Almighty, in the day of his burning anger.

ISAIAH 13:6–10, 13

This passage appears to describe some great final event, using language close to what we have seen in Mark 13. However, Isaiah makes it clear that it is a description of the conquest of Babylon by Persia (the Medes), which is seen as God's judgment. Verse 1 gives the heading, 'A prophecy against Babylon', verse 17 says, 'See, I will stir up against them the Medes', and verse 19 states, 'Babylon, the glory of kingdoms, the beauty and pride of the Babylonians, will be overthrown by God like Sodom and Gomorrah.' Earthly events can be 'the day of the Lord'.

The 'Son of Man' reference in Mark 13:24 is also complicated. It is a quotation from Daniel 7:

> *As I watched in my vision during the night, I looked and there was one like a son of man coming on the clouds of heaven. He came to the Ancient of Days and was presented before him. He was given authority, glory and reign, and all peoples, nations and languages will worship him. His authority is an everlasting authority that will not pass away, and his reign will never be destroyed.*
>
> DANIEL 7:13–14

Notice that the Son of Man is 'coming' not to earth but to the heavenly throne room. There he is given power and authority. He is given God's reign. Furthermore, Daniel 7 is a story of God's people suffering, and only after suffering receiving vindication. It is a story that Jesus himself uses to describe his death and resurrection.

So what do we have? We have a strong assertion that 'in the end' God will act with power. Not only does he cut short the days of suffering, but, as we have seen in the Old Testament, God will act decisively to bring justice, humbling the wicked and vindicating his people.

When?

> *'Learn the parable from the fig-tree. When its branches are tender and it produces leaves, you know that summer is near. It's the same for you. When you see these things happening, you know that it is near, at the door. I tell you the truth, this*

generation will not pass away before all these things happen. Heaven and earth will pass away, but my words will never pass away. Nobody knows about that day or hour—not even the angels in heaven, not even the son, only the father.

'Watch! Keep awake! For you do not know when it is time. It is like a man going on a journey. He leaves his home and gives authority to his slaves, to each his work, and the door keeper he instructs to stay alert. Therefore, stay alert! For you do not know when the lord of the house is coming, whether late evening, at midnight, at cockcrow or in the early morning. Otherwise he will come suddenly and find you asleep. What I say to you I say to everyone. Keep alert!'

MARK 13:28–37

We return to the disciples' original question in Mark 13:4. When? What will be the signs? Overall, Jesus' answer is a clear 'Nobody knows' and 'There will be no signs; just stay alert.' How does this sit with the parable of the fig tree? Well, if you think about it, the fig tree's leaves are not a very precise indicator of time. The leaves will tell you, 'Summer is coming' but they won't tell you, 'Summer will be here in 12 days, 10 hours and 43 minutes'. Of course they can't, because summer is not a precise event that 'arrives' at a certain moment. What we learn from the fig tree is that 'near' is as close as we are going to get. This brings with it two counterbalancing dangers, of which Jesus warns us. There is the danger of being deceived by people saying 'It's here' when its not, interpreting wars and disasters as 'signs of the countdown to the end' when they are just part of the suffering to be endured, and there is the danger of 'falling asleep'—acting as if it is not 'near', as if it will never happen. There are many important resonances in this passage.

Jesus' first proclamation was that God's reign 'is near'. We have already seen, in the parable of the tenants, that Jesus is like the final messenger (the son) of a master who has gone away but will come back, and his death will bring judgement. In the next chapter, in Gethsemane, Jesus will ask his disciples to keep watch and stay awake.

This brings us to the question: what are 'all these things' that will happen before this generation passes away? The language takes us back to Mark 9:1: 'Some of those standing here will not taste death before they see that God's reign has come in power.' It seems right to see these as roughly equivalent statements, expressed in different terms. God's reign will come in power. The Son of Man will receive power and glory from God. God will act decisively to save his people.

Confrontation

We will return to Mark 13 at the end of this chapter, as we try to fit the pieces together. For now, though, we will notice some details in the story of the crucifixion that touch on our theme.

Then the high priest stood up in the centre and asked Jesus, 'Have you no answer to these accusations?' But he remained silent, giving no answer. Again the high priest questioned him, 'Are you the Messiah, the Son of the Blessed One?' Jesus said, 'I am, and you will see the Son of Man sitting on the right side of the Power and coming with the clouds of heaven.'

The high priest tears his robes and says, 'Why do we still need evidence? You heard the blasphemy. What do you think?' They all condemned him as deserving to die.

MARK 14:60–64

We studied this passage at some length in Chapter 5. It's a confrontation between Jesus and the high priest, in which the high priest has physical power (he, with his allies, can condemn Jesus to death) yet Jesus claims that God will vindicate him. Moreover, Jesus says, 'You will see' (which is not in the quotation from Daniel). I always imagine Jesus saying this while poking his finger at the high priest. The logical conclusion is that the high priest will see the vindication of which Jesus speaks. Again, the 'son of man' scripture seems to be referring to something in the lifetime of those present.

> *The crowd came up and began to ask him to do what he usually did for them. Pilate replied, 'Do you want me to release for you the king of the Jews?' For he knew that the chief priests had handed him over because of jealousy. But the chief priests stirred up the crowd so that instead he would release Barabbas for them. Pilate again asked them, 'What then do you want me to do with the one you call king of the Jews?' They shouted back, 'Crucify him.' ...*
>
> *They put a purple robe on him, twisted thorns together to make a crown, and placed it on him. Then they started saluting him, 'Hail, King of the Jews!' They were hitting him round the head, spitting at him and kneeling down, worshipping him...*
>
> *The placard showing his crime read, 'The King of the Jews'...*
>
> *The chief priests with the scribes mocked him to one another: 'He saved others, but he can't save himself! The Messiah, the King of Israel, should now come down from the cross so we can see and believe!'*
>
> MARK 15:8–13, 17–19, 26, 31–32

The whole of the crucifixion story is shot through with the idea that Jesus is the king and hence it resonates with our theme of the reign (kingdom) of God. Pilate and the Romans present him as the king, presumably not as a comment on Jesus himself but as an assertion of Roman dominance, effectively saying, 'Jews, this is what happens to any Jewish "king". The only reign around here is Caesar's.' The religious authorities' mockery is based on a different logic: the fact that he is being crucified proves that he is not the king. The people incited by those authorities find themselves demanding that their king should be crucified. God's reign is rejected. We saw earlier that response is crucial: response to Jesus seems integral to 'entering God's reign'. Here we see the opposite played out—rejection of Jesus and of God's reign.

> *At midday, darkness came over the whole land until mid-afternoon...*
>
> *Jesus gave a loud cry and died. The curtain of the temple was torn in two from top to bottom. When the centurion who stood facing him saw how he died, he said, 'Truly this man was the Son of God.'*
>
> MARK 15:33, 37–39

We should note the connections between these events and the predictions in the 'Son of Man' passage in Mark 13:24–26. The sun is darkened. The tearing of the temple curtain is surely a sign of God's judgement against the temple, the first step towards its destruction and the shaking of the 'powers in heaven'. The centurion gives Jesus the glory destined for the Son of Man. The final shaking of the powers in heaven, and vindication of Jesus as Son of Man, will follow with the resurrection.

Putting it together

What can we make of all this? From our study of passages from Mark 1 to 12 earlier in this chapter, and from our work on parables, it has emerged that, to a large extent, God's reign can be entered immediately by responding to Jesus. God's reign is, in some fashion, bound up with the person or presence of Jesus, and Jesus' arrival was, in some sense, the arrival of God's reign. Responding to him brings us 'into' that reign. God's reign is not in the distant future; in Jesus' ministry it was 'near' and people needed to grab hold of the opportunity to listen and respond. They needed to live in accordance with God's reign.

However, throughout these passages there is also the suggestion of something more—not just seeds growing, but harvest, some kind of final state. There is also the claim that those around Jesus would see God's reign come in power in their own lifetime. Mark 13 is not crystal clear regarding God's reign, but a number of themes emerge from it. There is a strong sense that God's reign is near; that God's reign will come in power; that the Son of Man will receive power and glory from God; that God will act decisively to save his people; and that this will happen in the lifetime of those with Jesus. It is expressed in language that speaks of suffering, 'earth-shattering' events and the destruction of the temple (although the use of this sort of language elsewhere in the Bible cautions us against taking it strictly literally).

In Mark 15—16 we see terrible events in which God's reign is rejected, judgement falls on the temple, and Jesus receives vindication and glory.

All of this fits into a coherent overall picture.

- God's reign is present in Jesus. By responding positively to Jesus, we enter immediately into God's reign. Our external physical situation might not change dramatically, but we are living in a new way, by new values, understanding God's purposes and accepting his rule.

- God acted decisively in Jesus' death and resurrection to bring in his reign. This involved Jesus, as the Son of Man, being vindicated by God and receiving power and glory. His vindication was public: the judgement on the temple and the resurrection of Jesus were visible. This was the predicted 'God's reign come in power': it demonstrated the Son of Man 'coming (to God) with the clouds' and receiving power and glory within the lifetime and sight of those around Jesus.

- There is still more to come, although its nature is not expressed very clearly: Mark focuses on the events of Jesus' life, death and resurrection. However, we can't ignore the idea of a future harvest and the call to endure *for now*. Furthermore, although God might have acted decisively to save his people in the life, death and resurrection of Jesus, God's reign is still not universal. We still need to avoid being deceived and to stay alert.

To return to the opening of this chapter, and the question 'When does Christmas come?', we can quite easily cope with the idea that a carol service can be both Christmas and a sign that Christmas is on its way. We can, at one and the same time, be enjoying the Christmas spirit, celebrating Christmas and looking forward to Christmas. Maybe the different aspects of God's reign are not so alien after all.

CHAPTER 9

THE DEATH OF JESUS

Everyone was saying it was a tragedy, but she knew. She had been there. The newspapers said it was not unknown for people to drown at that beach, although it hadn't happened for many years. A young man, aged 30, they were saying. So sad. They said it was a tragic accident, a terrible loss of life. He must have misjudged the tides. It's a cruel world in which a mistake can kill you.

But she knew better. She had seen him notice the two boys cut off by the approaching tide. There'd been a moment of calculation, a flash of realisation passing between her and the... hero... and he'd been off, running down the beach. All she could do was watch. It had seemed so futile as he'd started to stride out into the grey ocean towards the sand-bank on which the two children were trapped, still oblivious to their fate. She'd tried shouting but there was no way they could have heard.

The water was up to his chest as he battled through the waves to reach the children. By then they had realised and were panicking. She could see them running round the ever-shrinking sandbank, looking desperately for a way out. She could only hold her breath as he picked up the smaller one and started to wade back towards the shore. Time seemed to stand still as he pushed the kid into the shallows and turned back for the second one. Now he was swimming and the other child barely standing against the waves. For a moment she thought it would be OK. He was swimming back, holding the boy, and she saw him half-throw the child towards the beach. In a split second the wave hit, and the boy caught the surf that rolled him up the beach. But the man was caught by the breaker and plunged under. Surely? Surely? But no, he didn't surface again.

People die. When someone dies young, the word 'tragedy' easily comes to our lips, but sometimes there is more to say. The woman thought that the man who rescued the boys was a hero, not a tragic figure. He had gone into the water deliberately. It was no mistake. He had gone in to save them.

The children at first hadn't realised the danger they were in. When they did, it was too late. There was nothing they could do. He saved them, yet he was the one who died. He was only a man, after all, not a superhero from a film. He couldn't stand against the tide.

Had he known he was risking his life? Maybe he thought it would work out fine. Maybe he miscalculated. If he had known how it was going to end, would he still have rushed in? Are people actually willing to give their lives for others?

The long shadow

Finally we come to what might be considered the central topic of Mark's Gospel—Jesus' death. Mark doesn't finish his account with a series of resurrection appearances: the climax of the book is Jesus' death. However, we also have to admit that most of the book, most of Peter's preaching, is not about Jesus' death. In fact, the number of passages that discuss it are rather small.

Over 100 years ago, the biblical scholar Martin Kähler described Mark's Gospel as a 'passion narrative with a long introduction'. Of course, that is a gross simplification: there is much more than the passion narrative (the account of Jesus' suffering and death) in Peter's preaching. However, it is true that, from very early on, Jesus' approaching death overshadows the Gospel.

The first clear allusion to it is in the illustration of the bridegroom. Mark 2:20 reads, 'But the days are coming when the bridegroom will be taken from them—then on that day they will fast.' For anyone who knows anything about Jesus, this points towards his death. Shortly afterwards, we find this passage.

> *Jesus entered the synagogue again. There was a man there who had a withered hand. They were watching him to see if he would heal him on the sabbath, so that they could accuse him. Jesus says to the man with the withered arm, 'Get up; come into the middle.' He says to them, 'Is it permitted on the sabbath to do good or to do evil? To save life or to kill?' They were silent. Angrily he looked round at them, upset by how hard-hearted they were. He says to the man, 'Stretch out your hand.' He stretched it out, and his hand was restored. The Pharisees went out and immediately started plotting against him with the Herodians about how to destroy him.*
>
> MARK 3:1–6

This passage comes at the end of a sequence of six 'conflict stories' in which Jesus has offended the religious establishment of his day. This sense of a clash is highlighted right at the beginning, in the contrast between him and other teachers (1:22: 'They were shocked at his teaching, because he didn't

teach like the scribes; he taught as if he had authority').
The healing of the man with the withered hand clearly fits
the pattern and is presented as the final straw that led the
Pharisees and the Herodians to decide to destroy Jesus. But
why? What was the offence?

Perhaps the offence was that he healed a man on the
sabbath, on the grounds that healing is work. However,
even with a Pharisaic interpretation of the law, it is not clear
that what Jesus did was work. Indeed, it seems as if he carefully planned to avoid doing any work in the healing, for
all he actually did was to speak. He didn't touch the man.
He didn't make any ointment. He did nothing. It would be
very hard to argue that speaking is work. Nor can he be
accused of encouraging the man to work: it was permissible
to stretch on the sabbath! There is a far stronger case that
the disciples' plucking corn on the sabbath (Mark 2:23–28)
and Jesus' eating with sinners (2:15) broke the law, and
some of his earlier words could be seen as threatening the
law (for example, 2:10 on forgiving sins and 2:27 on the
sabbath).

Perhaps more significantly, this was a very public confrontation. It happened on the sabbath in the synagogue: we
could not find a more public and significant arena for religious controversy. It gives the impression of a set-up: the
Pharisees knew that the disabled man was there and they
were watching. Jesus responded by challenging his accusers
openly and reacting with anger at their silence. The events
were taking place in Galilee, far from the temple, and in
a land ruled by a Jewish king, Herod, not directly by the
Romans. Thus the Pharisees and the Herodians (Herod's
officers) represented religious and secular power combined.
They stood for the status quo.

If this is right, their desire to kill Jesus was not really because of his teaching or actions, but because he presented a direct public challenge to their personal authority. This seems strangely fitting and implies that they did understand Jesus, for his teaching, as we have seen, was also personal: it was all about him. Thus, the clash on this occasion was not about religious teaching; it was about authority and power. Who had it? Who spoke for God? Who were the leaders of God's people?

The 'prophetic' role of challenging authority has been an important function of Jesus' disciples at various times in history. Often it has led to opposition, sometimes to death. Is it an important element of your faith or of your church's role?

John's death

After Mark 3:1–6, there is no mention of any threat to Jesus or of conflict with the authorities until the middle of chapter 6. As we noted earlier, this is probably a reflection of the way in which Mark has arranged Peter's preaching. He has brought together similar material in sections, focusing on different issues at different times. The theme of conflict has been established, and then the focus moves to miracles, the parables, the disciples and Jesus' identity. In the midst of all this, we are told about John the Baptist's death.

> *Now King Herod heard, because Jesus' name had become well known, and he said, 'John the Baptiser has been raised from the dead. This is why these powers are at work in him.' Others were saying that he was Elijah, and others that he was*

a prophet like one of the prophets of old. When Herod heard, he said, 'John whom I beheaded has been raised.'

For Herod himself had sent soldiers, seized John and imprisoned him, because of Herodias, his brother Philip's wife, whom he had married. For John had said to Herod that he was not allowed to have this brother's wife. So Herodias had a grudge against him and wanted to kill him, but she wasn't able to because Herod was afraid of John. He knew that he was a righteous and holy man and so protected him. When he heard him he was greatly troubled, yet he liked to listen.

Then an opportunity came when, on his birthday, Herod gave a banquet for the nobles, the military officers and the leading men of Galilee. His daughter Herodias came in and danced and pleased Herod and his guests. So the king said to the girl, 'Ask me for whatever you want and I will give you it.' He swore to her earnestly, 'Whatever you ask me for, I will give to you, up to half my kingdom.' She went out and asked her mother, 'What should I ask for?' She said, 'The head of John the Baptiser.' She immediately rushed back to the king and asked, 'I would like you to give me the head of John the Baptiser immediately on a plate.'

The king was very sad to hear this but did not want to refuse her because of his oaths and his guests. So the king immediately sent an executioner with orders to bring his head. He went off, chopped John's head off in the prison, brought his head on a plate, and gave it to the girl. The girl then gave it to her mother. When John's disciples heard, they came and took his body and placed it in a tomb.

MARK 6:14–29

The context of this passage within Mark is not a coincidence. Structurally, it provides an interlude between the accounts of Jesus sending the Twelve out to preach, heal and cast out demons (vv. 12–13) and their return to him (v. 30). Something would be lost if he sent them out and then, in the very next verse, they returned. In passing, we can also note that, presumably, Peter didn't know what Jesus was doing during the period while the disciples were away, because he was with them. But there is more. As the Twelve are sent out, we are faced with the likely consequences of their mission: speaking out for God is a dangerous occupation.

Jesus was closely connected with John. Most historians would say that Jesus emerged from the movement surrounding John; certainly the Gospels give that impression (for example, see Matthew 3:13–17; 11:2–19; John 1:19–40; 3:22–23; 4:1–3). Luke's Gospel tells us that their mothers were related. It is commonly said that they were cousins because the King James Bible uses the word 'cousin' in 1:36, but the Greek word is rather more vague, meaning simply 'a relative'.

The story of John's death is introduced with this note of relationship between John and Jesus, through the lens of King Herod's thoughts. Herod believes that there is a connection—in fact, that Jesus and John are 'really' the same person. There is a touch of paranoia about Herod's thoughts, in the idea of the holy man he has murdered coming back to haunt him. Then we are presented with the story of John's death. It's a memorable tale—a bit of sex and violence always spices up a story—but why is it told here? What does it add to the story of Jesus?

John was a holy man who challenged the powerful. They wished to stop him but feared him because of his holiness. John also had a significant public following. In the end, though, John was killed because someone who hated him

(Herodias) manipulated the person in authority (Herod). The person in power could have resisted but didn't bother, and so John was killed. The story is colourful, but anyone hearing it would recognise how shameful it was for a holy man to be killed because the king got drunk, was proud and liked a pretty girl.

This storyline is almost identical to that of Jesus in his last days in Jerusalem. He challenged the temple authorities and the religious establishment. They wished to stop him but feared the crowd. Therefore, they manipulated Pilate in a shameful way, but Pilate also showed no interest in saving him and had him killed.

What difference do these parallels make? First, they mean that this story acts as a further 'passion prediction': as we read about John, we are reminded of what will happen to Jesus. Even though we are still in the first half of the Gospel, the shadow of the cross deepens. Second, they cast a certain light on the events in Jerusalem at the end of Mark, implying that we should not talk of a 'trial' before the high priest and the Sanhedrin. Jesus' appearance there was just part of a manipulative process though which those whom he had challenged managed to engineer his death. Pilate, through the lens of Herod, emerges as a pathetic figure, so tied up with his own reputation and his need to appear strong that others are able to manipulate him. (Interestingly, Pilate was eventually sacked in AD36 for his failures as governor.) It is no kindness to Pilate to suggest that he was manipulated into killing Jesus, for it would be a grave insult to any Roman governor to suggest that he was both as weak and as callous as is suggested of Herod here. This is a clever and wise way for Peter to make veiled comments on Pilate's character, preaching as he was within the Roman empire and even in Rome itself.

Third, we should notice the one contrast with the death of Jesus. John's disciples came and took his body away for burial. They stayed true to their master, whereas Jesus' disciples fled and let a stranger bury him (Mark 15:43–46).

The passion predictions

After the hinge point in the Gospel, the discussion of Jesus' identity on the road to Caesarea Philippi (Mark 8:27–31), much of the second half is strongly coloured by the approaching passion, until we arrive at 14:1: 'It was two days before the Passover…'

Three times Jesus predicts his suffering, death and resurrection (Mark 8:31; 9:31; 10:33–34), and each time is similar, though not identical. Conventionally these are known as the 'passion predictions', meaning predictions of the suffering and death that Jesus was going to undergo. ('Passion' in medieval English, drawing on French and Latin, meant something you 'suffered'; nowadays it is used to mean strong emotions that overcome us.) Here we will look at the third of these predictions.

They were on the road going up to Jerusalem with Jesus leading the way. They were astonished, and those who were following were afraid. Again he took the Twelve and began to tell them what was going to happen to him. 'We are going up to Jerusalem and the son of man will be betrayed to the chief priests and scribes. They will condemn him to death and hand him over to the Gentiles. They will mock him, spit on him, flog him and kill him. Three days later he will rise.'

MARK 10:32–34

The word 'prediction' points to a difficulty posed by these passages in Gospel scholarship. Can we believe that Jesus predicted his death or, at this point, must we suggest that the Gospels contain material from the period after Easter, which has been put back into a pre-Easter setting? The latter view might be uncontroversial if we are talking of material that is presented as interpretation or comment, such as the note 'Saying this, Jesus made all food "clean"' in 7:19, but here we are talking about words directly attributed to Jesus.

We need to be careful. We should remember that, in Mark's Gospel, we have Peter's preaching—material that Peter used time and time again after Easter, when he and many of his audience were fully aware of the story's end. Furthermore, Peter's preaching will have been an edited version of what happened, and Mark will presumably have shortened it further. Jesus would have been a very peculiar figure if, on the road, he had only said these 61 words. The process of remembering, editing and translating happened after Easter, so it is not surprising if some post-Easter influence is seen.

However, it is not impossible to expect that you may die or to predict that you are likely to die. Given all that had happened in Galilee, and the knowledge of what had happened to his relative John and to others who had challenged Rome, if Jesus was approaching Jerusalem intending to attack the temple at Passover in the way that he did, his death would have seemed a likely outcome. Also, as we have seen, the phrase 'Son of Man' appears to have been Jesus' chosen self-description—a phrase that, in various places, is linked explicitly to Daniel 7 (Mark 8:38; 13:26; 14:62–63). Daniel 7 is a story of the people of God, represented by a human figure ('son of man'), undergoing great suffering before they are vindicated by God. If this text guided Jesus' sense of his mission, then a prediction of suffering followed by vindication would be hardly surprising.

Aside from such historical concerns, how does this passage speak to us? Its impact is similar to the thoughts of the onlooker in the story of the hero that opened this chapter. It makes clear that Jesus' death was not a tragedy. It was expected, faced and even planned for, not something that took him by surprise. For me, the challenge comes down to the contrast between Jesus' courage (he was 'leading the way') and the fear of those (like me) who are following. We know that God will vindicate us in the end, just as he did Jesus, yet do we have the courage to face suffering? I hardly seem to have the courage to face a bit of discomfort.

A ransom

In the two chapters between the first passion prediction and the end of Mark 10, Jesus teaches his disciples about the meaning of discipleship. Alongside the passion predictions, we have teaching about status, ambition, faith and the need for dedication. This teaching, in a sense, unpacks the passion predictions: this is what Jesus' calling means for his followers. The section concludes, just before they reach Jericho, with a discussion of status, power and servanthood raised by James' and John's request to sit at Jesus' right and left in his glory. We discussed that passage as part of our study of 'following on the way' in Chapter 3. Now we need to consider the final saying about Jesus' death.

> *Jesus called them and says to them, 'You know that those regarded as rulers of the Gentiles lord it over them, and their*

> *nobles exploit them. It is not like this among you. Instead,*
> *whoever wishes to be great among you will be the servant of*
> *all. Whoever wishes to be the first among you will be the slave*
> *of all. For even the son of man did not come to be served but to*
> *serve and to give his life as a ransom for many.'*

MARK 10:42–45

The general point is clear: greatness comes through service of others, not through status. Power is to be used for the good of the weak. This is an important message, strengthening what we found in Chapter 3. However, what about Jesus' death? The passion predictions demonstrated that Jesus faced his death willingly and trusted that God would vindicate him. However, that does not give a purpose to his death, and purpose matters. The onlooker in the story that opened this chapter knew that the man had died not as an accident but because he wanted to save the boys. So what does it mean to say that Jesus gave his life 'as a ransom for many'?

Whole books have been written on that one phase. What is its background? What does it mean? We will focus on four possible strands of interpretation.

First, there is a connection point in the literature circulating in Jesus' day about the Maccabean martyrs, who had died 200 years earlier. They were religious revolutionaries who rebelled against the rule of the Syrian-Greek king Antiochus IV after the king had tried to destroy Judaism by burning the books of the law, banning circumcision and defiling the temple. There is a celebrated story in which seven brothers and their mother die horrible deaths at the hands of Antiochus because they will not break the law by eating pork. In the story, the younger brother says, 'I, like my brothers, give up body and life for the laws of our ancestors... to bring to an end the wrath of the Almighty that has justly fallen on our whole nation' (2 Maccabees 7:37–38).

The martyrs' death was to bring an end to God's wrath, which had fallen justly on the nation. We have already met the idea that Israel had, in some sense, remained in exile because of her sin. Here we find the idea that this sin was being atoned for by some Jews who were willingly under-going suffering and death. Thus, the idea of a willing death achieving a purpose was known within the Judaism of Jesus' day. Against this background, Jesus' death is solving the problem of God's anger at the nation's sin. As Peter puts it in his first letter, 'He bore our sins in his body on the cross, so that we might die to our sin and live to righteousness. By his wounds, we are healed' (1 Peter 2:24).

A second strand is that the word 'to ransom/redeem' is used in the Old Testament to describe God's rescue of the people from Egypt and from exile in Babylon. This links Jesus' suffering to the great acts of salvation in the Old Testament that led to the formation of the Jewish people. Jesus is giving his life to rescue the people, just as God did of old.

Third, another possible background to 'ransom' is the slave-market. This brings in the idea of a payment made to 'buy out' another person from slavery, as opposed to the story of the exodus, which uses the word 'redeem' in a rather vaguer sense, effectively equivalent to 'save'. It is not dissim-ilar to the main use of the word 'ransom' in English today in the context of kidnapping and hostages. Something valuable is paid over in order to get the captured one released.

Finally, some see a connection with the 'suffering servant' in Isaiah, particularly Isaiah 53, which speaks of a death for others and includes the words 'he bore the sin of many' (v. 12). Peter certainly quotes Isaiah 53 in his letter (1 Peter

2:22), so it might be fair to assume that he had this passage in mind in his preaching (although that isn't the same as saying that Jesus was thinking of it when he spoke).

What do we make of these multiple possible connections? Some scholars argue at great length to try to decide which is 'correct', but it is not particularly clear what 'correct' would mean in this case. If, when Jesus spoke these words or when Peter preached them or when Mark wrote them down, none of them were thinking of the exodus, does that mean God cannot speak to us now through that link? It is fruitful to allow these meanings to sit alongside each other as we contemplate the multifaceted nature of Jesus' death, united in the idea that it was a willing death, it was for others, and it achieved a great rescue.

A new covenant

Jesus was famous for eating. The archbishop of York, John Sentamu, once commented that the only way we show our faith and love for each other is with 'prayer and parties'. Jesus certainly engaged in both, but it was his eating that caused a stir. He welcomed people, including the 'wrong sort' of people, to eat with him. He fed the people in the wilderness. Then, on the night before he died, he met with his followers to celebrate the Passover (Mark 14:16–17). This was a very important night, on which Jews remembered God's rescue of his people from slavery in Egypt. Significantly, the Passover was not centred on the temple but on a gathering of family, neighbours and friends around a meal. We don't know as much as we would like, nor as much as some people claim, about the details of a Passover meal in Jesus' day, since most of our evidence comes from several centuries later. However, it is clear that the Passover meal included many symbolic actions and rituals set around a meal. It is in this context that we should understand what Jesus said and did.

> *While they were eating, Jesus took bread, praised God, broke it, gave it to them and said, 'Take it, this is my body.' Then he took a cup, gave thanks and gave it to them. As they were all drinking from it, he said to them, 'This is my blood of the covenant, which is being poured out for many. I tell you the truth. I will never drink the fruit of the vine again until that day when I drink it new in God's reign.'*
>
> MARK 14:22–25

This passage, along with its equivalents in Matthew, Luke and 1 Corinthians, is the starting point for the development of one of the most central and distinctive aspects of Christian worship and community. The ceremony has different names in different traditions, such as the Mass (derived from the final Latin words of the ritual in the Roman Catholic Church, '*Ite, missa est*'), the Eucharist (from the Greek word for 'thanksgiving'), Holy Communion or the Lord's Supper, and it gives rise to one of the richest interfaces between theology and spirituality. However, here we will focus on the bare words given to us in Peter's preaching, quoted above.

What happens with the bread is very limited. During the meal, a single loaf is broken and shared, with the words 'This is my body'. What would this mean? It becomes a little clearer with the cup, for here there is more detail: it represents not just 'my blood' but blood 'of the covenant' and 'poured out for many'. Jesus is enacting a new covenant ritual. 'Blood of the covenant' occurs in Exodus 24:8, when the covenant between God and those he rescued in the Passover is sealed with blood at Sinai (see also Zechariah 9:11).

> *Then Moses sent young Israelite men, and they offered burnt sacrifices and sacrificed young bulls as fellowship offerings to the Lord. Moses took half of the blood and put it into bowls, and the other half he threw on the altar. Then he took the Book of the Covenant and proclaimed it in the hearing of the people. They responded, 'We will do everything the Lord has said; we will obey.' Moses then took the blood, threw it on the people and said, 'This is the blood of the covenant that the Lord has made with you in all these words.'*
>
> EXODUS 24:5–8

In Exodus, the blood of a sacrificial animal is sprinkled on the people to seal the covenant (agreement) between God and the people he has rescued. In Mark, the 'blood' of Jesus is drunk by the people to seal the new covenant between God and the people. If we allow the parallel to guide us, various features emerge.

First, Jesus seems to be standing in the place of the sacrificial animal. It is Jesus' blood that seals the covenant. Coupled with the fact that Jesus has just torn up a loaf of bread while calling it his body, this sets a clear expectation that he is going to die. He is going to die as a sacrifice, and his death is going to be the seal of this new covenant.

Second, the blood is drunk, not just sprinkled (and the bread/body is eaten, too). In the parts of the Old Testament that speak of a 'new covenant' or God's new relationship with his people in the future, there is a focus on God's being *within* the person.

> *'The days are coming,'* declares the Lord, *'when I will make a new covenant with the house of Israel and with the house of Judah. It will not be like the covenant I made with their ancestors when I took them by the hand to bring them out of the land of Egypt… I will put my law inside them and write it on their hearts. I will be their God, and they will be my people.'*
> JEREMIAH 31:31–33

> *I will give you a new heart and put a new spirit within you; I will remove from your body the heart of stone and I will give you a heart of flesh.*
> EZEKIEL 36:26

This focus is a continuation of an approach found within the prophets and psalms, which pointed out that God was concerned not with the blood of animals and religious rituals but with the heart (see, for example, Psalm 51:16–17). It is not a coincidence that the new covenant is sealed in a ritual that involves us symbolically taking God inside us. The new covenant is better than the old because it changes our hearts of stone and puts God inside us.

Third, Jesus' blood is poured out 'for many'. It is hard to pin this phrase down, but it conveys expansiveness: the covenant is for more than just the disciples, more than just a small group, even perhaps more than just the Jewish people. The phrase also connects this passage with Mark 10:45 and the idea of a 'ransom for many'. The new covenant is marked by its breadth, not its limitations. This echoes what we have seen in Jesus' own ministry. He has welcomed those who others saw as 'beyond the pale'. Even when he went into Gentile lands, he helped the people. The Syro-Phoenician woman's insight was right: God's goodness is not just for the 'children';

it overflows to the 'dogs' (Mark 7:28). 'Many' is not 'all', and we have seen some people reject Jesus, yet 'many' is an open word. Given Jesus' focus on response and the challenge 'If you have ears to hear...', it effectively means 'for as many as want it'.

The final oath intensifies the whole, for it brings a sense of imminence. The covenant ritual in Exodus was enacted after the rescue from Egypt, and after the sacrifice. Here, the equivalent events still lie in the future. Nevertheless, Jesus' oath not to drink wine again until he drinks it new in God's reign implies that God's reign must come soon, for drinking wine was a regular part of life. They have arrived in Jerusalem; it is Passover. Now is the moment! This confirms what we saw in the previous chapter. God's reign is declared to be 'near' in Mark 1:15 and, in a real sense, 'comes in power' at Jesus' death and resurrection.

Jesus is going to die. He has told his disciples so, three times before. Now we see that his death is going to be a sacrifice, not a tragedy, and it is going to bring in the longed-for new covenant—God's reign. Moreover, it is going to happen very soon.

The crucifixion

Within a few hours of that final meal, Jesus is arrested, condemned and killed. I think it is useful to give the whole of the crucifixion narrative in one block, since here Mark's Gospel seems no longer to be 'pearls on a string' but a single powerful narrative.

Straight away, early in the morning, the chief priests, with the elders and scribes and the whole Sanhedrin, made a plan. They tied Jesus up, took him out and handed him over to Pilate. Pilate asked him, 'Are you the King of the Jews?' Jesus replied, 'You say so.' The chief priests made many accusations against him. Pilate questioned him again. 'Have you no answer? See how many accusations they make.' Jesus made no further reply, which amazed Pilate.

In honour of the festival, Pilate would release for them one prisoner at their request. Now a man called Barabbas was in prison with the rebels who, in the rebellion, had committed murder. The crowd came up and began to ask him to do what he usually did for them. Pilate replied, 'Do you want me to release for you the King of the Jews?' For he knew that the chief priests had handed him over because of jealousy. But the chief priest stirred up the crowd so that instead he would release Barabbas for them. Pilate again asked them, 'What then do you want me to do with the one you call King of the Jews?' They shouted back, 'Crucify him!' Pilate said to them, 'Why? What crime has he committed?' They shouted all the louder, 'Crucify him!' Pilate wanted to please the crowd, so he released Barabbas for them and had Jesus flogged, and handed him over to be crucified.

The soldiers took him out into the courtyard (which is the Praetorium) and gathered the whole company. They put a purple robe on him, twisted thorns together to make a crown, and placed it on him. Then they started saluting him: 'Hail, King of the Jews!' They were hitting him round the head, spitting at him and kneeling down, worshipping him. When they had mocked him, they took off the purple robe and put him back in his clothes. Then they led him out to crucify him.

A certain Simon from Cyrene (the father of Alexander and Rufus) was passing by, coming in from the fields. They forced him to carry his cross. They bring him to the place 'Golgotha' *(which translates as 'The place of the Skull'). They gave him wine mixed with myrrh, but he would not take it. They crucified him, and divided up his clothes, throwing dice for them, for who would take what. It was mid-morning when they crucified him. The placard showing his crime read, 'The King of the Jews'. Alongside him they crucify two bandits, one on his right and one on his left.*

The people passing by insulted him, shaking their heads, saying, 'So! He's the one who would destroy the temple and build it in three days. Save yourself! Come down from the cross!' In the same way, the chief priests with the scribes mocked him to one another, 'He saved others, but he can't save himself! The Messiah, the King of Israel, should now come down from the cross so we can see and believe!' Even those crucified alongside him insulted him.

At midday, darkness came over the whole land until mid-afternoon. Then Jesus cried out in a loud voice, 'Eli, Eli, lema sabakhthani!' (which translates as 'My God, my God, why have you abandoned me?')

Some of the bystanders heard him and started saying, 'See, he is calling Elijah!' One ran and filled a sponge with bitter wine, put it on a reed and gave it to him to drink, saying, 'Leave him alone. Let's see if Elijah comes to take him down.' But Jesus gave a loud cry and died.

MARK 15:1–37

Within the richness and horror of this passage, I would draw attention to three points. First, we ought to take in the repulsive, horrendous suffering—the casual mention of flogging (v. 15), sufficient on its own to kill; the piercing with thorns (v. 17); the mockery (vv. 18–19, 29–32); and finally the long, slow, agonising suffocation of crucifixion itself (v. 24). We have perhaps grown so used to the idea of 'the crucifixion' that we forget what it actually involved, and we use words like 'sacrifice' glibly. Furthermore, a standard human reaction is to 'look away' from horror and pain, but if our calling is to follow Jesus, surely we must follow him, at least in our mind's eye, all the way to the cross. Paul later wrote:

> *I want to know Christ and the power of his resurrection and the sharing in his sufferings, becoming like him in his death, so that somehow I might achieve the resurrection from the dead.*
> PHILIPPIANS 3:10–11

> *We share in his sufferings so that we may also share in his glory.*
> ROMANS 8:17

Second, we can notice the theological irony in the passage. Jesus is proclaimed 'King of the Jews' by both the Romans and the temple authorities (vv. 18, 26, 32). They all think that the title is laughably ironic, since how could a dying man be king? Perhaps we might think the same—that Jesus can only be king when the shame of the cross has been wiped away by resurrection. Similarly, the idea that Jesus could be the Messiah, that he would destroy the temple and save others, is thrown back at him. These ideas were in the air and provided the context for his arrest, trial and condemnation; but again it is assumed that his death must prove these claims false. It is a picture of the finality of death, making a mockery of hopes and dreams.

However, we should remember Jesus' discussion with James and John (Mark 10:35–40). They asked 'to sit, one on your right hand and one on your left *in your glory*', to which Jesus replied, 'To sit at my right and my left is not for me to grant—it is for those for whom it has been prepared.' I believe that this connection is the reason why Peter bothered to provide the detail that one bandit was crucified on Jesus' left and one on the right. If so, then the crucifixion is not a tragedy and a shameful event; it is Jesus' glory. This interpretation is certainly developed in John's Gospel, where the idea of Jesus being 'glorified' seems to be connected with his death (for example, 12:23; 13:31), and in Revelation, where Jesus is given glory because of his death (5:9–12). His death, far from proving that he is not the Messiah, actually proves that he is, for, as he said numerous times, his death was necessary and he was prepared to go through it.

Third, there is the darkness—physical (v. 33) and, more importantly, spiritual darkness (v. 34) as Jesus cries out that he has been forsaken. There have been some attempts to claim that, since this is the first line from Psalm 22, Jesus really had in mind the hopeful way in which the psalm ends. But if that was the meaning that Peter wanted to give us, why did he not quote the ending? No, if we read the text straightforwardly, we see Jesus experiencing the horror of feeling utterly alone and forsaken, even by the God he called 'Father', whose will he accepted (14:36). Gone is the confidence of the passion predictions, as the true horror of a pain-filled, torturous death is faced.

Many people, understandably and even rightly, are frustrated or angry with God because he doesn't seem to answer their prayers in times of suffering. Here we see what has been called 'the most unanswered prayer in history'. God did not answer Jesus' cry of pain and frustration as he hung dying. Jesus knew the agony of feeling that God had turned his face away from him. The rest of the story demonstrates that God had not actually abandoned him at all, but at the time, even Jesus could not hold on to that truth.

How can we respond? First, we can express thankfulness and awe at the depth of love that was willing to endure even this agony to welcome us back to God. We should remember that Jesus had known and told his disciples, weeks before, what would happen when he reached Jerusalem. However, we are also reminded of the terrible pressure brought by insults and apparent failure. We see it often enough in the media; maybe we know people going through similar experiences; maybe we have endured it ourselves. There is no answer, but there is one consolation—that in such experiences we model Christ.

Done

Jesus' final words in John's Gospel are 'It is finished'—words which bring together both the cry of the broken, tortured body entering the release of death and the cry of victory as God's saving work is achieved. These words are not expressed in Peter's preaching, but the same sentiment is there.

> *Jesus gave a loud cry and died. The curtain of the temple was torn in two from top to bottom. When the centurion who stood facing him saw how he died, he said, 'Truly this man was the Son of God.'*
>
> MARK 15:37–39

We have already considered this passage because this is the first time that a human recognises Jesus as 'Son of God'. We have also noted the divine judgement against the temple (represented by the torn curtain), whose authorities had rejected Jesus and arranged his death. Nevertheless, we cannot end a study of Jesus' death without revisiting Mark's words here.

Jesus' death—not his resurrection—is seen as the place of revelation, of judgement and of victory. Again we must say, if you want to see what Jesus is really like and what 'Son of God' really means, look at the man dying on the cross.

A strong, consistent message is coming through from our study. Jesus faced his death willingly. He knew what was coming; he could have escaped it easily, but he didn't. His death was 'for many': it was a ransom, a sacrifice. It was God's great act of saving power; it brought about the new covenant and it brought about God's reign.

Jesus' death in Peter's preaching can be summed up that easily. However, its implications are so enormous, so central to Christian theology, spirituality and mission, that a further book could be written unpacking them. For now, though, let us consider three final reflections. Dare we follow Jesus' and John the Baptist's example in challenging power, despite its potential cost to us? Can we grasp the fact that Jesus' sacrifice was for many, not for a few? Can we hold on to the assurance that Jesus has experienced the pain of insult, abandonment and apparent failure himself, but that it was not the end of the story?

CHAPTER 10

MARK'S GOSPEL

'He's amazing,' the man said to his girlfriend on the way out of the comedy club. 'All he did was tell a few stories and I don't think I stopped laughing for two hours.'

'I know,' she gasped, still trying to control her breathing. 'I couldn't believe that one about the...' and broke down in hysterics again. 'It's the way he tells them.'

Peter's preaching: Mark's Gospel

Do you like to read? What sort of books? I enjoy a good thriller—a real 'page-turner'. Of course, it can be a curse at times, reading too late into the night because you desperately want to know how it ends. Other people, I know, like something slower, something to be chewed and digested, where the beauty of the language is celebrated. We could have the same conversation about TV. Even within one genre, such as detective/crime programmes, there is a massive spectrum, from Sherlock Holmes patiently working out the clues to the modern police action drama.

Comedy, books and TV all agree: it's not just about the content, it's about how the story is told. So far in this book, we have been enjoying and learning from the way Mark has written down the individual episodes of Peter's preaching. As we have examined it passage by passage, we have encountered the dialogue, the detail and the drama. We have become familiar with the style in which Mark has written Peter's preaching, and his distinctive vocabulary.

In Chapter 1, we came to the conclusion, based on the available evidence, that Mark was probably Peter's translator/interpreter and wrote down Peter's preaching 'accurately but not in order'. If that is right, we might reasonably expect that, when reading Mark, we are hearing 'Peter's voice', yet we can't be 100 per cent certain about the origins of any particular word or phrase. We need to remember again that Jesus will have said and done 100 times more than Peter remembered and preached about, and Mark will have managed to capture only a small proportion of what Peter said. Nevertheless, we are still hearing Peter's voice.

The same is not true of the overall order and structure of the book. Papias seems clear that this did not come from Peter but was created by Mark. We have noted a few cases where two incidents appear to be intimately woven together—such as the bleeding woman and Jairus' daughter, or the fig tree and the temple incident—and we might suppose that the intertwining of these stories goes back to Peter. There are also some longer sections—Mark 13 and the passion narrative. Nevertheless, in general, we have approached Mark on the basis that the arrangement of the passages is secondary to the material itself: it comes from Mark, not Peter. That understanding has partly justified the thematic approach of this book. Since the contents, but not the structure, goes back to Peter, it made sense to reorder the contents thematically to allow us to focus on each of the key themes of Peter's preaching in turn.

I believe we have been able to grasp more clearly the message of Peter's preaching because of this thematic reordering. It has allowed us to chart the descent of the disciples, from their initial dedication through misunderstanding and fear to betrayal and abandonment. At the same time, a hopeful message has emerged. Our past commitment offers no guarantee that we will not fail in the future, but failure, however serious, does not bar us from being true disciples once more. We can pick ourselves up and meet Jesus again.

We have also been able to tease out what it meant to be 'following on the way'—the call for humility and courage. The call to be 'with' Jesus showed the importance of loyalty and companionship. It was about the challenge to reject status and self-interest, just as Jesus himself did—to let go and embrace security in God.

Gathering the miracles together helped us to realise that, in Peter's preaching, the miracles are not primarily about demonstrating Jesus' divine power; they are about his compassion and the relationship between Jesus and the one healed. The miracles seem to focus not on the power but on the person helped, or the faith or understanding of the others present.

This connects well with what we saw in Chapter 5, as we considered the question 'Who is Jesus?' He was affirmed as the Son of God and Messiah, with authority in teaching and over nature, sickness and evil spirits. He seemed to stand in God's place, bringing God's rescue and forgiveness. Nevertheless, more importantly, we saw that his true nature—what 'Son of God' might mean—was displayed in his death on the cross. As in our study of the miracles, our focused attention allowed us to see that power is a distraction from what really matters. Our ideas about God are often dominated by the language of 'miracles' and 'omnipotence', asking, 'If God exists and is good, then why does he allow this, or why won't he do that?' We think that power is what matters, but, in Peter's preaching, compassion and self-sacrifice are far more important.

The material within Peter's preaching on the law was complicated. In some passages it sounded as if Jesus was challenging the Jewish law head-on, while in others it was clear that his conflict was with a particular interpretation of the law or, indeed, just with people who used the law to emphasise their own importance. Taken together, the passages seemed to convey that the law was simply not so important—no longer the dominant factor in the relationship between God and humanity.

The parables within Peter's preaching are a strange bunch. We have a couple of classic parables, such as the sower and the tenants in the vineyard, but also quite a few short ones, as well as other pieces of teaching that are often not seen as parables, although they are clearly labelled as such—for example, the discussion of Satan, and the parable of the sewer. We were able to see that, although the parables do teach us things, they are designed more to provoke and challenge than to explain. Moreover, their overriding theme is Jesus himself and what God is doing in him. They are, in a sense, a commentary on Jesus, and the response they call for is not just a response to their message but a response to him.

God's reign was also a tangled knot to unpick, although it was helpful to consider all the relevant passages together. As with the law, we could easily have allowed one strand to dominate—for example, the idea that God's reign is present now in Jesus—yet we saw that there are three aspects of

God's reign in Peter's preaching. God's reign is present in Jesus, and responding to Jesus means that we enter into God's reign. God's reign also came decisively in Jesus' death and resurrection: this was its public inauguration, the crucial moment. In addition, though, there is more to come. We need to watch and not be deceived as we wait for God's reign to become universal.

Finally, we brought together the passages that speak of the death of Jesus. Here we saw that 'tragic' is definitely the wrong word to use. The long shadow of his death over the first part of the Gospel, plus the repeated predictions, makes it clear that Jesus could have avoided his death but chose not to. Instead, his willing, self-sacrificial death is the climax of the book. It was a ransom, a sacrifice, 'for many'. God's great act of saving power brought about a new covenant and also God's reign.

However, as we noted at the beginning of this chapter, 'the way he tells it'—the pace and style of narrative—does matter. If Mark's Gospel is 'pearls on a string', we must recognise that they are indeed 'on a string'. Mark's Gospel is a necklace, not a basin of pearls. The different passages have been carefully arranged with a particular order and structure. It is Mark's Gospel—this particular 'necklace', this arrangement of the pearls—that has been recognised across the millennia and across the world as scripture through which God speaks. Indeed, as we saw, Matthew and Luke largely maintained this arrangement, supplementing Mark but keeping his basic structure. It is not something to be discarded easily.

So let's take a step back and consider Mark's Gospel as we have it. What can we learn from the particular way in which Mark tells the story? In fact, we have already benefited hugely from his structure. If you think back, you will realise that, in almost every case, we have considered the passages on a particular theme in the order in which Mark presents them. Thus, within each of the themes, we have already been guided by the way in which Mark chose to order the material. This was most apparent in Chapter 2, on the disciples. There we saw a steady descent from initial wholehearted response, through the three worsening incidents on the boat, to open clashes and arguments, and on to betrayal and abandonment, with a final scene where even the women fail. Much of this 'theme' has emerged from the ordering of the material—although, of course, a considerable amount may be a reflection of how it happened originally, with the disciples' commitment fraying as Jesus turned towards Jerusalem.

We have also noted, a number of times, the sense of a 'hinge' in the middle of the Gospel, with Peter's 'confession of faith' on the road to Caesarea Philippi and the transfiguration (Mark 8:27—9:8). We should pause and consider these scenes a little further. They are at the centre of the Gospel, and I do not think that this is a coincidence. Furthermore, as we noted in Chapter 5, the 'hinge' provides a key moment in the development of our understanding of Jesus. The first half of Mark's Gospel stretches from the baptism, where God's voice tells Jesus that he is his beloved Son, to the transfiguration, where God's voice repeats this message to Jesus and the three disciples. The first half is dominated by the question 'Who is Jesus?' The disciples are called and then start to struggle with this question, which is highlighted by the miracles. Stories of Jesus' conflict with the religious authorities raise another question: 'Who does he think he is?' The parables call for a response to him. Even Herod joins in the conversation.

The 'hinge' then moves us on. In one sense, Peter gives the right answer—'You are the Messiah'—but this only opens up a deeper question: what do we mean by 'the Messiah'? What does it mean to be a follower of the Messiah?

This question is the focus of the second half of the Gospel. Here we find far fewer miracles—really only the story of blind Bartimaeus on the road to Jerusalem, with its message about having courage. The point about Jesus' power has been made, and now we have to face the harder message that he is not going to use power to save himself. On the way to Jerusalem (Mark 9—10), we consider the nature of Jesus' calling and, hence, our own calling. This culminates in the declaration that he is going to give his life as a 'ransom for many'.

Then we reach Jerusalem, and here conflict erupts. People try to trap Jesus. He tells parables 'against them'. The crowd becomes a mob, both in favour of Jesus and turning against him. Division—the moment of response—has come. Finally, we face the willing, self-sacrificial death, which reveals what God is really like, as well as bringing about God's reign, Jesus' vindication and the judgement of his enemies.

One structural element that we can surely attribute to Mark is the lack of resurrection appearances, for it is hard to imagine that Peter never preached about them. Nevertheless, Mark has chosen to end the story with the fear and silence of the women. The ending is open, not 'happily ever after'. It calls for a response: Jesus has gone ahead of us, too, so will we follow? Will we speak or say nothing because of fear?

This amounts to a particular Christological structure ('Christology' meaning 'discussion of who Jesus is'): the key structuring element is given by the titles, such as Messiah, and the idea of Jesus as God's Son. However, the same structure guides the 'descent' of the disciples, the culmination of the conflict with the authorities and the call for a response. The order of Peter's preaching in Mark is deliberate and important. It may not go back to Peter, but it is no accident.

The Gospel

We are still in danger, though, of missing Mark's crucial contribution to Christianity. He may have turned Peter's preaching into the first, trendsetting, never superseded Gospel, but he also invented the very idea of 'a Gospel'. We looked at some of the evidence for this in Chapter 1, but we skipped over a more siginificant point. Why does 'a Gospel' have this particular shape? We learnt that 'gospel' originally meant the good news about Jesus, and that it also became the word for a text, a book, which told the good news. We saw that it is quite probable that Mark's Gospel was the key driver for that movement to a Gospel book.

We may be used to the fact that 'a gospel' means 'an account describing the life, death and resurrection of Jesus of Nazareth' (as I have just read on Wikipedia), but it is not at all obvious that this is the right way of telling the gospel message. Many of the letters in the New Testament tell us the gospel message: they tell of God's love for us and the sacrifice of Jesus that can bring us back to God, and they call us to respond. Indeed, we might say that the gospel message comes across more clearly in the careful theological presentation that we find in the letters than in the rough-and-tumble of Jesus' life and the misunderstandings of his disciples. Also, as you might know, there are other Gospels besides Matthew, Mark, Luke and John, such as the Gospel of Thomas. In all likelihood, that book dates from at least a century later than Mark and seems to be written from the perspective of a divergent Christian group, but it is also different in the sense that it is a compendium of Jesus' teaching, not an account of his life.

So we could give 'the message of Jesus' in different formats: we could tell the message in a letter or doctrinal treatise, or we could gather a compendium of Jesus' teaching. But Mark didn't do this. He invented 'the Gospel'—the idea that the way we tell 'the message of Jesus' is by giving an account of Jesus' life, death and resurrection, in which we have Jesus' teaching alongside stories of how he met people. We have become used to it, but that just proves how dominant Mark's invention became.

What difference does this make? It reinforces one of the key points that emerges from Peter's preaching: Jesus is not just the messenger but the message as well. The parables are not pieces of teaching; they are calls for response, and response not so much to the parable as to Jesus. He is the secret of God's reign. Responding to Jesus' call to 'follow me' means that we enter God's reign and understand the parables. It's in comparison to the need to respond to Jesus that the law seems marginal. If the miracles have a function beyond helping the individuals concerned, it is to reveal Jesus: miracles fade out in the second half of the Gospel because there are more important things to be revealed about Jesus than his power.

How do we encourage response to Jesus? We tell stories in which Jesus meets people and they respond or, in some cases, fail to respond to him. This is the genius of the Gospel format that Mark invented. The text does not just tell us about Jesus; it presents Jesus to us. As we read about his meetings with people, we put ourselves in their shoes and he meets with us. As he calls them to respond to him, we hear that call directly ourselves. The genius of a 'Gospel' as we have it in Mark, Matthew, Luke and John, and one that we can, with reasonable confidence, attribute to Mark himself, is that it makes Jesus real to us.

This cuts to the heart of the Christian faith. We are followers of Jesus. Yes, we may believe some doctrines; yes, we may behave in certain ways and not others; but what matters is our relationship with a person—Jesus Christ. Mark's Gospel presents that person to us and calls us to respond to him.

Christians across the centuries have recognised that Mark got it right—that presenting Jesus in this way should be at the heart of Christian spirituality and mission. This recognition is demonstrated in the adoption of Mark's format by Matthew, Luke and John, and by the dominance that these Gospels gained over other 'Gospel texts' which told the message of Jesus in a different way—for example, by simply giving his teaching. It is demonstrated, too, by the dominance that the Gospels following Mark's pattern came to have in the church's worship, its art and its private devotions and prayer. The Old Testament and the New Testament letters, the Acts of the Apostles and the books of Revelation are all scripture, but the Gospels have a central place. It's here that we meet Jesus.

It's impossible to split this genius between Mark and Peter—and, of course, we may say that God was behind it all. Peter's preaching, written as Mark's Gospel, created the centrepiece of Christianity. The medium fitted the message perfectly. The message is a call to respond to Jesus, and Peter's preaching, written as Mark's Gospel, focuses our attention unflinchingly on that message. We do not have resurrection appearances; we do not have the Lord's Prayer; we do not have infancy narratives. What we have is material chosen, written up and structured to lead us to respond to Jesus. Each time Jesus meets someone, we are drawn into the text. What would we do if we were that person? In what ways are we like them? How would we respond if Jesus met us like that? At the climax, do we respond to Jesus as the high priest did, or as Peter, the women and the other disciples did, or as the centurion did?

The last words spoken in Mark's Gospel are these. They refer to Galilee, the place where the disciples first met Jesus, the place of their ordinary lives—their families, their friends, their work and their homes.

> *'You are looking for Jesus the Nazarene who was crucified. He has risen… He is going ahead of you to Galilee. You will see him there, just as he told you.'*
> MARK 16:6–7

How will we respond?

About the author

The Revd Dr Jeremy Duff has taught New Testament at Oxford University and a number of theological colleges and courses, and is a vicar in an urban parish in the Diocese of Liverpool. For ten years he was one of the commissioning editors for BRF's *Guidelines* Bible reading notes and his book *The Elements of New Testament Greek* (2005) is Cambridge University Press's bestselling religion title. He is also the co-author, with the Revd Dr Joanna Collicutt McGrath, of *Meeting Jesus: human responses to a yearning God* (SPCK, 2006).

Enjoyed

this book?

Write a review—we'd love to hear what you think.
Email: reviews@brf.org.uk

Keep up to date—receive details of our new books as they happen.
Sign up for email news and select your interest groups at:
www.brfonline.org.uk/findoutmore/

Follow us on Twitter @brfonline

By post—to receive new title information by post (UK only), complete the form below and post to: BRF Mailing Lists, 15 The Chambers, Vineyard, Abingdon, Oxfordshire, OX14 3FE

Your Details
Name _____
Address_____
_____
Town/City _____ Post Code _____
Email _____

Your Interest Groups (*Please tick as appropriate)	
❏ Advent/Lent	❏ Messy Church
❏ Bible Reading & Study	❏ Pastoral
❏ Children's Books	❏ Prayer & Spirituality
❏ Discipleship	❏ Resources for Children's Church
❏ Leadership	❏ Resources for Schools

Support your local bookshop
Ask about their new title information schemes.